Asking the Fathers

AELRED SQUIRE

NEW YORK

MOREHOUSE-BARLOW CO.

1973

til den svevende

First published in America, 1973,
by Morehouse-Barlow Co., Inc.,
14 East 41st Street, New York, N. Y. 10017

SBN 8192-1164-8
Printed in the United States of America

CONTENTS

εἶναι δέ, μᾶλλον ἤ δοκεῖν, Θεῷ φίλον.
To be, rather than to seem to be, a friend of God.

Gregory Nazianzen,
Carmen de vita sua, 324

1

FINDING OUT WHERE ONE IS

If you open this book at this first page and begin with this first sentence, you can decide whether to continue or to stop. But what you cannot do now is to cease to experience what you have experienced. It affects even your ability to lend yourself to anything that breaks in upon your attention. These words must share the fate of any other sight or sound. Here in these hills a stream falls endlessly over rocks in a gulley, between fir trees that stand in their own living silence as far as the blue barricade they make against the changing sky. A moment ago a hawk hovered in the sunlight, searching, and is gone in the lighter, irridescent blue.

Is all this ambient nature kindly? Or is it sinister? Or merely indifferent? Already in 1867 Matthew Arnold in his poem *Dover Beach* was expressing a post-Christian reaction to the experience of nature which, with the passing of a century, has become almost universal. He invites his companion to a window above the sea in full tide under the moon 'where the cliffs of England stand, glimmering and vast, out in the tranquil bay'. But a far from tranquil thought at once intrudes upon the mind through the experience which enters by the ear.

> ... from the long line of spray
> Where the sea meets the moon-blanched land,
> Listen! you hear the grating roar
> Of pebbles which the waves draw back, and fling,
> At their return, up the high strand,
> Begin, and cease, and then again begin,
> With tremulous cadence slow, and bring
> The eternal note of sadness in.[1]

And what is this note of sadness that the sea's harsh music on the shore brings in? The thought of an absence, where a presence has been too long taken for granted.

> The Sea of Faith
> Was once, too, at the full and round earth's shore
> Lay like the folds of a bright girdle furl'd;
> But now I only hear
> Its melancholy, long, withdrawing roar
> Retreating to the breath
> Of the night-wind, down the vast edges drear
> And naked shingles of the world.[2]

We have, many of us, gone far beyond Arnold's provisional answer to this terrible absence; human love often proves little more than a make-shift barrier against the blind forces of a world 'where ignorant armies clash by night'.

But, in a stanza from a less successful poem of the same date, Arnold hints at the possibility of a state of mind, difficult to live with, yet invigorating enough to be explored. Certain that there is nothing directly to be done about his disillusionment, the poet climbs to visit the Carthusian solitaries of the Grande Chartreuse,

> Wandering between two worlds, one dead,
> The other powerless to be born
> With nowhere yet to rest my head.[3]

Is Arnold mistaken in feeling a certain kinship of spirit between himself in his predicament and the lives of the silent monks into whose thoughts it is only too evident he altogether lacks the equipment to enter? His instinct was sounder than he knew. It is certainly no accident of history that the Christian monastic movement was born at the very moment when, apparently, the sea of faith was about to go lapping round the known world. Often inarticulate in their doubts and reserves about what was happening, many thousands of Christian men and women withdrew from the seemingly comforting prospect of an established Christianity and, with nowhere yet to rest their head, set out in search of a comfort of a rather different kind. It was in their circles, and in the circles of those connected with them, that the first great Christian masters of the things of the spirit emerged.

Even in the minds of many practising Christians the very mention of these people calls up a world that is strange, remote, and irrelevant. To those whose aspirations have understandably kept them aloof from Christianity in any of its established forms, it seldom occurs that any of those who are at least nominally venerated by the traditional Churches could have anything pertinent to say to their problems and needs. To both the one and the other, the teachings of the Christian spiritual masters are frequently inaccessible on account both of the languages and of the forms in which they have come down to us. Too much work and too many explanations seem likely to be necessary if one sets out to investigate them unguided and unequipped. What this book will attempt to do will be to initiate a dialogue between the teachings of these masters and any of those who, like Matthew Arnold, and like them, find themselves wandering between two worlds, one dead, the other powerless to be born, with nowhere yet to rest their head.

But it must from the outset be insisted that there are certain conditions apart from which such a dialogue cannot genuinely and fruitfully occur, and the first of these may strike the modern reader as unusual. He will be accustomed to supposing that one can read what one likes and how one pleases, and from one point of view this is true. Yet—as we shall find more than one of them saying— this principle cannot be applied to the teachings of the Christian spiritual masters. Our Lord Jesus Christ himself is reported in the Gospels to have said: 'My teaching is not my own; it comes from him who sent me. Anyone who is willing to do his will will know whether this teaching comes from God, or whether I am speaking only on my own authority.'[4] In other words, it is the man who lives a certain kind of life who is in a position to understand the doctrine. There are some kinds of knowledge to which experience is the only key. Teaching of this kind rests upon foundations which, it is seldom safe to suppose, are any longer properly understood and appreciated. Our God, says the letter to the Hebrews, is a consuming fire,[5] and if this is so, those who approach him presumptuously may expect to be burned. Yet those who are disillusioned with what their Christian faith has so far offered them, and those who are accustomed to feeling lost in any case, may take the rough, but honest comfort that, if they are prepared to pay the price for it, the true doctrine of the great teachers will never shut them up within a world that is safely bounded by notions that are easy to master in any odd, spare moment. These teachings define the frontiers of the unknown, and they do not pretend anything else. The security they offer—which is the only one there is to be had—is that of always being ready to pass beyond what one imagined one understood.

3

They ask nothing less than a total renunciation, of a kind with which it will be necessary to become acquainted, and teach a way of life at which one cannot merely play. To say this is to say that one can only prepare oneself to listen to their teachings by being ready to change one's state of mind. One must be willing to learn—to devote one's best attention to different things from those which formerly occupied it. In this enterprise it is no small thing to be able to begin from where one actually is. There is, indeed, nowhere else to begin.

It is rare, as we pass from one place to another, not to find ourselves remaining almost rootedly somewhere else. A sound, a shape, a colour, the way the light falls, a turn of phrase in conversation will awaken, or force us back upon impressions, desires, and fears that have made, and continue to make, a more vivid impact upon us than the place where it would be most correct to say we 'happen to be'. Nor will any artificial attempt to bring that attention back, even supposing we desire to do so, meet with any notable success. Everyone knows that we can sit on a chair in the presence of someone else and even be vaguely aware of the sound of his voice rising and falling, and of our own returning answers of some kind, and yet remain so preoccupied as not to know very clearly what he or we have said. Were we to look into similar experiences with insight and understanding, we should already know, at least by implication, much of what the first half of this book is going to try to make explicit in terms which have only been forgotten and neglected because they are, like life itself, too demanding to be merely comfortable. Yet, if we can only be patient with them, they will force us to find a new value in everything we are. They will encourage us to allow our immediate experience constantly to break in upon our preconceived notions with such fresh news that we find ourselves suddenly where we actually are, in a world quite different from the one we supposed it to be, and with many a burning bush among what we always thought to be a waste of dry shrubbery.

With a quiet, persistent courtesy the old books insist that there is a distinctive pathway to be found in these matters, a 'royal road' which stretches from the days of the Apostles to our own. Their view of the continuity of the tradition to which they thus refer does not inevitably involve a belief in a continuity that can be historically demonstrated. We now know, better than they sometimes did, that there are many gaps along that line. They were, in any case, thinking of a continuity of life, and were not concerned primarily with

4

the set forms and shapes in which it might manifest itself. For them, tradition is not the dead hand of the past, but the living wisdom of a master who himself responds authentically to the spiritual fulness of his immediate situation and helps others, who wish it, to do the same. This point is made quite clear in the context in which the notion of the 'royal road' first occurs in the *Conferences* or *Conversations* of the great early fifth-century writer John Cassian, the classical interpreter of the desert tradition to the West. This 'royal road', is the standard by which to judge of the soundness or wisdom of a given doctrine or practice. That there is no set formula for this standard, no certain secret of success, is the point of a story which occurs near the beginning of the second *Conference*.[6] The speaker, Abba Moses, is describing an all-night discussion in the desert at which he had been present as a youth. Anthony the Great, the symbolic pioneer of the way of the desert, was then still alive. It was he who summed up an argument in which different parties had variously contended for fasting or vigils, silence or solitude, as the ultimate secret of the perfect Christian life. When Anthony opens his mouth, we realize why he enjoyed such a reputation for giving wise advice, not only to monks, but to the enormous number of those living ordinary lives in the cities who consulted him. There is a lot to be said for all the points of view put forward, says Anthony. Yet, why is it that one has seen people, pursuing their chosen path with enthusiasm, who suddenly go to pieces and end up in spiritual confusion and ruin? There cannot, he says, be any other reason for their collapse than that, owing to insufficient formation by the *seniores*, 'the elders' or experienced ones, they were never able to acquire that authentic discretion which, avoiding all extremes, teaches one to keep to the 'royal road'. On the one side of that road lies the exaggerated pursuit of right purposes which, in stupid self-confidence, exceeds the bounds of all reasonable restraint, and on the other an equally dissipating latitude about everything. Anthony thus refuses to be caught in the snare of discussing any particular activity, however good in the abstract, as though it could be valuable in and for itself, and puts the discussion on an entirely different footing. He points to that self-authenticating tradition of doctrine and life which, when properly understood, is flexible enough to make something valuable and sanctifying of any human situation and commitment that is not of its nature evil. For the moment it is not necessary to enter into the subtler implications of what Anthony is here saying on the recurrent theme of 'dis-

5

cretion', but it suffices to note his sense that the authentic tradition about how to live needs to be imbibed by converse with those in whom it is at work, not as a theory in their heads, but as an experience in their lives. The motive of those who would understand this tradition must be, not intellectual curiosity, but a desire for a satisfaction more complete than that which can come to the mind alone. Hence within this desert tradition the masters do not set themselves up as systematic teachers. Their doctrine is drawn from them by the questions of their disciples. Thus, early in one of the great collections of the replies of experienced men, a book commonly referred to as the *Verba Seniorum*, or *Sayings of the Elders*, a reply, which obviously bears some relation to the discussion with Anthony reported by Cassian, is introduced by the words: 'What is so good that I may do it and live by it?' This is the common question which all these little nuggets of doctrine in the form of stories or brief sayings presuppose: 'Speak to me a word, father, that I may live.'[7]

This is the tradition into which this book attempts to enter, taking as its 'fathers' not simply Anthony the Great and his desert companions or even those who are in the more technical sense Fathers of the Church, but a wider range of people, both in patristic times and since, whose claim upon our attention will be precisely that in their own day, and later, they have been recognized, in some way or another, as transmitting an unbroken tradition of Christian life. Though its ideas are documented, this book is not addressed to scholars. It seeks rather to present to anyone who may wish to submit themselves to a similar discipline a vision which has seemed to emerge from the prolonged business of asking the 'fathers' of the Christian life for a little light on many dark matters. It may, incidentally, serve as an introduction to many of the great Christian masters, as they are known to us through their writings, but it is not intended as a history of spirituality. That must be sought in other places by those who have a taste for it. Here the witnesses speak as and when their voice seems to be particularly significant for the topic that forces itself upon our attention. For one of the striking features of the doctrine of the great desert Fathers, as of all in every century who have reached their spiritual stature, is how little the substance of that doctrine is tied to any external form of life. They often speak to us with an immediacy that is clinically disturbing. If we give them the serious attention they deserve, we shall often have to rectify

6

our previously misguided views. For, as Abba Abraham says in Cassian's final *Conference*: 'It is evident that it is *we* who make rough with the irregular and unyielding stones of our desires the plain and easy ways of the Lord; who are so crazy as to forsake the royal road...'[8]

If, groping after this, to us nowadays, often lost pathway defines the sense and shape of this book, we shall frequently find ourselves having to cast aside conventional patterns of thought, particularly those we have picked up from a desiccated Christianity reduced to maxims of conduct and rules of thumb. We shall have to allow our minds to be freed from those cramping limitations upon our insight which might otherwise prove to be grave obstacles to all real progress; and since it is often necessary in these matters to talk in parables, the mood and method of our undertaking may perhaps be suggested by two images.

It is a summer day in Burgundy, where the light has a vibrant clarity quite unlike that of English summers. Sitting at the long white table in the shaded room with its slatted shutters, we seem to be enclosed within that mysterious and complicated world in which, by eating and talk, man transforms what comes to him by way of his senses into his own distinctive life. But, as those who are waiting at table come and go with the dishes, there is revealed through the long doors, in bursts of limpid sunshine, another world of *things*, clear and triumphant in their independent existence, stones and plants and trees, insistent upon being seen in the exactness of their contours, defining themselves in colour and form and movement, simply, gloriously and beyond all argument *being*. In such a setting only the most insensitive eye could fail to note the challenge of all in the world that *is*, that carries in it a truth and rightness that determines it to be just this and not that. Men of scientific training, whose business it is to work with this world of things, normally acquire that instinctive respect for and appreciation of creation which is also the mark of gifted gardeners, cooks, artists, and poets. Often it is only people who imagine themselves to be religious who treat this whole vista with the profoundest contempt. Yet these have so frequently upon their lips the, for them, evidently meaningless words 'consubstantial with the Father, by whom all things were made'. Their own tradition shames them. One would rightly expect to be able to gather examples of every kind of strained and unusual austerity from the desert sources. How gratifying it is, then, to hear a scholar, with a trained and experienced eye in this field, remarking when he comes to Anthony the Great's reaction to his first sight of the Interior Mountain, where he was for so long to live: 'Note this love for the place', and going on to cite Anthony saying: 'My book, O philosopher, is the nature of created things, and it is present when I will, for me to read the words of God'.[9]

Neither Anthony in the context of his hard life, nor anyone who grasps what is really at issue here, can rightly be assumed to be adopting a self-indulgently romantic attitude to created things. This superficially romantic attitude is, indeed, commonly implicit in the shallow religiosity against which the way of life of the Fathers would put us on our guard. When it chooses, this easy religion sees the world in the bright, patchy, and blurred tones of the cheap Christmas calendar, rather than in the sure, clear, and definite forms that emerge for the disciplined observer of nature. Anthony and his like are brave with recalcitrant material. Professor Alec King has made the essential point admirably in his book on *Wordsworth and the Artist's Vision*, where he is incorporating some of the poet's own words:

> What is necessary first for visionary power is an undaunted appetite for liveliness—to be among the active elements of the world and to love what they do to you, to love 'to work and to be wrought upon'; to be 'alive to all that is enjoyed and all that is endured', to have the loneliness and courage to take in not only joy but dismay and fear and pain as modes of being without bolting for comfort or obscuring them by social chatter.[10]

This, as Professor King goes on to say, is not a frail gift which can flourish only in the seclusion of a beautiful world. It is rather, in Wordsworth's own words, 'the mind working in alliance with the works which it beholds'.

This is, in its way, very close to the spirit of the desert contemplatives. We are not here concerned with the making of a creative artist, but we are concerned with that mode of understanding by which we are able to let, or to help, the things that *are* make their true impact upon us. It may hitherto have seemed a matter of small importance that we should like some things and dislike others, that we should see some things and not see others. But if we exert this capacity to choose as a way of imposing *ourselves* upon the world that is, then we shall deserve the inevitable and inseparable punishment that follows, namely that the world

8

brings us no message of God. That real world only disturbs a little our private day-dreams in its desperate striving to put us in touch with the God who is, and who consequently is as utterly unacceptable to us as the things he creates. We must, in a word, have a practical confidence in the consequences of the dogmatic truth which St John proclaims when he says of the Word of God: 'It was through the agency of the Word that everything else came into being. Without the Word not one single thing came into being'.[11]

This is the best of all reasons for seeing the world as it actually is, even if we cannot at first read its message or value it as God values it. We need not aim at being wise and learned in all the arts and sciences; for there, too, we shall have to submit to what is, in ourselves. But we must avoid like the plague that selective egotism which begins by censoring the world, goes on to miss out half the Bible, and finally, and predictably, takes flight and scandal when in the end it has to meet an uncensored God. It will certainly be best, if we are going to come into relationship with the God who is, not to think that we can know in advance what he will be like. There will be something very wrong both with the theology and the theologian that does not approach the mystery of God through a deep reverence for the mystery of what he has made. It can never be too often said that one of the first traps set before the man who desires to pray or to study the theology of prayer is to set it in a world apart. The man of prayer cannot be a man of two minds. If our attitude towards the least of the creatures is wrong, so will our attitude to God be wrong. We might remember that, in the right hands, a little of the common earth, upon which men walk without reflection, can open the eyes of the blind.

If, then, a little dazzled by the divine sunshine upon things, we stumble indoors again, it would profit us to find ourselves in a delightful little house that King Christian iv of Denmark built in a park not far from the centre of Copenhagen. The Rosenborg Palace is too modest and too domestic to conform to the common view of what a palace should be. It is, in fact, a comfortable royal lodge of a kind of which there were once similar examples in England, though all have now disappeared. From many points of view, the Rosenborg, like much of the art of the incredibly fertile mid-seventeenth century, is almost the physical embodiment of the thought and feeling of an age that was still in vital contact with many of the common insights of the medieval world. These insights are often clearer and easier to grasp for us today in their late-received form than in their older originals. Now the Middle Ages found a special fascination in the idea of mirrors, and so did many people in the seventeenth century, and for much the old reasons. Thus Christian IV included in the house, which he is believed personally to have designed, a small room in which one might stand with one's feet on mirror-glass and see oneself reflected, all about and up and down, in other mirrors. The mirrors are now dull, but the essential effect remains, and something graver than either vanity or tomfoolery held the imagination of those who took pleasure in such artifices. None of the mirrors in this room are trick mirrors and the whole thing corresponds to a certain appetite for the truth, even when that truth is a mystery. There is, after all, a sobering possibility of holding a mirror up to life, of remembering what manner of man one is. Deeper down in the recesses of the Christian memory there is the revealed truth that man himself is in some mysterious way a mirror or reflection made, in whatever sense the words are to be understood, in the image and likeness of his Creator. Here, then, though we may be baffled by it, we are once again standing upon what ought to be for us confident ground. If all things bear the marks of their maker, of none of them, save man, is it said that it is made in his image. Evidently, then, the man who would draw near to God would do well to attend to what he can see in his image. Once he has taken up this standpoint, he will eventually discover himself in a mirror-filled room. For, apart from what God holds up to him in the universal features of his human nature, there is that other portrait of himself that God holds up to man in holy Scripture, where we shall find not only God revealing himself, but also the features, comely and unpleasant alike, of man to whom the revelation is made. We too often fail to realize that one of the primary purposes of holy Scripture, considered as a vital whole, is to show man to himself, as he was made and as he has become, as he acts and reacts in relation to his maker, with *nothing* left out. Hence the violence and crudity and sensuality that God there pushes in front of our noses, even if we would, to our very great danger, prefer to turn away. The God of the Bible does not whittle down the truth, and we must not try to do so either. Then, beside these mirrors, universal in their validity, there are others for our more particular information, held up to us by those in the past or the present whose development we are personally best prepared to understand and, surer still, those additional portraits of ourselves that we are daily making in the actions and thoughts which mirror what we individually are. Even those who imagine they know themselves will often be surprised at what they see, if they have the courage to look honestly into *those* mirrors. From those, particularly, we shall often prefer to look away. But from time to time, in a moment of grace, which we can either accept or refuse, we shall be forced to look, and then we shall either be humbled and led back to the God of inexorable truth, or turn angrily away and lose ourselves in lies.

Yet the living Truth, the great breaker of idols and destroyer of false gods, is ultimately easier to live with than the most comforting of lies. It is better to lose the God we found it easy to envisage, and the faith that was only a protection from our fears, and stand naked and unknowing in the presence of the One who can only really be known when he is lived with. At least with that God we can and, indeed, must begin from where we are. There can be no becoming which does not start from something that already is. Similarly, we shall discover that we already know, however confusedly, enough to take us on the next step to what cannot properly be known before we come to it. If a book like this must speak of *some* things to which some people will never come, that must not trouble them. We read in the *Sayings of the Elders*:

> Abba Anthony was baffled as he meditated upon the depths of God's judgements, and prayed thus: 'Lord, how is it that some die young and others grow old and infirm? Why are there some poor and some wealthy? And why are the rich unrighteous and grind the faces of the righteous poor?' And a voice came to him: 'Anthony, look to yourself: these are the judgements of God, and it is not good for you to know them'.[12]

This kind of advice applies to everyone who is merely curious about spiritual things. The other way follows fancy and merely stimulates and intrigues the mind.

To say this is to touch upon the oldest notion of what it is to be a theologian. If St Gregory Nazianzen, who undoubtedly had one of the ablest minds of any fourth-century writer, was traditionally referred to as 'Gregory the Theologian', this honorific title was not a tribute to his outstanding intellectual capacities. He was 'the Theologian' in the same sense as the author of the Fourth Gospel was called 'the Theologian' on the *graffiti* of the ancient church at

Ephesus, and in the dedications of so many old English parish churches. Probably many passers-by no longer realize that St John the Divine means 'John the Theologian'. His was the learning of the man who leaned on the breast of his master at the Last Supper and knew what he knew by the closest possible intimacy. The contrast between this kind of learning and mere book-knowledge, valuable though that may be, is instructively brought out in the medieval West in the account, by a friend, of the conversion of the thirteenth-century St Gertrude of Helfta, which occurs in the first book of her *Revelations*. Gertrude had received a good literary and religious education in the convent which she entered, as some girls do, almost as a matter of course. She could express herself with clarity and a certain charm and, as a finished 'grammarian', a phrase which may be taken to refer to her entire humane education, she felt happy and at home in a civilized household where the liturgy was performed with dignity and beauty. It was all innocent enough and Gertrude never realized anything was missing until a few weeks before the Christmas of her twenty-fifth year, when the bottom of this sophisticated little world seemed to drop out. The feeling was more serious than a passing depression and culminated, in the dormitory after Compline on the last Monday in January, in a totally unawaited encounter with our Lord, who quoted the familiar liturgical texts of the foregoing Advent season in a manner which was at once an invitation and a cure.

What matters is not so much the nature of the encounter, which Gertrude herself elsewhere describes with her customary attention to colourful detail, but its effect, which tradition is unanimous in regarding as the only sure test of an experience of this kind. This effect her friend and biographer describes in a single, simple phrase. It was thus, she says, that from being a grammarian she became a theologian.[13] Naturally this does not mean that Gertrude suddenly lost all feeling for a correctly turned sentence, or that she ceased to be able to see and appreciate all the things in books and in the world that she had formerly enjoyed. Everything, indeed, goes to show that from this point of view Gertrude remained essentially the same. It was simply that a fundamental change of perspective had occurred. As a 'theologian' it was now the 'word of God' rather than any other words that absorbed and pre-occupied Gertrude. By this, as a study of the *Revelations* for anyone who finds them accessible would show, we must understand nothing bookish. This 'theologian' knew her Bible well, but she also found the world all about her alive with the 'words' of the same God who speaks in Scripture.

Gertrude's world and way of expressing herself is hardly one that most modern readers would find it easy to enter, and there is no reason why they should even try. It is enough that we should understand that it is possible in *our* world and in *our* way to become a 'theologian' in the same legitimate sense in which Gertrude became a theologian, since the same 'word of God' is still being spoken and is still operative if we can only learn how to attend to it. When this attention grows it will lead naturally into prayer and even sometimes *be* prayer. In any case three facts about our situation may be regarded as certain. Whether any of us has ever been, as we say, 'aware' of the presence of God or not, it is certain with the certainty of faith that he is present to us *in some way* at this moment since, were this not so, we should not even be here. It is also equally certain, on the same grounds, that we all of us stand in some definite relationship to that divine presence, whether we have any inkling of what that relationship is or not. God at least knows what it is, and all traditional theologians would believe that there will always be *some* things about that relationship that we can never know for certain in this world. On the other hand, we do know for certain that God wishes that relationship to come alive *at our end*, as something that can be humanly known and responded to, since he has revealed himself for no other purpose than that he should be known, with all that that implies in a relationship between persons. In so far as the awareness of this fact has reached us as an individual, it already constitutes an invitation to respond in some personal way to God's self-revealing. There may, nevertheless, be all kinds of obstacles in the way of our doing this. In fact there normally will be. If modern people with a troublesome thirst for spiritual things often cast wistful glances over their shoulder at the ages of faith, it is frequently because they do not realize that obstacles of exactly the kind they rightly feel they encounter have always formed an inseparable part of the preoccupations of traditional spiritual training. To be asked to pray or to expect to be able to pray without taking these obstacles, and also certain equally invariable assets, into consideration is like trying to fly before one has learned to walk. On the asset side of the balance are the underlying convictions which have been proposed in an extended way in this chapter and which form the essence of what St Paul had to say to the Greeks in the Areopagus at Athens:

> The God who made the world and everything that is in it is the Lord of heaven and earth. He does not have his home in man-made temples, nor can he be served by human hands, as if he stood in need of anything that men could give him. It is he who gives to all men life and breath and all things.... He created them to seek God, with the hope that they might grope after him in the shadows of their ignorance, and find him—and indeed he is close to each one of us. In him we live and move and are.[14]

Hardly anyone would take this address seriously when it went so far as to suggest that everything about man could find its ultimate significance in this context of thought. But the few who did give it their attention, both then and since, found that there was more to be said for it than at first appeared.

2

IN THE IMAGE OF GOD

For me the initial delight is in the surprise of remembering
something I didn't know I knew. I am in a place, in a situation,
as if I had materialized from cloud or risen out of the ground.
There is a glad recognition of the long lost and the rest
follows. . . .[1]

The American poet Robert Frost is here describing the experience
by which a poem comes into being, a kind of creative recognition
of what is already somehow obscurely known. It may seem a
somewhat startling leap to make, but to the great spiritual masters
of the undivided Church, the revealed doctrine of man as having
been made in the image of God universally inspires this feeling
of glad recognition. They go on, in fact, to take it seriously for what
it claims to be, a long lost memory of their true selves, and from
that all the rest they have to say follows. Their doctrine is concerned to arouse in their disciples a sense of the implications of a
memory they believe could not have been initially reawakened
without a divine intervention. The factors likely to prevent the
personal realization of this truth determine the form of their teaching. It will be necessary to look somewhat later at the capacity of
holy Scripture, as understood in the apostolic tradition, to fit the
case of the one who lives with it, as though it spoke to him directly
out of the depths of his own being. Time and again, its words give
shape to his unformed awareness, answering, as it were, to his
own experience. It suffices for the moment to recognize that, from
the earliest times, whether in the East or the West, the great theologians of the spiritual life are unanimous in the importance they
attach to the doctrine of man's imagehood. In the West the last
firm expression of this universal tradition is to be found in St
Bernard and the other twelfth-century writers who came more or
less directly under Cistercian influence. They were all men involved

in a conscious return to the spirit of the Fathers, both Greek and Latin, whose teachings they studied and digested, as far as they could get hold of them, putting them to the test of experience with an integrity impressive in some of its more tangible results.

After them, the lamentable effects of the division between East and West begin at last to be felt, and even mirrored, in an increasingly divided theology which promotes the attempt to lead 'a spiritual life' no longer necessarily integral to the concerns of the professional theologian and hence often at variance with his theoretical convictions. Only the very greatest teachers transcend these divisions, and it is significant that to none of them can one so readily appeal for light on matters of fundamental principle as to the earlier saints and writers. Twice only has a reaction to the earlier standpoint opened up the possibility that fundamental theological insights might once again become central to the Christian life. In seventeenth-century France the patristic studies of Cardinal de Bérulle, begun for controversial purposes and continued for their own life-giving sake, place him at the theological hub of a circle of spiritual influence that extends beyond the limits of the Catholic Church, and most notably in England. Both he, and his better-known contemporary and admirer, St Francis of Sales, with a sound instinct for the situation of the Church in the modern world, take a distinctively Christian doctrine of man as the basis on which to construct their spiritual teaching. It would seem that it was a similar instinct which led the Second Vatican Council to begin its document on the *Church in the Modern World* with a statement on the doctrine of the image of God in man unique among conciliar documents. Couched in language which studiously avoids committing itself to Augustinian speculations, it modestly reports what is undoubtedly common to Greek and Latin theology alike. That its statement that 'it is not permissible to despise the bodily life' should have been necessary,[2] is the measure of how far the things of the spirit had become disincarnate in the West, and with what care the credentials of commonly-received ascetic doctrine often need to be examined. Nothing short of a positive restatement of fundamental principles is likely to break the fatal combination of admirable intentions and thoroughly unsound ideas, which often passes undetected. If all the ends of the earth need to remember and turn to the Lord, it is only when man remembers what, according to holy writ and the teachings of the Fathers he is, that this is likely to happen.

Much has occurred within the last fifty years to alter the ordinary man's impressions of the physical universe of which, as a bodily being, he is himself a part. Whether he looks to the animal world with which, on one side of his being, he has so much in common, or goes further afield in space and time, the contrast between his own relative size and vulnerability and the universe, which he is piecemeal mapping out and learning in so many ways to know, is striking. 'If I look up to your heavens, made by your fingers, at the moon and stars you set in place—what, then, is man that you should spare a thought for him, the son of man that you should care for him', wrote the Psalmist.[3] Even landings on the moon itself cannot modify the humbling thoughts these prospects must inspire, though they do, on the other hand, something to strengthen the conviction of the succeeding verse of the same psalm: 'Yet you have made him little less than God'. The Hebrew word here translated 'God' is sometimes translated 'the angels' and there is Greek New Testament support for taking it this way, though the same word is at issue when, quoting another psalm, our Lord answers those who accuse him of making blasphemous claims, with the words: 'Does it not stand written in your law: I said you are gods?'[4] However the words in question are translated, such phrases are clearly saying that man is a special case among created things, a being with a resemblance to that which lies beyond what can be seen and admired, and St Paul quotes with approval a phrase of the Greek poet Aratus: 'We are his children'.[5]

The mystery which is thus alluded to, a realization which is the cause of awe rather than of arrogance, is envisaged in two important and interconnected ways in the Bible, and some notion of Hebrew ways of thinking is necessary for the proper understanding of either. We are generally accustomed to thinking of the ideas of soul, spirit, and flesh as distinct *things*. Although the Hebrew language could and did make these distinctions, it did not think of them as actually *distinct*. In other words, the Bible does not draw a distinction between psychic functions and physical ones. These functions can be both material and immaterial at one and the same time. For the Old Testament, the bodily parts, the shadow, even a man's possessions, are all indications of the *person*. Thus the hand or the heart can stand for, and even *be*, the soul and the spirit. There is absolutely no sense of dualism in this way of looking at man; he is not made up of several things. Thus when, in the most primitive account of the creation of man in Genesis we read:

'Then the Lord God formed man from the ground and breathed into his nostrils the breath of life; and man became a living being',[6] we have a description of a person which it is of the greatest moment not to interpret in our conventional way of looking at things. As the Danish scholar Pedersen, on whom all other writers on this subject depend, has noted:

> It is not the object of the narrator to analyse the elements of man, but to represent his essential character. The basis of its essence was a fragile, corporeal substance, but by the breath of God it was transformed and became a *nephesh*, a soul. It is not said that man was supplied with a *nephesh*, and so the relation between body and soul is quite different from what it is to us. Such as he is, man, in his total essence, is a soul.[7]

Yet, as Pedersen will go on to point out later, it is equally true to say that the body is a perfectly valid manifestation of the soul.

> The man of clay was a dead thing, but by the breath of God he was entirely changed and became a living soul. Soul and body are so intimately united that a distinction cannot be made between them. They are more than 'united'; the body is the soul in its outward form.[8]

This is an insight to which the Christian ascetic tradition will constantly and inevitably be brought back by reason of its belief that the whole person, body and soul, has an ultimate destiny.

If, with these observations in mind, we return to the Hebrew conception of soul, it will be clear that we could, according to our way of speaking, often write 'person', where the Hebrew would write 'soul'. Yet if we look at the account of man's creation with which the book of Genesis opens, we shall notice that the animal world is also a world of souls. What distinguishes man from animals is that he is a living totality with a peculiar stamp. Thus the soul is at one and the same time something visible and something invisible. Hebrew, in other words, demands to see the impression a person makes in their total context. Nor is the word 'soul' the only Hebrew word for that indefinable thing the person. From other points of view a person is also spirit and heart. The heart is the soul in its inner value, the soul as character. Hence our Lord is using a wholly Hebrew way of thinking when he says:

Do you not realize that everything that goes into a man's mouth goes into his stomach, and is evacuated into the drain by natural processes? But what comes out of his mouth comes from his heart, and it is that which defiles a man. For from the heart come evil thoughts, murder, adultery, fornication, theft, lies about other people, slander. These are the things that really defile a man.[9]

'Spirit', on the other hand, is the soul as motive power. Thus, in the book of Exodus we are told: 'They came, every one whose heart stirred him, and every one whose spirit moved him, and brought the Lord's offering'.[10] Soul, then, is everything a person is, living and acting.

Thus man does not have a soul, he is a soul. He is also a cluster of relationships, and it is with these that we come to what is properly theological in the Bible's account of man. For, although the book of Genesis gives us a doublet about man's creation, both accounts in their rather different ways make essentially the same point about man. What makes man distinct is his quite special relationship with his creator, and this relationship is expressed in the notion that he is made in the image of God. If we take what is generally regarded as the later account of man's creation where it now appears, first, in our present form of the book of Genesis, we read: Then God said:

Let us make man in our image, after our likeness; and let them have dominion over the fish of the sea, and over the birds of the air, and over the cattle and over all the earth. So God created man in his own image, in the image of God he created him; male and female he created them.[11]

'Man' in these verses is the common word for mankind and is probably connected with the idea of being taken from the earth. The Hebrew word for 'image' relates to the root idea of something that is like another in the way that a man's shadow is like him as, in bright sunlight, it falls on the ground, a clear and concrete shape. One of the Fathers will, as we shall see, work very fruitfully, and with complete theological propriety, even with the very physical implications of this word. Most will tend to distinguish— naturally without claiming any linguistic basis for the difference— between image and likeness. Even the Hebrew allows some room for a slight distinction, the word for 'likeness' being the more ab-

19

stract and normally denoting the link between the idea or plan in a man's head and its outward expression. In either case, a relationship is suggested between something which is primary and that which resembles it in a striking and intimate manner, such that the one cannot be correctly conceived without the other. In a later chapter Adam will become the father of a son 'in his own likeness, after his own image'.[12] Although the notion of 'image' in these two contexts is in neither case given a defined content, the latter usage confirms the implication of the first that what is at issue is a distinctive kind of life.

This impression is strengthened when we look at the more primitive account of man's creation told in the manner of a folktale.[13] We are shown the maker of everything carefully preparing a specific kind of body into which he breathes the life-giving spirit, so that it becomes animated with a life that is unlike that of any other creature. This becomes clear to man himself when, in establishing his relationship with animals, he expresses his rule over them by giving them names. In Hebrew thought, as in the fairy tale of Rumpelstiltskin, to know the name of something is to have power over it. It is, then, in this act of naming that it becomes evident, we are told, that among animated things there is 'no counterpart to man'. He thus recognizes the uniqueness of his situation, as God himself gives recognition to it, in making the woman with the same kind of life to be man's companion.

Relationship is, then, written into the very nature of man. As the Bible sees him, you cannot think about man without recognizing that he is, as it were, made for relationship. God crowns his work of making by creating someone to whom he can talk, as we see when, after the story of the Fall, man hides himself and is afraid to meet and speak with God, as apparently he was formerly accustomed to do. Man also lives a shared life with the woman. They are not just part of that world with which, as creatures with a bodily life, they have the closest links. For, although before the Fall the world is a friendly place, it does not provide them with the companionship which they find in each other. Indeed, perhaps we may even say that the very friendliness of the world depends upon the ability of the man and the woman to recognize their relationship to and responsibility for it. We shall not fail to remark that the garden is committed to man's care long before his relationship to creation begins to cause him the trouble of sweat and thorns and thistles.

We must further note, before we consider more clearly what it might mean to say that man is made to God's image, that while we can plainly say that the image of God in man is intimately connected with a dynamic relationship to God and his creation, it is theologically and biblically certain that we can no longer, from our present situation in a fallen world, see fully what this means. This is a matter of the greatest contemporary relevance. What is God like? It is sometimes supposed that these early biblical pictures of the meaning of man really, in effect, put man up in heaven and seat his own likeness on the throne of his creator. But this is certainly not what they are designed to do. On the contrary, they claim to tell us what *man* radically is like. Of God their word is considerably darker. Not only does the God of the Old Testament consistently forbid images of any kind to be made of him, he even refuses to communicate his proper name to man in his fallen condition.[14] As St John of Damascus will point out, the only images of God that are allowed in Old Testament times are those which God himself makes.[15] In the mystery of man, God guards his own mystery. To this sense that God himself is utterly beyond our conceiving, the doctrine of the Fathers is faithful, as the word of scripture requires. Like Job we may enter into relationship with God through his intervention in history, but then it is God the incomprehensible we meet, God the breaker of the heart's idols and the confounder of edifying talk. He is what he is.

The first words of Scripture about man are therefore dark with the admirable darkness of poems and parables and, by not pretending to be ordinary history, cannot rightly be taken as expressing a kind of truth that does not concern them. Seen in the context of Hebrew anthropology, they sufficiently insist upon man's solidarity with the rest of creation while isolating the mystery of his distinctness from it. They have, moreover, a New Testament complement which sheds on them a light bright with the divine darkness itself. Of Christ in his letter to the Colossians St Paul writes: 'He is the image of the invisible God, the first-born of all creation'.[16] 'First', clearly, not in a sense that is measured by history, though it is in and through history that this becomes known, but in a sense which gives Christ a priority of another kind. 'For in him all things were created, in heaven and on earth, visible and invisible and in him all the fullness of God was pleased to dwell'. Thus, although it can be said of man that he is 'the image and glory of God',[17] what is unveiled in the gospel, or good news, of Christianity is that Christ is this likeness of God in a primary and unique sense, as the opening verses of chapter four of the second letter to the Corinthians maintain. Hence, too, St Paul is even ready to speak of a first and last Adam. Quoting the words of the second chapter of Genesis, he writes: 'The first man, Adam, became a living being; the last Adam became a life-giving spirit. Just as we have borne the image of the man of dust, we shall bear the image of the man of heaven'.[18] Thus the mystery which reveals itself later in time than the appearance of men in the world comes before time itself in the dynamism of the making of all things. Through the mystery of the one for whom it is claimed that he was, and is, truly God and truly man, everything returns into the mystery of God 'that God may be everything to everyone'.[19] This claim that somehow or another the person of Christ enters, from the very beginning, into what is meant by saying that man is made in the image of God can no more be a piece of ingenious mystification than truth itself can be deception. It is too completely harmonious with the dark hints of Scripture taken as a whole to be a merely human invention. It can, of course, be rejected, as Christ himself was rejected, but its challenge cannot lightly be dismissed. It is all the more impressive for occurring in a context of thought that, far from attempting to spiritualize away the reality of the body, is constantly underpinned by that thoroughly Hebrew anthropology without which St Paul, although writing in Greek, cannot properly be understood.[20]

Irenaeus, who through his contact with the martyr-bishop, Polycarp of Smyrna, was in close touch with the spirit of the apostolic age, inherits both its vocabulary and its theological convictions. It is he who most lucidly brings together in a single statement the two major elements in the biblical doctrine of man's likeness to God.

In times past it was said that man was made in God's image, but this was not made evident. For the Word, after whose image man was made, was still unseen. And this was why he so easily lost the likeness. But when the Word of God was made flesh he established both the one and the other: he displayed the true image by himself becoming what his image was; and he made the likeness secure by uniting manhood to the likeness of the unseen Father by means of the visible Word.[21]

In other words, Irenaeus believes with Paul and John, whose

22

ardent faith in the truth of the Word made flesh he reiterates and shares, that it is only in the Person of Christ that it becomes clear what was meant by saying that man was made in the image of God. In Christ man sees himself in one who was truly man. Irenaeus is therefore not embarrassed by the notion of including the body in the belief that man is like God. Indeed it is because the one who is truly man is also truly God that, at least in the person of Christ, the living likeness of humanity to the unseen God is permanently secured in one and the same person. This idea, grounded in the belief that God truly appears and acts in history, also has the merit of not disposing of either the mystery of man or the mystery of God, who still remains ultimately inconceivable. Christ becomes the living embodiment of man's meaning and destiny. As Irenaeus says elsewhere:

> This is why the Word became the dispenser of the grace of the Father for the profit of men, for whom he performed such redemptive work. Displaying God to men and man to God, he preserved the invisibility of the Father, that man should never come to despise God and might always have some goal towards which to move. At the same time he made God visible to men by many acts of mediation lest man should be so utterly deprived of God that he should even cease to be. For the glory of God is a living man; and the life of man is the vision of God. If, then, the manifestation of God by creation gives life to all who live on earth, how much more does the revelation of the Father by the Word give life to those who see God.[22]

It will at once be evident that if the goal towards which human life needs to move is the realization of our godlikeness in a living relationship with God which is finally vision, Irenaeus, like all the Fathers, is quite unable to think of the life of the spirit as a matter for theories and experiments divorced from the basic facts which alone make its existence possible. The union of the human and the divine which is a fact in the person of Christ, is a task to be achieved for men at large, and God's gesture of love in becoming man is both the sign of our destiny and the source of the only means of its fulfilment. This conviction is expressed in the simple and bold formula that Jesus Christ our Lord, God's Word, 'on account of his measureless love became what we are that he might make us in the end what he is'.[23] Athanasius, the great fourth-century champion of orthodox Christology, uses a similar phrase the Greek of which may be literally rendered, 'he was humanized that we might de deified'.[24] Gregory of Nyssa affirms the same in his Great Catechism.[25] None of these Fathers thinks that man literally becomes divine by nature. The creature remains the creature, but transformed by its share in the life of the creator through consent and co-operation.

No one is more insistent upon this process of transformation as a process of growth and maturation than Irenaeus is. The imagery he uses for it is, like all his language, memorably biblical, and the precondition that it should occur is the right use of man's freedom. Irenaeus, in common with many later Fathers, is explicit in seeing man's capacity for free choice as a primary mark of his godlikeness.[26] One readily sees how he appreciates its connection with the true nature of love.

> That saying 'How often I have wanted to gather your children together and you did not wish it', admirably illustrates the ancient law of the liberty of man [he writes]. For God made man free, having from the beginning his own autonomy and his own soul that he might use the counsel of God freely and not under constraint from him.[27]

God never does violence to the creature he has made this way. The purpose of this loving forbearance on the part of God is that 'one day man should be mature enough to see and grasp God'.[28] Far from thinking, as some later theologians do, that man started as a kind of intellectual giant, Irenaeus believes that man began his career rather like an infant whom God meant, in any case, at the right time and in the right manner, to grow up.[29] If his is a case of arrested development, this is in part because he often refuses to recognize his true situation.

> Knowing neither God nor themselves, insatiable and ungrateful, they are unwilling first to be what they were made, men liable to passions; over-riding the law of the human condition, before even being men they want to be like the God who made them and see the difference between the uncreated God and the newly created man disappear.[30]

This shrewd observation applies to many people with ardent spiritual aspirations, and the disastrous consequences that follow from refusing to recognize the laws of the human condition are the subject of many of the sayings and anecdotes of the old masters. Irenaeus, however, produces one passage of unique insight and beauty on this theme. The symbolism of the passage comes from the opening chapters of Genesis, but what it speaks of is still going on.

> How shall you be god who have not yet been a man? Or how shall you be perfect when you have scarcely been created? How shall you be immortal when in your human nature you have not obeyed your creator? For it is necessary in the first place to keep to your position as a man, and only then to receive a share in the glory of God. For it is not you who makes God, but God who makes you. If, then, you are God's workmanship, await the hand of your maker, which does everything at its proper time, opportunely however, in relation to you who are being made. Offer him a supple and docile heart, and keep the form which the artist has given you, having in yourself the water which comes from him, and for want of which, in hardening yourself, you would resist the imprint of his fingers.[31]

Thus Irenaeus sees God as still at work on the making of man. As our Lord is reported to have said in St John's Gospel: 'My Father goes on with his work until now, and I go on with mine'.[32] In order to profit from this work, it is necessary to remain as responsive to it as moist clay, by allowing the grace that comes to us as the result of the redemptive work of Christ to penetrate and soften us. But it is equally important to see that we shall only permit this to happen by being content to be faithful to the intentions of God in making man. There is an unusual sense of equalibrium about the insistence of Irenaeus that it is necessary first to be a man, if one is not to be swept off one's feet by aspirations which lead one higher. Like every wise master, he brings us back to the earth on which we stand as the condition of our starting out on our spiritual journey with any solid hope of making progress. His consistent teaching has implied that while all men are made in the image of God, not all men are actually living in that likeness to God which is possible for, and appropriate to them, with the help of grace. He says elsewhere: 'According to nature we are all sons of God, since we have all been made by him. But according to obedience and doctrine we are not all sons of God, but only those who believe in him and do his will'.[33] There can be no doubt that this is evangelical teaching, which finds its place in St Matthew's Sermon on the Mount:

> I tell you
> love your enemies,
> and pray for those who persecute you.
> If you do that,
> you will be like your Father in Heaven,
> for he makes his sun to rise,
>   on the bad and on the good alike,
> and he sends the rain
>   on saint and sinner.[34]

There can be no doubt either that Irenaeus would see our habitual failure to be like our heavenly Father as something likely to affect our judgement about the very nature of God himself, in the long run. If the harmony that should exist between the created image and the God it should be like is too completely broken down, the God who is and the man who *should be* often almost disappear from view. But this is a fact of contemporary experience and has been neatly expressed in a pair of verses by Robert Frost, where a connection is made between the absence of God to man. and the absence of man from God which is too little considered:

> I turned to speak to God
> About the world's despair;
> But to make bad matters worse
> I found God wasn't there.

> God turned to speak to me
> (Don't anybody laugh)
> God found I wasn't there
> At least not over half.[35]

The Fathers have a good deal to say about this business of not being where one is, and it is now necessary to examine it.

3

IN THE LAND.OF
UNLIKENESS

'Know yourself first', says Gregory Nazianzen, who often pauses
to consider the baffling commingling of soul and body, and wonders
how one can be both dust *and* the image of God[1] The mood is
caught by Hamlet in one of the most familiar of his speeches,
where Shakespeare, at the dawn of the seventeenth century, ex-
poses the humane convictions of the Christian centuries to a draught
of sharp despair:

> I have of late—but wherefore I know not—lost all my mirth,
> forgone all custom of exercises; and indeed it goes so heavily
> with my disposition that this goodly frame, the earth, seems to
> me a sterile promontory; this most excellent canopy the air,
> look you, this brave o'erhanging firmament, this majestical roof
> fretted with golden fire—why, it appears no other thing to me
> than a foul and pestilent congregation of vapours. What a piece
> of work is a man! How noble in reason! how infinite in facul-
> ties! in form and moving, how express and admirable! in action,
> how like an angel! in apprehension, how like a god! the beauty
> of the world! the paragon of animals! And yet, to me, what is
> this quintessence of dust?[2]

Perhaps it is true that 'no one else has felt so strongly the absolute
meaninglessness of human life' as Shakespeare.[3] Yet one can verify
that Gregory Nazianzen, who earned for himself the unique title
of 'the Theologian' among his great fourth-century contemporaries,
knew by temperament and experience well enough the apprehensions that lead to this feeling. He felt within himself, as every true
theologian must, the sublimity and the humiliation of man together.
For if one is not haunted by the sublime about man, one does not
know the humiliation either. One does not feel the Fall. A text-

book theologian might once have objected that naturally one cannot feel the Fall since the claim is made for this doctrine that it can only be known by revelation. Yet the Second Vatican Council felt able to say that 'what revelation tells us here is in accordance with experience itself'.[4]

It is difficult to see how anyone could think otherwise. By the very fact of having been born at all, we are all of us involved in a state of tension between two apparently incompatible facts. On the one hand, simply as human, and not as monkey or cat, or even rose, we have a special and unique sublimity. The now respectable hypothesis of evolution has, partly by reason of the yawning gaps that still remain in its chain of explanation, done little to modify this conviction and a good deal to strengthen it. An ethologist of distinction has written, 'only the person who knows animals, including the highest and most nearly related to ourselves, and has gained insight into evolution, will be able to apprehend the unique position of man'.[5] The biblical apprehension of this situation, as seen through the eyes of the New Testament, is that all that God has made is good, and very good, but only man is, as St Paul says, 'the image and glory of God'.[6] This is God's first and, as it will be necessary to see, his last word about man, and anything that may have to be added to it by way of explanation must always be seen against this background.

Yet, on the other hand, that it is necessary to add an observation which would seem to be a direct denial of all this was as clear to St Paul as to the ethologist or to any ordinary, honest man. If it is in any serious sense true that man is the image and glory of God, then this sense must take into account the inescapable fact that something has evidently gone unaccountably wrong with him. St Paul's way of saying this explicitly refers the matter to its context within the doctrine that man was made in God's image when it declares that we all 'fall short of the glory of God'.[7] No translation of his Greek which does not bring out St Paul's notion of failure to measure up to a norm can be regarded as satisfactory. The 'glory of God' of which we fall short is clearly not some merely external law, however exalted, but something intrinsically appropriate to our being human, some dynamic wholeness that we can see could and should be ours. It is not the theologians alone who find themselves having to talk about a norm to which no one can confidently point in the world of beings that exist. Psychology has never been able to escape from this need for some standard of judgement, a fact which is, at the very least, some kind of reason for considering the merits of the traditional explanation of why we are haunted by the notion of normality. This explanation is more complex and subtler than is commonly appreciated, and it is bound up with the different ways in which we find ourselves involved in what the Bible calls 'sin'.

Sin is always a failure to measure up to what should be, either by excess or defect. Experienced in its global effects which touch us socially and personally, both from without and within, it is baffling enough to be called a 'mystery' in its own right.[8] Our bewilderment before it is partly to be explained by a feeling that, whatever our personal responsibility for the moral evils we know of, there is an area of moral evil which goes beyond anything we could attribute to anyone to whom we could point. Traditional Christianity recognizes this distinction as just. The sin situation in which we are all alike involved, though its effects upon us individually may be varied, is that in which we become involved by the mere fact of being human. We are in it by way of origin rather than by anything we do. Hence it is called 'original sin'. The general notion is sufficiently clearly described by Gregory of Nyssa when he writes:

> As by the succession of offspring in a given species the nature of animals is passed on, so that what comes into being conforms to the nature of that from which it was born, so man is born from man, the implicated from the implicated, the guilty from his like. Is not this, then, the way sin comes into existence with those who come into being, being produced with them and growing with them, and going down with them at the limit of life?[9]

This statement may be taken to contain all the elements of the doctrine of original sin about which traditional Christianity is undivided. It will be noticed that it commits itself to no view about the connection between original sin and the physical processes of generation, but simply refers to the way its inheritance bears a similarity to the law that like begets like. Man who is already out of true begets those who find themselves in the like condition. In other words, contrary to much popular misconception, original sin is not called 'sin' as being something of which we could by any stretch of the imagination be regarded as the cause. It is a situation of disharmony in which we *find* ourselves, as opposed to that in which we can *place* ourselves by our personal choices. In saying that the mark of original sin is to be 'implicated', Gregory of Nyssa

29

is using the notion of empathy, which enables one to identify one-self with someone or something and thereby understand it from within, in a sense which is *wholly unfree*. Through the passions we are, in our fallen state, pulled apart *in spite of ourselves*. Although it will be necessary to discuss in some detail the ways in which original sin is normally taken to affect our experience, it may for the moment be said that its common feature is that it presents us with an inability to do or achieve something which we can see ought, in principle, to be physically or morally possible for us. Each of us finds himself, in some respect or other, to be flawed in a way which is clearly not our fault, even when allowances are are made for anything we may have done to make ourselves worse. Hence the effects of original sin are visible even in the sorrows and difficulties of childhood, as the poet Gerard Manley Hopkins tells Margaret, a little girl grieving:

> Now no matter, child, the name:
> Sorrow's springs are the same.
> No mouth had, no nor mind, expressed
> What heart heard of, ghost guessed:
> It is the blight man was born for,
> It is Margaret you mourn for.[10]

We all of us mourn for ourselves and, because not all this sorrow has its source in anything we have done, the older theologians often draw a distinction between the image of God in the soul which remains, and the likeness which, as a living reality has, in fallen man, been lost. Our capacities remain; it is when they begin to function that we discover that something is amiss. We have lost that adaptation to right action which is called virtue. The situation is implicit in the remark of St John of Damascus, where he says that to be made 'to the image' refers to the capacity to understand and be self-determining, while to be made 'to the likeness' refers to the actual virtue which really fits our capacity.[11]

It is particularly the writers of the Latin West who explore and explain the great primal sorrow of the lost likeness which man discovers when he honestly contemplates himself as he is. The thought often returns in St Ambrose, as when, commenting on a verse in the psalms which says: 'Why, Lord, have you gone so far away?' he adds,

He is right to be afraid, who knows himself to be a man; he begs that we who were far away may begin to be nearer and know that we are men, to the image and likeness of God, to whom, through the child-bearing of the Virgin, Christ too was conformed'.[12]

St Ambrose's brilliant convert, St Augustine of Hippo, takes up the thought in his own characteristically personal way in his *Confessions*:

I discovered I was a long way from you in a land of unlikeness. And it was as if I heard a voice from above saying, 'I am the food of the fully grown: grow and you will feed on me. But you will not change me into you as you do your ordinary food. Rather, you will be changed into me. And I recognized that you have corrected man for his iniquity and made my spirit vanish away like a spider's web. And I said, 'Is truth, then, nothing at all, since it is not spread out in space finite or infinite?' And your voice called from afar, 'Yes, I am he who is'. I heard as one hears in one's heart, and there was no further room for doubt. I could more easily have doubted that I myself was alive than believe that Truth not to be, which is known to be by the thing he made. Who can understand this, he says later, and who can talk about it? I am filled both with awe and with ardour: I am overawed in the measure that I am unlike him; I glow with fire in the measure that I am like him.[13]

It is St Bernard of Clairvaux, in the twelfth century, who draws the traditions of East and West on this subject together in passages which clearly reveal the influence of Gregory of Nyssa:

See, we are before him as though we were not, as nothing and emptiness. In this land of unlikeness what business are we engaged upon, Lord God? I see the human race from sunrise to sundown circulating in the traffic of this world; some seek wealth, some run after privilege, others are captivated by the gratifications of popular favour.[14]

These are depressing words to describe a dismal condition, that of losing one's true human dignity in being pushed and pulled hither and thither by one's own uncontrolled and often uncontrollable drives. The Fathers are all agreed that human nature is profoundly wounded by the Fall, but they are equally agreed that it is not destroyed by it. Hence the experience of deep disharmony in those who become aware of their true possibilities, their true selves. This experience is a genuine ground of hope. St Bernard's convic-

31

tion, like that of the entire tradition, is that in the unlikeness to God which we find in man after the Fall 'the soul has evidently not put off the form it was originally given, but has put on, over it, a false one. The latter is added, the former is not lost, and that which covers it is only able to hide the original but not destroy it'. The human tragedy is that 'what makes the soul unlike God makes it unlike itself; hence it is compared to senseless beasts and becomes like them'. Its opportunity occurs when it realizes that this has happened to it. 'The more it is disgusted with the evil in itself, the more it urges itself towards the good which it equally sees in itself and longs to become what it was made, simple and upright'.[15]

It is in this way that traditional Christianity does justice to man's nostalgia about himself, not offering him a false comfort which denies a situation of fact common to human experience, yet insisting that his aspirations are also grounded in a persisting reality, and that *both* must be seen together in any spiritually mature way of living. It will be necessary to discuss in a more extended way the practical significance of this view of the human condition which refuses to choose between a light-headed optimism and a misanthropic pessimism, but one final aspect of this overall picture must first of all be grasped. The thought of St Bernard, like that of all the great masters, moves naturally in the direction of the divine intervention in the human dilemma. For neither human nature as it now is, nor human effort as it can now be made, can achieve a resolution of that dilemma, though both have an important part to play. As St Bernard observes, 'like seeks like, even in the realm of nature'. It is the Christian belief that in the relation between God and man this has been and continues to be a reciprocal affair, and St Bernard is particularly insistent upon this conviction as the very foundation of his account of the developing life of the spirit.

If a great good is not to be twisted into a great evil it is of paramount importance for every one among you who seeks God to understand that he anticipates you, and that you were being sought before you sought him. The soul seeks the word, but it was first sought by the Word. For ... when once it had gone forth or been cast forth from the presence of the Word ... I would not say that the soul which longs to return and desires to be sought is completely unprotected and abandoned. For whence comes this desire that is in it? If I am not mistaken, it must be that it has already been visited and sought by the Word.[16]

32

It is in this belief that the theology of St John and St Paul in the New Testament meet. In this theology, although the idea that man is made in the likeness of God is taken entirely seriously, it is insisted that he is not that living likeness itself. He is not the image in the most ultimate sense in which that word can be used. Only in and through Christ have we access to the God who tells us that he is 'He who is'. Only in and through him does God's glory unmistakably stream out upon the world, as once it did upon the mountain of Transfiguration, where the privileged three were, for a moment, caught up in the bright cloud which overwhelmed and overawed them. There, as St Leo says in his great sermon on this subject, 'the foundation of the Church's hope was laid, that the whole body of Christ might realize the character of the change it would receive, and that his members might promise themselves a share in that honour which had already shone forth in their head'.[17] What does this really mean in the context being discussed? The Second Vatican Council states it succinctly when it says:

Our Lord Jesus Christ is perfect man, who restores to the sons of Adam the divine likeness. He is, if we may say so, the image when it is alive with God's own life. In him God sees himself actually reflected, and the one in whom he sees himself reflected is perfect man. This recent council, like the earlier councils of the Church, insists upon the unity of the two natures, human and divine, in their integrity in Christ. And 'since in him human nature is assumed and not annihilated, by that very fact it is also raised to a sublime dignity. For by his incarnation the Son of God in a certain way united himself with every man'.[18]

The mountain of Transfiguration may seem a very exalted point from which to view the meaning of man, yet, seen in its context in the Gospels, we can be confident that it is Christ himself who will deliver us from the danger of delirium. If we can, for a brief moment, see in Christ what we were first meant to be from what, in him, by the free gift of grace we can in the end become, we may be sure that it is in his company that we shall be led down the mountain. We shall be *brought* down, and made to walk about in the world, as he walked about in it, eating, drinking, sleeping, really working with our hands, thinking, choosing, loving—all of which can be truly asserted of him. In fact we are going to have to insist so much in this book upon his wholeness and our own wholeness as human and this-worldly in our immediate considerations

33

that there could be—and probably at this period in history there is—some danger of our forgetting what the glimpse on the mountain ought to have taught us. Yet it is very important for us to retain this point.

First and foremost, we must recall that, for the one who is made in the image of God, the true centre of his life is not to be found in himself as something he can possess or fully comprehend in its wholeness. All the great masters make it clear that there is nothing so much like a second nature as grace is. Yet, just as the three disciples in the bright cloud on the mountain experienced a bewildering combination of reverential awe and complete happiness *together*, so grace, in restoring our lost relationship with God, and thereby putting our ultimate centre outside ourselves, leaves us in a situation which, in practice, often baffles our limited understanding. For it must yield to what it cannot always, of itself, see. Here lies the cause of an apparent contradiction in much that this book is going to have to say. The redemption is, on any traditional showing, a restoration of nature, and hence we must never forget: no nature, no grace. There is no such thing *for man* as the *purely* spiritual. Man is not an angel and he never becomes one. Hence, redeemed man, in common with every man of good will, will have to do a good deal of hard thinking about what human wholeness is, and even make a great deal of positive effort to achieve that wholeness. But he will also, in practice, constantly have to give that wholeness up and, apparently, die to it too, because his true centre lies in being *at all costs* open to relationship with the One who is so eternally and abundantly alive that he can snatch life out of death. Man finds his life ultimately by losing it. This is the distinguishing mark of the Christian way.

That the cross is the way through to the glory is an idea already explicitly present in the story of the Transfiguration. Our Lord calls Peter and James and John apart 'to pray', St Luke tells us.[19] And what happens, happens as he prays. It is no accident that it is the same three who are called apart to pray in the garden of Gethsemane. Perhaps the subject of the prayer was on both occasions the same. At least we know that the Transfiguration not only followed a prediction of the Passion, but that it is about this coming Passion that our Lord is speaking with Moses and Elijah when they appear. As St Leo sees it, the glory of the Transfiguration is from one point of view the preparation for the scandal of the cross. Certainly, according to our Lord's own word, the story of it is only to

34

be told when the three on the mountain and in the garden can see the two together in the light of the resurrection. In both cases, although the prayer takes place 'apart', it is intimately bound into a life that is developing in the way that God wills. *That* way goes beyond what man, in and of himself, can fathom. Hence in the Garden of Gethsemane the genuine human nature of our Lord is in a state of agony and upheaval that causes a sweat falling like great drops of blood. This we are also meant to know for our understanding of what the restoration of man's likeness to God can entail, even for us. Thus, as the Second Vatican Council says, 'in suffering for us, our Lord not only gave us an example that we should follow in his steps, but he inaugurated a way, in following which, life and death are sanctified and given a new sense'. It is this new sense that we must cleave to, for it is always going to be present, penetrating right through the most positive things that we, as true Christians, do in this world. In other words, because God has made the world good and ourselves noble, we are going to have to value that world, and above all the people in it and the life we live with them. We can only evade doing this at the price of spiritual death. But in the concrete we are also always going to have to be aware that the value we give to man's world cannot ultimately be measured by something from within itself. Already, in and through Christ, by the grace of God, man is being raised to ends beyond what he can discover or conceive in and of himself. The recent Council will say: Whoever follows Christ, the perfect man, becomes himself more a man.[20] The words are in complete harmony with an observation made by Archbishop Ramsey in one of the few seminal theological studies written in the twentieth century.

> In Christ mankind is allowed to see not only the radiance of God's glory, but also the true image of man. Into that image Christ's people are now being transformed, and in virtue of that transformation into the new man they are realizing the meaning of their original status as creatures in God's image.[21]

Thus we are both like and unlike God at one and the same time and in different respects, 'Why is it', asks St Augustine, alluding to the old Stoic maxim also quoted by Gregory Nazianzen, 'that it is enjoined upon the soul that it should know itself?' 'I suppose', he answers, 'that it may consider itself and live according to its nature'.[22] What exactly does this involve?

4

THE HUMAN SITUATION

Pascal, one of many in seventeenth-century France who strove to find again the personal significance of the living tradition of Christian belief, still continues to break in upon us with a disturbing, contemporary voice.

> Let each of us examine his thoughts. He will find them entirely occupied with the past and the future. The present is never our purpose. The past and the present are our means; only the future is our purpose. And so we never live, but rather *hope* to live and, since we are always getting ready to be happy, it is inevitable that we never actually are.[1]

This sense of life as a relentless process of development, in which the only opportunities for influencing its course so easily slip through our fingers, was as real to Gregory of Nyssa in the fourth century, or St Bernard and his contemporaries in the twelfth, as it must be to anyone who recognizes that the Christian account of man's predicament deserves to be taken seriously. Pascal also draws attention to the fact that if all action upon the only moment we are given is not to be either perverse or ineffective, it is necessary to hold a balance between the two aspects of man which our previous two chapters have considered. 'Christianity is odd. It tells man to recognize that he is base and even loathsome, and also that he must want to be like God. Without such a counterpoise, this eminence would make him disgustingly conceited and this abasement frighteningly cowed'.[2] Indeed, if the traditional Christian view of man is sometimes considered to be so naïve as to have been superseded today, it is largely because this view is assumed to involve a choice between two equally implausible extremes. The doctrine of the undivided Church is, as Pascal insists, subtler than this and more exacting in its consequences upon the mystery of the here and now.

Man is only a reed—the weakest thing in nature. But he is a reed that thinks. It is not necessary for the whole universe to arm itself to crush him: a mist, a drop of water, is enough to kill him. But if the universe crushes him, man will still be nobler than that which kills him, since he knows he is dying, knows of the power of the universe over him, of which the universe knows nothing. In thought, then, our entire dignity consists. It is on this we must draw and not on the conquest of space and time, with which we should not know how to cope. Let us, then, work at thinking straight; that is the foundation of conduct.[3]

The practical consequences of the relationship between the doctrine of man we have been considering and Pascal's observation that most people live either in the past or in the future become clear in the awareness that it is, in fact, very difficult to live in the present, where we actually are. And the root of the difficulty, the Christian believes, is in the sin situation in which we are involved by way of origin. The biblical picture of man at his creation is of a being whose basic call is to relationship, relationship first and foremost with God and with others, and then relationship to the universe at large through understanding and care. We are, as it were, born for openness, for that shared life which is the mark of those who are capable of knowledge and love. Only the orthodox doctrine of the Fall clearly asserts how intimately every other relationship, inner and outer, is bound up with the maintenance of the living relationship with God which, mysterious though it be, is an ineradicable need of man's nature. A condition of things which is most dramatically and definitively displayed in the separation and dissolution of death reveals itself also in a general tendency to a breakdown of relationship at every level of our being. It will be convenient to refer again to the summary of these commonly received notions agreed upon by the Second Vatican Council, rather than build them up from earlier witnesses. We must realize that if these basic doctrines have been discredited, it is nevertheless part of their merit that they explain why it lacks overwhelming persuasiveness, as Gregory of Nyssa explicitly saw. Here, at least briefly stated, that traditional doctrine is:

> Man, established in uprightness by God, abused his liberty from the very dawn of history, as a result of the influence of the evil one. Raising himself up against God, he desired to attain his goal outside God. *Although they knew God, they did not honour him*

37

as God, but their senseless minds were darkened and they served created things rather than the creator. What revelation makes us aware of coincides with experience itself. For man, looking into his heart recognizes that he is inclined to evil and sunk in many ills which cannot come from his good creator. Often refusing to acknowledge God as the source of his being, he also breaks with the necessary relationship to his final destiny and likewise with his relationship whether to himself, to other men, or to all created things. Thus man is divided against himself. And so the entire life of man, whether personal or collective, witnesses to a dramatic struggle between good and evil, light and darkness. Man finds himself to be, of himself, incapable of successfully combating the assaults of evil so that everyone feels himself to be, as it were, bound with chains. But the Lord himself came to free and strengthen man, renewing him interiorly and casting out the prince of this world, who had held him in bondage to sin. Sin, however, diminished man, preventing him from pursuing his fulfilment. The lofty calling and the profound wretchedness which men feel simultaneously find their ultimate explanation in the light of this revelation.[4]

It is an immediate implication of this general statement of belief that, even where man's fundamental relationship with God is restored at least by a desire to accept God's loving intervention to rescue man from himself, traditional Christianity does not believe that all the other areas of lost relationship are automatically restored. This the Church does not even believe of the effects of the sacrament of baptism, which is the normal way, within the Church, of signing and sealing a personal belief in the redemptive work of Christ. Our total reintegration is left before us as something to be achieved. In other words, our life's task is, with the help of God, to give our response to our call to relationship a full and truly human shape, a response that involves, progressively, the whole of us, right down to the tips of our fingers. The Christian believes that this work is, at root, God's work. But at the same time it is not God's work without our consent and co-operation. We must therefore personally desire it and work towards it. The dialogue which reopens as a result of what the Greek Fathers liked to call God's 'philanthropy', his friendliness towards man, is not a dialogue in which the script for one side is written by the other in advance. We have each to find our own words and actions to make this relationship meaningful. The possibility which comes from God is *our* opportunity.

Gregory of Nyssa has a particularly striking way of saying this, which he uses more than once. In his *Great Catechesis*, a work specifically designed to show his Greek contemporaries that the claims of Christianity are at least not contemptible, he is very insistent that the sacrament of baptism should not be treated as though it were some kind of exalted magic which leaves us with nothing more to do. As he says in his concluding paragraphs:

All other births are dependent upon the impulse of the parents. But spiritual birth is in the power of the one who is born. Since, then, in this matter, where everyone is free to choose, there is a risk of failing to hit upon what suits our case, I think things work out satisfactorily if the one who is about to bring himself to birth considers in advance whom it it suitable to have as a father, and of what sort of nature it would be better to be composed. For, as I have said, in this kind of birth we are free to choose our own parents.[5]

It is thus that Gregory links the initiation of baptism with the personal development that ought to follow it. 'For it is evident to everyone that we receive the saving birth for the purpose of renewing and transforming our nature.' This task of renewing ourselves, of bringing to life again in us the likeness of the one in whose image we are made, is the task of Christian training or ascesis, of which Gregory gives a picture in his explanation of the symbolic meaning of the life of Moses. There again he insists that 'we are, in a sense, our own parents'.[6] There are indeed few who will not recognize the justice of believing that, when allowance is made for all the obscurities in which we have to work out our salvation, we never become what in fact we do become, unless deep down in ourselves we have chosen and desired it, and gone on doing so for a lifetime.

To be persuaded of this is not incompatible with allowing a large element of truth in the feeling that there is much in every life about which there is really no choice. It is not necessary to believe that *all* human problems are explained by heredity to believe that we owe our parents more than the specific bodily and temperamental constitution with which we find ourselves endowed. As we have seen Gregory of Nyssa saying,[7] the mere fact of being born involves us in an overall situation in which 'virtue is hard to accomplish', and this is what the traditional view of the effects of original sin means by saying that it 'diminishes' man, making him, as it were, less than himself and placing him in a state of conflict. It is not part of this view to believe that this condition of things is the personal fault of anyone immediately known to us. Jesus is reported to have said in answer to those who asked about a man born blind: 'Rabbi, was it this man's sin, or was it the sin of his parents, which was responsible for the fact that he was born blind?' 'The reason for this man's blindness is neither any sin of his own nor of his parents; the reason is to allow the activity of God to be displayed in him.'[8] This reply appears both to accept the nature of the problem and to suggest the answer to it. If there is sin in this situation, it is not *personal* sin, not the sin that a man does, but rather that which he suffers. And, if unmerited suffering requires a reason, it must be found in the intentions of God which can make the deprivation the occasion for an enhancement of life which far outweighs the adversity. There is every reason to suppose that St John, whose report is here quoted, is recounting a genuine miracle of physical healing but, in common with the other evangelists, he deliberately raises it to the level of a sign of universal spiritual significance, which can be recognized as occurring even when physical healing is not its immediate natural accompaniment.

Physical handicaps are, after all, only one of the forms in which the continuing effects of original sin manifest themselves and, as experience frequently shows, there are also handicaps which are primarily psychological and moral. It is particularly in relation to personal limitations of this latter kind that the universal effects of original sin are best appreciated. In asserting that man remains radically as God made him and that his dignity and capacities are inalienable, Christian belief is not inconsistent in maintaining that these capacities are damaged in the way they work. For this is exactly what experience verifies. It is not in man's nature, but in his activity that the wounds of original sin manifest themselves. They manifest themselves in every aspect of his life as someone actually knowing and loving and, at least to some extent, freely choosing and, further, as embodied and hence with appetites rooted in instinctual drives. From the cradle to the grave we are, either consciously or unconsciously, involved in activity, whether that activity is externally manifested or not. It is also in our activity that we are all the time becoming what, at any given moment, we are. Under stimulus from without or from within, our life perpetually erupts into activity, and then it is that we see how things lie with us. How very different, and significantly different, we all are, and yet how much in the same general situation.

Thus St Augustine, who has very real claims to be regarded as the father of modern psychology, sees himself in the baby who takes his revenge for his unfulfilled wishes by bursting into tears. 'I have learnt by observation that this is how babies behave and, better than those who brought me up and know it all, they have, without knowing it, shown me that this is how I was myself'.[9] As St Augustine points out, here in these childhood tantrums we see in embryo that irrational disharmony which often arises between the claims of a need, sound in and of itself, and the total good of the whole. The brother who grows pale with jealousy when he sees that his brother at the breast wants his mother's milk, even when he does not need it, and wants it all and only for himself. If this condition of things runs its course, and the child becomes father to the man—as in some ways it inevitably must—then there is a real danger that it will become not only insufferable to others, but also a painful burden of frustration to itself. These impulses in children before they can speak are not voluntary and hence, of course, cannot be personally sinful. They thus ideally manifest the ordinary effects of the wounds of original sin as they continue to be experienced by us even in adult life. Our human situation is one in which our individual powers and capacities, left to themselves, simply tend to run away with us. It is often assumed that it is only the so-called 'lower powers' that are envisaged in this picture of human inner disharmony. But Augustine, who was never more maligned in any other matter than in this, was the last to believe any such thing. For him, the over-riding tendency to iniquity was that powerful substitute for sex which is the peculiar prerogative of the spiritually-minded, 'the desire to dominate'.[10] In what he has to say of this form of *libido* as a perversion of authentic love, he thus contributes a shrewd personal insight to a tradition about the wounds of original sin which were normally characterized in the ordinary catechisms of more recent times as being darkness in the mind, weakness in the will, and lust in the appetites. This is simply to say that, as a result of original sin, it tends to be more difficult to grasp the truth, to act upon it when we see it, and to free ourselves of compulsive drives in the basic instincts of love and aggression. Any one of these facets of our total make-up acting automatically and, as it were, in the saddle, can pull us apart and make us less than the whole human being who is called to relationship with God and his fellows. For instance, someone who for fundamentally egocentric reasons has, as he would boast, 'a firm grip on himself', can become a monster of inhumanity and utterly incapable of the real love that many apparently weaker people are constantly and bravely pouring out. To recognize that the apparently strong can often be the really weak and blind, and the apparently weak sometimes the brave and genuinely far-seeing, is to see that, while the wounds of original sin are found in all of us, they take on, in each and all, an entirely individual force. In the thirteenth century St Thomas Aquinas, was already explaining why this happens, and much of it he had learned from earlier observers of individual differences like St Gregory the Great. St Thomas says:

When the tie or original uprightness, by which all the powers of the soul were held in order is dissolved, each power has an inclination to its private movement; and the stronger the power is, the more potent the inclination. It happens, further, that certain powers are stronger in one man than in another on account of differences of bodily constitution.[11]

Those who would feel disposed to deny this theological explanation would be unlikely to reject the observation of fact with which it is linked.

The admission of this fact by so representative a Western theologian and so careful a reporter of the tradition behind him as a reminder that this teaching about the wounds of original sin must never be shorn of the refinements which it has always been understood to imply. Far from being a blanket explanation for any awkward difficulties which might mar some ideal picture of the human condition, it actually draws us back to the uncomfortable particularities from which it does not believe that the grace of God exempts us. We may, perhaps, with the help of God, learn to transcend them. By-pass them we cannot, if we are ever to reach the fulfilment for which, inexpressible though it be, our whole being, even in its disintegration, craves. This concrete reality of our personal situation we can and must know in peace and simplicity, like the psalmist who speaks not of his knowledge of God, but of God's knowledge of him. 'Lord, you examine me and know me; you know when I sit down and when I rise up'.[12] From this, he sees, there is no escaping. It does not matter whether I am still in the womb of my mother or in the nightly womb of my bed, God knows me through and through. The experience of waking up in the morning, the mere fact of being alive, is the sign of God's knowledge of me, whether I am conscious of him or not.

'That I may know you, and know myself' was the project the young St Augustine had set before himself at the beginning of his career as a Christian.[13] If it has seemed right to speak of the moment of recognizing the godlikeness in man as being the bringing to light of a long lost memory, this is because it is the orthodox Christian belief about man's inalienable dignity. But to say that the image of God in man can never be *eff*aced as long as a man lives, is not to say that it can never be so gravely *de*-faced as to be almost unrecognizable. This is because, as we have already seen, the living likeness of the image of God in the human soul only becomes evident when the natural capacities to know, love and freely choose are actually being exercised in harmony with the deepest laws of a universe in which a right relationship with God determines the right place of everything else. And precisely because the image is rooted in that which is dynamic about us, because it is rooted in our distinctively *human* kind of life I must, if I am alive at all, from moment to moment become more like that of which I am the image or more unlike it. There is no middle road in this matter. For even *not* to act in some respect about which I have a choice is really to act. Whether I lie on my bed or run a mile, I can rightly be said to 'do' either or both, since it is I who am the source of the running or the lying. Naturally, in the abstract, either or both may be good and sensible, and it is only when seen as part of the total process of becoming that their full human significance stands revealed. It is enough, at this stage of our exploration, to see that *some* becoming is inevitable, if we are human at all. It is also inevitable that this becoming always takes place in a context in which there is a simple alternative of becoming, through our knowing and loving, more God-like and consequently more genuinely free, or less God-like and so more deeply determined. To speak in a language which will later need further exploration, if we are not willing to be made whole by that mysterious governance of things which is called divine providence, we shall *have* to be destroyed by fate. This is the human situation.

At a time when the value of charms and horoscopes is again as widely credited as it was in the late classical world a Christian may, like the Fathers before him, hesitate to use a word like 'fate' in connection with this ultimate human alternative. Yet, with Thomas

Aquinas, who admits the unfavourable patristic reaction to the term, he may feel an inescapable constraint to discuss the notion.[14] All writers of any penetration in the long tradition necessarily find themselves compelled to say something of those aspects of the notion of fate which are an undeniable reality about the human situation. In St Augustine, for instance, the entire matter is always implied in the use of the heavily-loaded word *necessity*, which is, he says, 'the mother of all human activity'.[15] Thus, whether I choose to do it today or tomorrow, I shall have to plough and sow *some* day, if I am to eat any bread. Such things are an ordinary consequence of life in this world. But in St Augustine's writings as a whole, the notion of necessity is often richer than this. Frequently he will remark on the fact that it is not external factors alone that drive us, nor ordinary natural needs. Thus he will say that 'when our desires are strong and when we serve them, they are termed necessities'.[16] St Augustine is here referring to that way in which we are all radically necessitated as a result of original sin, as his allusions to St Paul's argument in the letter to the Romans make clear enough. As a result of original sin it is a fact that each of us individually finds that he or she is driven either too strongly or too weakly in certain directions to be able to achieve spontaneously that adjustment to life which even natural convenience often requires. Further if, from time to time, we yield in the direction in which the push is strongest then, even without our wishing it, we strengthen the force of that particular 'necessity' over our lives. It is not difficult to see, as St Augustine vividly does, that a man who makes himself the servant of the forces of disintegration within himself by yielding every time he experiences their drive, is inevitably more and more necessitated in every aspect of his life. It is not that he ever radically loses the capacity to see the truth about his situation or to desire what would be genuinely good and choose it; but more and more he becomes less and less disposed to see that truth, to want it or to choose it. As time goes on it requires nothing short of a miracle of grace and conversion to break the chain which we ourselves have been steadily forging, link by link. Buddhism also has its own technical term for this terrible phenomenon, which it calls *karma*.

To admit the validity of these notions is not to deny that the forging of the chain of personal necessity may begin from a bias which is entirely involuntary, a natural necessity in the sense that it is suffered and not chosen, something which has genuinely

44

'happened' to us, though it may be quite personal to us and not necessarily everyone's lot. Many sexual anomalies are fairly obviously of this kind. This kind of bias is the form that the wounds of original sin take in all of us, a particularity which is nevertheless universal. It is a question, the theologians would say, of a defect in the adjustment of our radical human capacities to their appropriate activity. To use the traditional language in this matter, we are by original sin deprived of the virtues. But if the classical notion of virtue is to be meaningful to anyone today it normally needs to be seen in the quite concrete setting with which the development of psycho-somatic medicine has made us familiar. This branch of medicine has been forced into existence by the need to see the individual patient in the round, by the recognition that failures of psychological or, one may broadly say, spiritual adaptation are often intimately connected with symptoms which would at one time have been treated as a purely physical affair, and vice versa. Thus many doctors have come to feel that quite tangible physical occurrences bear witness to something that the theologians ought not so often to have forgotten, namely that nothing in man is so purely bodily that the spirit has nothing to do with it, any more than of course, anything in man can be so purely spiritual that there is nothing bodily about it. These complementary observations are a practical consequence of what is also a theological conviction, that man is inseparably one thing in this world. The soundest tradition of Christian asceticism is based on this view; but that in practice this tradition has often and long been mislaid is suggested by the fact that the Second Vatican Council found it necessary to reassert it with some force.[17] A conscious redressing of the ascetic balance is inevitable, from time to time, necessary in an overall view which nevertheless believes that what determines the specifically *human* character of man's life comes from the side of the spirit. It is these spiritual capacities which make man God-like in a unique sense, just as they also mark him off from every other kind of animated being. Man is more than a splendid animal,[18] though he may often be that too!

Thus it is of the essence of the human situation that man exists between the naturally limited and limiting world of the body at the physical end of the human scale and the naturally unlimited world of the spirit at the opposite pole. Hence man can pretend to himself, and sometimes to others, that he is either an angel or a beast, and at least try to behave accordingly. Why is it that he is in this dilemma, and sometimes in it for half a lifetime and more, without realizing that it is a dilemma at all? Why is it that we do not find the right mirror into which to look? The theological answer to this question is 'because of the wounds of original sin'.

What, once again, does it mean to say this? The common tradition of undivided Christianity says something like this: At the Fall man was not stripped of his nature, which remains in itself intact, but the living relationship with God with which he was created was broken off. This is a break big with consequences for every aspect of man's life. The Fathers, both Eastern and Western, always regard man's relationship to God as something which is 'natural' to him. It is 'natural', not only in the sense that it was initially given to him with the gift of his distinctive nature, and hence was meant to be 'normal', but also because only in that relationship can man's natural capacity for the infinite, for the unlimited, ever really be satisfied. This patristic sense of perspective about man deserves to be borne constantly in mind, even though there is an obvious convenience of clarity in distinguishing between the rather different senses in which the word 'natural' may be used. Thus, speaking technically correct language, we should nowadays say that the gift of grace with which man was created, his share in God's kind of life, although meant to be 'normal' to man, was not in fact 'natural', in the sense of having its roots in his nature. However, it is as well to remember that to be without grace is not from a Christian point of view 'normal' for man—although today, in a further sense of the word, this is now 'natural' to us as fallen human beings. Further, the breakdown in man's relationship with God means, inevitably, the breakdown of man's own distinctive position in the universe to some notable extent. It is particularly in that which is most distinctive of man that this breakdown condition is most apparent. Thus, on this view, man still remains a creature with an appetite for and a capacity to know the truth, but the truth about his *own* condition is now beyond the resources of his own unaided nature. So, hence, are the judgements he needs to make about that condition in order to live with it as he should, though he may correctly make a number of them individually. By nature he lacks part of the evidence upon which the full range of such judgements would have to depend. Similarly, as a creature who always, in the last resort, moves himself, even when he yields to persuasion, man still desires his own good, in so far as he perceives it, but even *that* he does too weakly to achieve

46

it with perfection and consistency. In this statement of what it is like to be without the *virtues*, the nature and function of a virtue is already implied.

As we have already noted, at the physical end of the human scale, man exists in a naturally limited and limiting world. Thus, although we nowadays begin to find that even many of our bodily functions are not so limited to one kind of activity as was once supposed, it still remains true that not even the most advanced kind of therapy can at present enable the eye to hear. The eye appears to have been designed precisely to *see*. Nor have we any reason to suppose that the failure of the eye to hear is a defect consequent upon the Fall. Yet, at the same time, as anyone who has received any training in the fine arts will realize, few, even of those whose eyesight is physically perfect, see with very much precision. The human eye can in fact be trained to appreciate subtle differences of colour and form to which the eye of the amateur is virtually insensitive. This is to say that, over and above its natural capacity to see, the eye can, without mechanical aids, become better *adapted* to seeing, in a manner which, if the training is long and skilled enough, remains as permanent as the capacity to see itself. This adaptation of function which, purely by the processes of nature, gives that function a new precision and facility appropriate to its natural range, is the sort of thing a virtue is, even when it extends through and beyond what is rooted in nature. Thus a virtue is not a power or a capacity in the radical sense of those words, but a permanent adaptation of a given capacity either to the whole range of actions which are possible and appropriate to it, or to particular actions within that range.

If the advantages of favourable habits, which training at a physical or quasi-physical level leaves behind it, are self-evident, their vital necessity at the more distinctively human end of the scale ought to be no less apparent. Indeed, it may be remarked that the bodily capacities with their naturally built-in range of limitations, depend for their development, and even sometimes for their very survival, ultimately upon human capacities into which no such limitations are naturally built. To say this is, admittedly, not to imply that any human life starts as a blank sheet with no individual pre-dispositions. Both observation and the notion of the wounds of original sin exclude any such view. Indeed, both require us to note that not every 'habitual' adaptation of a natural capacity is necessarily built into it by the development of what we call habits.

47

One can be 'habitually' disposed to act in a particular sort of way without ever having done anything specific to bring this about. What is, however, being said is that, in so far as the being we are talking about is human at all, there is an area, beyond the given physical and psychological make-up with which he begins, where a man's future development as a whole is frighteningly dependent upon his free choice. In this area, however difficult it may sometimes be to isolate in practice, there is only one pre-existing limitation, namely that man is not free not to choose, since even not to choose is in itself a choice. Moreover, choices, in so far as they are free, depend upon man's capacities of knowledge and love which are not, simply in and of themselves, limited to moving in any particular direction. Hence, of course, the absolute necessity of adapting these capacities to activity. It is not possible for a human being, precisely as human, to live without developing either the virtues or the vices. If virtuous adaptation was given to us before the Fall as an achieved norm, it is only restored to us by baptism and the gift of grace 'in seed', as the old writers say, to be developed in a situation in which our powers, in and of themselves, are inclined to go off at a tangent. Hence the baptized, and all who open themselves to the help of God's grace, have before them the task of remaking their living human harmony, and their every act, internal or external, contributes to or detracts from that remaking.

If the limitless range of possibilities before man at the spiritual end of the human scale explains why he must inevitably develop either the virtues or the vices, it perhaps still leaves something to be said about what is involved in any action that can properly be described as human. What makes man unique in the entire world of change and development of which he is a part is that he alone is responsible for making his own distinctive world. By the simple fact of having the capacity to grasp the connection between purposes to be achieved and the means of achieving them, man is responsible whenever he can, and therefore should, use this insight as the basis of action. The point may be illustrated by means of an elementary example. If I have just eaten something my body will already be engaged in the process of digestion. It will not be a human failure on my part if I have forgotten to *decide* to digest the food, since this is a decision that is not possible for me, and therefore not required of me. Digestion is neither virtuous nor vicious. Eating, on the other hand, invariably is. If, knowing that I am the kind of creature that needs to eat in order to live and work and develop, I have deliberately chosen not to eat indefinitely, I am responsible for my death if I die. Similarly, if I start eating now, and go on eating for the next fortnight without stopping, I am equally responsible for producing the same result by the opposite means. There is an individually variable, but nevertheless discoverable norm about it. It requires no elaborate demonstration to show that even a decision about so simple a thing as eating will gradually affect the whole of life, not only for me, but also for others. Each individual time when, feeling the need to eat, I eat too much or too little will not perhaps be terribly good or bad. But cumulatively, in so far as I reinforce the habit of going to extremes, I bring about an adaptation of my natural capacities, which may lead to my own physical or mental break-down, or to other habitually vicious acts in respect of others. I simply cannot repeat the acts about which a truly human decision can and should be taken without moving either in the direction of the virtues, which enable me to do the right thing in the right way and do it more easily, or in the direction of the vices, which enable me to do the wrong thing in the wrong way and do it until it drives me with the force of a new need.

This is the framework of presuppositions within which Gregory of Nyssa constructs his picture of the developing life of the spirit in his explanation of the symbolic meaning of the life of Moses for everyone. 'Who does not know', he asks, 'that all things that are subject to change never remain identical with themselves, but pass continuously from one state to another, which is always for better or worse?'[19] Hence some choice is inevitable and 'just as the end of life is the beginning of death, so to cease to run in the way of virtue is to begin to run in the way of vice'. Within the area of genuine choice, if we follow Gregory's advice, the parents we should be wise to choose to bring about the birth, over which our liberty presides, would be the thoughts that father the virtues.[20] This notion leaves us with the entire equilibrium of the Christian life still to examine but suggests that, if Gregory is right in supposing that the royal road of the virtues is the same as the 'narrow gate' of the Gospels, which passes between the extremes, it will present us with no settled formula, but with a measure to be rediscovered in its living reality every day, according to our circumstances. For, where Gregory's thought represents the common tradition, as in fact it does, his expression of it is always fresh with personal insight, and never more so than when he says,

49

'the most paradoxical thing of all is that stability and mobility are the same thing'.[21] 'Perhaps the wish always to go further in the good is, after all, what perfection for man is'.[22] In the combination of openness and limitation which characterize the human situation, this is surely a growing freedom not, to be without norms of behaviour but, to remain supple enough to see that one's realization of them in the concrete needs continuous reassessment in the difficult actuality of the moment.

5

THE EMANCIPATION OF
OUR BODIES

Now I absolutely flatly deny that I am a soul, or a body, or a mind, or an intelligence, or a brain, or a nervous system, or a bunch of glands, or any of the rest of these bits of me. The whole is greater than the part. And therefore, I, who am man alive, am greater than my soul, or spirit, or body, or mind, or consciousness, or anything else that is merely a part of me. I am a man and alive.[1]

Any student of the conception of man in the Bible and in the tradition of the undivided Church must say 'Amen' to that. It is actually D. H. Lawrence writing an impassioned defence of the significance of the novel for generations that took his point, at least in their heads, while forgetting his explicit inclusion of the Bible in his broad perspective, and altogether lacking his informed conviction that it is 'really a book about man alive'. It does not, for the moment, matter that Lawrence proceeds from this position to others which not only professing Christians might find unacceptable. In his initial observation that 'we have curious ideas about ourselves' and in his insistence upon the need to overcome the dualism, not to say multiplicity, of our view of ourselves, he puts his finger upon the central difficulty of giving any satisfactory account of man, and consequently of offering him any really workable asceticism. It must be admitted that the difficulty has been a recurrent one within Christianity for reasons which are both psychological and theoretical. Every generation produces its instinctive Stoics and Epicureans, long before they begin to be reflective about the way they feel disposed to behave. More serious, from a theoretical point of view, is the fact that none of the philosophical systems which have influenced the way theologians express themselves can do justice to the subtle, unphilosophical unity of view about man with which the Bible presents us. The Christian disciples of Aristotle, who often delight in ill-founded jibes against Plato of which Aristotle himself would rightly have been ashamed, tend in practice to reach a no less overspiritualized account of the human situation than those from which they imagine they have emancipated themselves. Thus, in a controversy in which the intellectualism of the Latin West appears at its most odious, it is refreshing to find the fourteenth-century Greek writer St Gregory Palamas drawing the discussion back to what is undoubtedly a sound biblical and patristic starting-point.

> Brother, do you not hear the apostle saying: 'Are you not aware that your body is the temple of the Holy Spirit who dwells within us?' and again: 'We are God's house?' And God says, 'I will make my home amongst them, and I will move about amongst them and I will be their God'. How, then should anyone of sense think it unfitting that the mind should dwell where God is destined to have his dwelling? And how should God from the beginning have made the mind dwell in the body? Has he too, then, done amiss? People who say things like that, brother, talk like the heretics who say that the body is evil and a creation of the evil one.[2]

St Gregory must be allowed his point that here are theoretical difficulties which cannot be evaded though they commonly are, as Lawrence, who was obsessed by a closely-related intuition, maintains. That there is ultimately a question of Christian orthodoxy at issue here cannot be denied. St Thomas Aquinas may be permitted to state it, when he says: 'Our bodily condition is not the creation of an evil principle, as the Manichees imagine, but comes from God. And so with the affection of charity, by which we love God, we should love our bodies too'.[3]

It is easier vaguely to assent to this notion than to know in practice how to implement it since, as a contemporary French thinker, Merleau-Ponty, says, 'the experience of our own body discloses an ambiguous mode of existence'. Merleau-Ponty's statement of this ambiguity makes a serviceable framework within which to consider various aspects of traditional Christian ascesis. He says:

> The body is not an object. For the same reason, the awareness I have of it is not a 'thought'. That is to say, it is not something

I can take to pieces and put together again in order to form a clear idea of it. Its unity is always implicit and confused. Whatever it is, it is always something other—always sexuality at the same time as liberty, deeply-rooted in nature in the very moment of changing itself by culture, never closed in upon itself, yet never transcended. Whether it is a question of someone else's body or of my own body, I have no other means of knowing the human body except that of living its life, that is to say of accepting involvement in the action which passes through it and mingling with it. Thus I am my body, at least to the extent to which I have acquired one and conversely my body is, as it were, a natural subject, a provisional sketch for my whole being. Hence the experience of one's own body is the antithesis of that reflexive movement which disentangles object from subject and subject from object which only gives me the thought of the body or the body as an idea and not the experience of the body or the body in reality.[4]

With a subtlety that does no less justice to the body's complexity the great seventh-century master, Maximus the Confessor, thinks of the soul as endlessly transmigrating into the body, and the body endlessly transmigrating into the soul.[5] For the body simply as an idea or an abstraction the Bible equally has no place. With the vitality of the living whole the Hebrew of the Old Testament is so impressed that it has no proper word for the body, except when it is a corpse, something which is empty or hollow. It is what is left when the life is gone. When I am alive my body is quite properly *me* or, as Wheeler Robinson says, 'the Hebrew idea of personality is an animated body, and not an incarnate soul'.[6] The situation for the New Testament in general, and in particular for St Paul, is more developed and presents the greatest difficulties for the translator, as those who have to depend on translations alone need to remain aware.[7] Contrary to the impression that many people form on the basis of translations alone, St Paul has the very greatest respect for the body as essential to man's dignity. In order to grasp this point it is necessary to appreciate his use of the word 'flesh', which is not equal to that of the body, as his list of 'sins of the flesh' makes clear enough, including as it does things like idolatry, jealousy, and strife.[8] For him the essential contrast between 'flesh' and 'spirit' is not a straightforward one as between something material and something spiritual. St Paul's 'flesh' is not a physical substance such as one can cut with a knife. When in his letter to the Romans St Paul says that 'the mind that is set on the flesh is hostile to God', and that 'those who are in the flesh cannot please God', the context makes it evident that he does not mean that those who still lead a bodily life are necessarily hostile to God.[9] The kind of fleshiness of which he is speaking is plainly what we should call a state of mind. By changing one's state of mind one could be 'in the spirit'. To borrow a phrase of Professor C. H. Dodd,

> it is necessary always to bear in mind that by 'body' Paul does not mean anything material, but the organic principle which makes a man a self-identical individual, persisting through all the changes in 'substance' through which he realizes himself, whether material or non-material.[10]

Thus the New Testament leaves us with our attention focused on man as a vital whole, in whom body and spirit interpenetrate. The true sense of this elusive complexity, in which nothing is a matter of indifference, is one to which the great teachers must constantly help us to return. Without it the very conception of fasting or mortification as a part of Christian training, or indeed of any sane human living, is virtually unintelligible.

It is, then, in this very non-Greek climate of thought that we must understand the meaning of the answer to the tempter who suggests to Jesus in the desert that he should turn stones into bread : It is written, 'Man shall not live by bread alone'. Our Lord is genuinely hungry, but to the tempter he replies that man's life is not simply what in St Paul's language we should have to call a 'carnal' life. Although a bodily life, it is a life of the spirit. This answer to the devil is, however, a quotation and in the context of the Old Testament in which it occurs its true significance becomes clearer. The writer of the book of Deuteronomy is talking about the Jewish experience of wandering in the desert which must always remain, as it was for the Fathers, the symbol of what man's life as we know it is really about, the meaning hidden in the heart of its difficulty.

> And you shall remember all the way which the Lord your God has led you these forty years in the wilderness, that he might humble you, testing you to know what was in your heart, whether you would keep his commandments or not. And he

humbled you and let you hunger and fed you with manna which you did not know, nor did your fathers know; that he might make you know that man does not live by bread alone, but that man lives by everything that proceeds out of the mouth of the Lord.[11]

Thus being humbled, made supple, by hardship is connected with the manifestation of what is in the heart. It is by contact with the total reality of life and being kept down to the earth, even by a body that needs to eat, that man can discover his true nature. For 'everything that proceeds out of the mouth of the Lord' is not just the word of his revelation which goes forth. In Hebrew thought God's words are his actions; he speaks through events.

It is thus, following our Lord's own example, the belief of sound tradition in these matters that this is the purpose even of that discipline which is self-chosen: to open the heart to God, to awaken its awareness to the presence and action of God even under the most puzzling and deceptive appearances. In a manner that leads to a response of love the heart learns to live with the mystery of the apparent contradictions in which the bodily life already, in any case, involves it. This, it may be noted, is a very different task from that of cultivating the mind or of producing what is generally called 'a man of action'. It is, one may say, through choosing to renounce the resources of power which lie to hand under man's control that he opens himself to the experience that his true life, as fully human, has another and deeper source. The belief which makes this experience possible is to the devil, and even to many professing Christians, contemptible since its force is based on a faith and hope which, while not contrary to reason, transcend it. Yet it may well be asked how it is possible to prepare for properly Christian activity save by withdrawal to the presence and power of God, since all the means of that activity are essentially poor and simple. 'Take nothing for the road', our Lord tells the apostles when he sends them out. 'Don't take a staff or a beggar's knapsack. Don't take any bread or money. Don't have two shirts'.[12] And if not everyone can rise to such austerity, and is not even called to, only those who travel lightly-laden learn its more than human wisdom. There are no other convincing arguments in its favour.

But for its further comprehension it is necessary to be aware of the very positive setting in which primitive Christianity developed its attitude to physical austerity. The catacomb paintings of old Rome depict no mournful subjects. The bodies of the dead are surrounded with pictures of life and healing, and among the subjects which occur are little scenes of happy diners at a festival. While these may be intended to represent the Christian Eucharist, this is not invariably certain, and, in any case, there are always overtones of celebrations of another kind, endless holidays in good company. For the Christian fasting, whatever form of refraining it takes, precedes the banquet of God's presence and is the practical proclamation of a belief in the ultimate enjoyment of that which, like everything else about God in this world, can only be suggested by images for that which, in itself, is inconceivable. It is for this reason too that a properly Christian conception of self-denial is entirely consistent with an immense value being given to the body. Using the very Pauline vocabulary just discussed, Ignatius, the second-century martyr-bishop of Antioch, writes in one of his authentic surviving letters:

> The fleshly-minded cannot do the things of the spirit, or the spiritually-minded those of the flesh, any more than faith can do faithless things or faithlessness those of faith. Moreover, *the things you do in the flesh are spiritual* since you do them all in Jesus Christ.[13]

This theological paradox that 'the things you do in the flesh are spiritual' is in manifest harmony with the biblical conception of man's wholeness and is the clearest assertion of the belief that, in the reintegration of fallen man in and with Christ, the body is transformed with and by the interpenetrating spirit. In this theology the body is not the enemy of the spirit but a normal channel by which it expresses itself.

It must be admitted that the Christian record of more recent centuries has been by no means one of fidelity to these primitive perspectives. Particularly in the West, one of the unobserved consequences of the schism with the East was that, with the development of the scholastic movement, a schism between flesh and spirit was gradually established both in theory and in practice. Reinforced by the philosophy of Descartes and accentuated by the social results of the Industrial Revolution, this cleavage between the bodily and the spiritual has left us in our own period with a Christianity unbearably disincarnate. D. H. Lawrence, on whose mind the Bible made a profound and lasting impression, was only one of many who have felt the need to pass beyond Christianity in a desperate search for a reintegration that Christianity could and should have offered them. It is neither profitable nor necessary now to apportion exactly where the responsibility lies, but the fact is that, while orthodox Christians have gone on saying in their creeds that they 'believe in the resurrection of the body', St Bernard in the first half of the twelfth century is the last Western spiritual writer of undoubtedly major status to give that doctrine a clear and definite place in his vision of the meaning of the Christian life. It may well be thought that Western man in particular has now reached such a degree of psychological alienation from his body that to bid him fast and mortify his bodily life without helping him to change his attitude towards it is to try to push him further in a direction in which, left to himself, he must in the end inevitably accomplish his own destruction. While this lamentable state of affairs is clearly not the exclusive fault of professing Christians, their obligation to make a contribution towards the recovery of a true sense of the body is evidently a grave one.

There can be no doubt that this sense, for a Christian, is governed by his belief that man's destiny is the fulfilment of his God-given life *as a whole*. For this is what the doctrine of the resurrection of the body implies. Everything that makes me essentially what I am now, it asserts, will find its place in some flowering of my whole being in God which is beyond my present conceiving. St Paul is explicit on the sense of discomfort that we are bound to feel until this more than merely spiritual fulfilment is achieved. Of the many modern English translations of the New Testament probably only William Barclay's exactly renders what Paul is really saying when it makes him say: 'We too, even although we have received in the Spirit a foretaste of what the new life will be like, groan inwardly, as we wait longingly for God to complete his adoption of us, so that we will be emancipated from sin, both body and soul'.[14] If many Christians, like everyone else nowadays, find it difficult to make any sense of an ultimate fulfilment which explicitly includes the body, their difficulties are, it may be thought, largely imaginative. They are beset with the problem of collecting the bits and pieces on some strange day of general tidying-up and sorting-out. Why do they forget that they have within their ordinary experience a witness to the almost total irrelevance of particular raw materials to beings whose vitality enables them to replace their entire bodies every so many years, and yet remain always themselves? It is one of those daily marvels which St Augustine found more striking than miracles that the consumption of identical food at our meals should sustain the expressive individuality of such very different people. It could, naturally, be argued that the notion of the resurrection of the body poses a problem intrinsically more mysterious even than the results of the processes of digestion upon which anyone might ponder. In certain respects this is so, for the resurrection appearances of our Lord recounted in the Gospels describe a body capable of eating and being touched yet not, apparently, subject to the limitations of ordinary materiality. Yet, granted the survival of the vital spirit that evidently governs the ordinary processes of development familiar to us, is it really so extravagant to suppose that spirit, under circumstances and in a manner unknown to us, capable of acquiring a materiality of a significance as important for its completion as it is for its existence in the conditions we know? St Paul at least has his explanation for it all, as far as it will carry us:

> When you sow a seed, what you sow is not the body which it is going to become, but a naked seed, maybe of corn or some other grain. God gives it the body he has chosen for it, and to each seed he gives its own body.

So, he argues, it will be with us:

> What is buried in weakness is raised in power. It is a physical body that is buried in the ground like the seed; it is a spiritual body that is raised. If there is a physical body, there is bound to be a spiritual body. This nature, which is subject to death, must be clothed with the life that can never die.[15]

Those who cannot make the act of faith necessary to believe that this can and will happen must surely admit that it is a belief not unworthy of the strange nature of matter itself, at least as more recent scientific theory has been compelled to think of it; nor is it so very much harder to envisage. If in our own period 'the lovely, lively air' and all the sharp apprehensions of expressive human features no longer give so many people those intimations of immortality that they gave some of our seventeenth-century ancestors, the nostalgia for it is ineradicably there. It is, indeed, part of the anguish of Wilfrid Owen's memorable little poem about a young soldier just killed in the first World War:

Are limbs, so dear-achieved, are sides,
Full-nerved—still warm—too hard to stir?
Was it for this the clay grew tall?[16]

Everyone must return to himself some answer to this inevitable question in the face of the apparent futility of death and dissolution, however hard that answer may be to come by. The traditional Christian answer is not an answer suited only to the weak-minded and incurably idealistic, for it has repercussions upon life in the present, demanding enough to make the value it gives to the body something that can only be realized by the daily pursuit of a searching discipline.

When all the Fathers, in different ways but without exception, insist that the Christian life necessarily involves an alternation between action and contemplation, it is useful first of all to note that this view is one of the consequences of a humble and realistic acceptance of man's bodily condition. Even the theoreticians of a way of life on earth as 'spiritual' as possible always find themselves forced both by the Gospels and the plain facts of existence back to seeing their theories in the context of life as a living whole. As Ignatius of Antioch reminds us, even the things we do in the flesh are spiritual, and there is in fact no such thing in this world as a life of the spirit which is not also *in some way* a life of the body. It needs no argument to show that God has made it so, and experience confirms that we shall always live perilously if we do not look straight and true at what God has done, in this as in all other matters.

Not only should a properly Christian attitude to the body be permeated with a sense that the vital whole in *all* its aspects which makes a man 'a man and alive' will be of abiding significance, it must be an attitude which gives practical expression to the influence of the ultimate upon the here and now. Without this frame of reference all bodily discipline runs the risk of excess in one direction or another, or even of becoming an end in itself. Granted our modern knowledge of the relation between weight and health, for instance, keeping an eye on one's weight seems entirely worthy of inclusion among ascetic disciplines appropriate to sound living. Yet it seems that there are people who become so obsessed with this that they live to weigh themselves. Whether the motive for refraining be physical or spiritual—and the two are evidently not altogether separable—a sense of perspective is everything. We read

59

in the *Sayings of the Fathers*: Abba Anthony said: 'Some wear down their bodies by fasting. But because they have no discretion, it puts them further from God'.[17] God's intentions for man in relation to the ultimate are suggested in the formulation of one of the most fundamental laws of the spirit, the law of the sabbath. Like every other ascetic discipline, it needs a word of warning from the Gospels to remind us what it is really about: 'The sabbath was made for the sake of man, and not man for the sake of the sabbath'.[18] Of no ascetic discipline is it clearer from the very nature of the case that it is not designed for the disembodied. In giving man a permanent reminder of the needs of his spirit, God also reminds him how intimately those needs are linked with the needs of his body. The alternation between action and contemplation is linked with the alternation between work and rest. So much is this a law in which the world at large shares that it is, as it were, written all over nature. In the Old Testament it is commanded that the fields and the fruit-trees are to be rested, if they are to receive the blessing of fruitfulness.[19] This is the kind of wisdom that the rapacity of man is slow to learn so that, in our own period, he needs the unwelcome warnings of the ecologist that his disturbance of the balance and rhythms of nature may bring about his own destruction if he refuses to listen.

Within the primitive Christian tradition the sabbath law is apprehended in its fundamental spiritual significance. The Christian ought to do what God wants because God's laws are, as the prophets had wished, written on his heart. 'Nor', says Irenaeus in his *Proof of the Apostolic Preaching*, 'will he be commanded to leave idle one day of rest, who is constantly keeping sabbath, that is, giving homage to God in the temple of God, which is man's body'.[20] If organized Christianity eventually came to observe the cycle of Sundays and festivals in a manner which resembled Jewish sabbatarian custom, St Paul's explicit rejection of sabbatarian legalism[21] and the entire New Testament make it clear that no laws on the subject of work and rest can exhaust the Christian understanding of the true significance of the old command. Our Lord, while implicitly accepting the sabbath framework, is shown in frequent conflict with a merely legislistic interpretation of it. He, like his followers, healed and taught on the sabbath and permitted other breaches of custom, when this seemed right and reasonable. But it must also be noted that he saw to it that both he and his disciples withdrew from their public commitment from time to time for physical and spiritual rest and refreshment. He never behaved as though he were too busy for this, but his life and ministry, brief as it was, must be seen as an example of a life conducted according to its own inner laws. While the Gospels speak of pulling the ox out of the ditch, even if it does fall in on the day we intended to rest, they never deny that anyone who habitually and voluntarily ignores the inner significance of the law of the sabbath will suffer the old penalty of spiritual death, and be cut off from the people of God. In days as conscious of the need to do good to our neighbour as ours are, it often requires real faith to be true in a practical way to the spirit of this old law, and not to leave the other things undone. Yet even the quality of the service we offer our fellow men depends ultimately upon our willingness to live with this basic rhythm. Further, as the sabbath law reminds us, our body is in a special sense a determining factor in what it is desirable to try to attain in the life of the spirit.

Thus, although there may be general truths about the human situation, they apply to each person in particular. If it is part of the humility required in human living that we should take into account the determining factor of our bodies, then it is clear that, like the problem of holiness itself, this is not a general but, in each case, a quite unique problem. There is a delightful story which illustrates this point among the *Saying of the Fathers*. An evidently shrewd and humble old monk was visiting another, on whom sturdier men with tougher bodies had laid the burden of a severe regime as a cure for temptations that only grew worse as he grew weaker.

> When the old man heard this, he was vexed, and said: 'The fathers are powerful men and did well in laying these burdens upon you. But if you will listen to me who am but a child in these matters, stop all this discipline, take a little food at the proper times, recover your strength, join in the worship of God for a little, and turn your mind to the Lord—for this is a thing you cannot conquer by your own efforts. The human body is like a coat. If you treat it carefully, it will last for a long time. If you neglect it, it will fall into tatters'.[22]

There are always some people who need to be reminded of things like this. For, although God may have given us all a common calling to fulfilment, we are not now, and never will be, the same in spiritual or physical gifts. The touchstone of this factor in spiritual development, in so far as it is discussable at all is, it may be suggested, the 'chemistry' of the relation between our particular body and spirit. When we are considering the mysteries of God and the human spirit, we are, on the Christian view, considering the mysteries of two deeps that call to each other. For it is not God alone who is a mystery. We are mysteries to ourselves and to each other, and the body is an essential factor in this human mystery. From one point of view, indeed, the soul is nothing other than the body in activity. The point of view from which this can truthfully be said is that *empirically* soul and body are two different aspects of the same thing. Even if we include in our consideration those aspects of the human soul which make it something more than the vitalizing principle in man—which empirically it is—it still remains true that it is Peter and Paul, Mary and Anne, who are, on the Christian view, called *in their totality* to fulfilment in God.

We may even go so far as to say that it is this totality that we *are* that knows God, even before we begin to be reflective. It is commonly reported that St Thomas Aquinas suggests five ways by which one may validly conclude to the truth of the statement that a somewhat, whom all men call God, exists. But, in common with many others before and since, he also admits a sixth, where he says that to know God is, in a confused way, naturally given to all of us, in so far as what God is is man's fulfilment. For man naturally desires his happiness, and what he naturally desires, he 'knows'. But, he adds, this is the kind of confused knowledge which enables one to see down the street, as it were, that *someone* is coming, without being able to identify who.[23] Later, when he comes to examine this notion of desire in talking about human activity as purposeful, St Thomas concludes that man's final bliss can only be in some complete fulfilment of the capacities of the highest of his powers, his mind. But this conviction never leads even someone who is as much of an intellectual as he is away from the need to think about the body. For he is so convinced that the body is the means of the spirit's action that he teaches that there is no act, no matter how spiritual, in this world, for which the body is not, in some way, needed, even if its role be only that of supplying to thought the refined support which all thought presupposes. In this matter the empiricism of Aristotle appeals to him and he often quotes the Greek philosopher's observation that a sensitive body, with a subtle sense of touch, is the normal sign of notable intelligence.

To begin with, such indications are, naturally, merely signs of a latent capacity. No thought is possible in this view of knowledge, without a slow education of the whole body, beginning with perception, an education which we so often, unfortunately, neglect to continue into adult life. There are not, after all, so many people who, with or without spectacles, really see the world of things in its true sharpness with trained and observant eyes. A young baby starts out on this work of perceptual education by feeling and experimenting with the sensations of its own body. By this means he slowly constructs an image of his own body, and becomes conscious of himself, of his outlying promontories and distinctive possibilities. A process is starting, whereby soul and body contribute to each other's mutual awakening

This awakening, once it occurs, is capable of almost limitless development, but it never reaches a point where it becomes possible for the soul to be independent of the body. For it is not an isolated intelligence that thinks and experiences, but a man. Thus the body becomes not only the means of the soul's action, but also the source of its experience, and the channel for the expression of its inner reactions and life.[24] The signs of the nature of this life can never be permanently affected, as an actor can sometimes affect them by assiduous skill and practice. For in ordinary life the body tells a truth which is so unmistakable that it is almost impossible to make it lie. The twelfth-century Cistercian writers particularly notice this. As St Bernard says,

> When the truth shines out in the soul, and the soul sees itself in the truth, there is nothing brighter than that light or more impressive than that testimony. And when the splendour of this beauty fills the entire heart, it naturally becomes visible, just as a lamp under a bowl or a light in darkness are not there to be hidden. Shining out like rays upon the body, it makes it a mirror of itself so that its beauty appears in a man's every action, his speech, his looks, his movements and his smile.[25]

St Bernard is evidently thinking here of something more than the evanescent beauty of youth and innocence. It is the mature beauty of those who have climbed St Benedict's ladder of humility, a ladder which, as St Benedict says, has two sides into which the rungs are fitted, our body and our soul.[26] This ladder of ascent is like the ladder which Jacob saw in his vision and leads up to and down from heaven. Some people make the effective discovery that this ladder really has *two* sides later in life than they should, and sometimes through a personal crisis with which none of their previous training and resources have equipped them to deal. And it is only then—if they get through the difficulty as they should—that they are compelled to say like Jacob after his dream: 'Surely the Lord is in this place; and I did not know it'.[27]

In such a case, many would feel justified in saying that no one had ever really made them *see* the spiritual significance of all these things. Not only do a great number of 'spiritual' books seldom mention the body, but when they do they make us feel that they regard it as something rather indecent. The writings of even some of those who are venerated as saints are not always exempt from this criticism and can sometimes seem to inculcate a kind of life which is so much and so negatively a flight from the flesh that it is difficult to see its compatibility with sound Christianity at all. All through, orthodox Christianity has always maintained its stand against physical mutilation in the name of asceticism. But only the wise and genuinely brave and holy have seen that other kinds of human mutilation are possible. The difficulty in finding the balance is that the Christian life cannot be either a kind of materialism or a kind of angelism, and of the two the latter is often more tempting to the spiritually-minded and frequently deeply destructive both to themselves and to others. For it leads to what a singularly brave and good nineteenth-century French priest, Henri de Tourville, called 'a distillation of perfection, not simple but overstrained, an extract of all that was most particular to most unusual people. And then we are told that this applies to everyone'.[28] It is possible, as de Tourville saw, almost to kill oneself by persistent efforts in the wrong direction. All the great masters of all periods have had to rescue their disciples from this danger. It is, as St Benedict insists, part of the humility which God requires in human living that we should take account of the determining factor of our individual bodies, training them, naturally, but always within their particular possibilities. Thus the true nature of the spiritual equilibrium which God intends for each human being is something each must set himself to discover, in so far as this can be done by reflection, experiment and effort.[29]

If this chapter has dwelt upon all that is most positive about the bodily life in the sound tradition and shown the ways in which the body's needs must be met and stilled, this is because for Western Christianity of more recent centuries there has been an urgent need to redress a lost balance, as almost everyone recognizes. Yet, if our bodily life is an invaluable asset, it is also something that involves us in risk and it would be dishonest not to face that. Body and soul exist as an indissoluble unity in this world, but each has in its way an existence of its own, and neither is reducible to the other. The soul unites and concentrates, the body disperses and multiplies. The body-soul unity is therefore a unity of tension involving, in man's present condition, a possibility of conflict. What ought to be a conversation between them can become a mortal argument. This awareness makes some people so frightened that they aim, not at the virtue that would be appropriate to them, but at some ideal that would exempt them from the common lot of men. This is, inevitably, an illusion that must go before they can begin to grow as they should. The dignity of being a man in this world, as it is now, is that one can become progressively, under grace, the architect of one's own inner unity, once the nature of the work and of the materials with which it must be achieved have been accepted with humility. Normally this acceptance is a progressive thing, for the psychological personality which fits my individual make-up in its totality is not evolved at once. I shall not arrive at integration without passing through conflict. If, instead of realizing that it is precisely *in* the conflict, with all the fears and feelings of guilt and rebellion that will involve, that I must develop the virtues which calm the storms, I prefer to take to my heels and run, I shall be incurring a greater danger. The danger will be that the affective life, the life of feeling, which I should have integrated will become hidden and autonomous, and one day slay me with a sword of unexpected power. We should not imagine that God will let us off the harder road of the virtues which we ought to take, because we offer him the sop of what we imagine to be bodily mortification.

Mortification is only true and real when it is appropriate to the total context of living. St Basil, with characteristic penetration, goes straight to the heart of the matter in his answer to the first of a series of questions about fasting: 'The question does not seem to me to be rightly framed. For abstinence does not consist in refraining from material foods, whereby the severity to the body condemned by the Apostle results, but in the complete giving up of one's own will'.[30] St Augustine, like St Basil, correctly interpreting the thought of St Paul, equally insists that 'the man who makes the soul's nature the greatest good and rejects the body's as

65

evil, evidently desires the soul in a carnal way, and flies from the body in a carnal way. This gives the impression of being human folly rather than divine truth'.[31] In other words, the deepest conflicts can exist on a higher level than that of the organic affectivity which results from my particular temperament and constitution. There is, after all, a conflict between a 'carnal' and a 'spiritual' self, in St Paul's sense of those words, a conflict between egoism and generosity, which is commonly excited by and intervenes in the conflict that results more directly from the bodily condition. It is, one may suppose, in the problems connected with human love that the more exacting trials about all this normally occur, and it would be as well to take an honest look at those. They can sometimes save us from the fall of Lucifer.

6

THE ART OF ARTS

The flowers grow, and the sun it shines
The Earth is fully at ease;
Over the hills and vales the dew
Drifts from the sky in a breeze.

So it goes with the human heart
When it has ease and relief;
If it meets its dearest friend,
They laugh away their grief.

These happen to be stanzas from a sixteenth-century Danish song-book.[1] But something rather like them could be found almost anywhere in Europe at the same period, and they have an ancestry that goes back at least as far as the twelfth century, the period when it is normally thought romantic love as a notion first took popular shape. It would, we must remember, have struck anyone from the ancient civilizations of Greece or of China as odd that in these verses the word 'friend' should be employed indifferently of both the boy and the girl in the song. Women to look beautiful when young, and then to keep the hearth warm and bear children, to wait and to weep, this in earlier times would have been understood from Scandinavia to the Pacific Ocean. Thus St Augustine is no poker-faced Church Father when, reflecting upon the mystery of the creation of woman, he says: How much more satisfactory for the sharing of life and talk are two friends rather than a man and woman living together'.[2] He is simply stating what for the bulk of the time-span of human history would have seemed a truth so obvious as to require no more discussion than he gives it. Nor need we suppose of a man who had, in his time, kept a mistress and fathered a son that his acceptance of this point of view was due to an inability to respond sexually to women. It has taken us very much longer than most people realize to grow used to the idea of a woman as a genuine companion and to find it natural to suppose that the need of her companionship is the first and most obvious meaning of the observation of the Creator in the book of Genesis that it is not good for man to be alone. It may, indeed, even be wondered whether the influence, at a popular level, of the immensely important work of Freud has not proved to be profoundly retrogressive in this respect. For if he, more than anyone, has opened our eyes to the diverse ramifications of sexuality, he must also be regarded as bearing some measure of responsibility for our contemporary obsession with genital satisfaction. As an intelligent and witty woman writer in a light-hearted essay on middle-aged companionship has remarked, 'sex is so fashionable that no other form of intimacy gets a chance'.[3] It is thus also comprehensible that the criticism by the ablest of his disciples, Carl Jung, of the dogmatic status Freud gave his distinctly personal obsession, should be suffering what must surely be only a temporary eclipse. For it is not necessary to believe that Jung was right in everything he said to feel that he was entirely justified in his conviction that sexuality is 'an essential—though not the sole—expression of psychic wholeness'. Jung understandably felt that he ought to make it his 'main concern to investigate, over and above its personal significance and biological function, its spiritual aspect and its numinous meaning'.[4]

If, in Merleau-Ponty's phrase 'the experience of our own body discloses an ambiguous mode of existence', there can be little doubt that our sexuality is one of the focal points of that ambiguity, and that to try to reduce what, after fifty years of study, is still an inadequately defined area of our existence to a matter of deprivations, fulfilments and techniques is to renounce not only the true complexity of sexuality itself, but to close the door upon most of the more enriching possibilities of being human. It is probably only our contemporary preoccupation with sexuality as implying physical relations between men and women that prevents our acknowledging with the necessary frankness that there can be no personal relationship between two people, whether of the same or of the opposite sex, into which sexuality enters *in no way at all*, and that this state of affairs is as entirely normal as the inevitable involvement of the colour of our eyes and the shape of our bodies in everything we do. Our relationships, even when heterosexual, begin to take on the proportions of pathological difficulty only when the psychological polarity between male and female in areas other than

68

purely physical ones is either lost or destroyed, as it can be as well within marriage as outside it. It was probably St Augustine who first observed the vital significance of the characteristic masculine and feminine functions within one and the same personality and noted the possibility that, as in the story of the Fall, the one might betray the other.[5] It is precisely because, in the relationships we cultivate, our own inner equilibrium as well as that of others is always at stake that the concerns of the psychologist and the moralist inevitably overlap. It would in our own period be disastrous if the insights of the two disciplines did not benefit from each other. In fact it may even be said that traditional Christian morality has always implicitly required this cross-fertilization in so far as it takes it as axiomatic that no judgement about a particular human situation can be morally sound, unless the knowledge of the relevant factors that could and should be present is actually there. Today, required knowledge for an educated adult certainly includes an awareness of the more commonly agreed findings of the psychologist. How grave a deprivation it would be were some of the wiser insights of an older tradition to get lost and forgotten. For they often remind us of matters less central to the interests of the psychologist but no less vital to human wholeness. As a psychiatrist uncommitted to a specific school of thought has observed, 'in earlier Freudian writings one might be forgiven for assuming that the achievement of satisfactory heterosexual intercourse was the final aim of human relationship'. It may be added that this is perhaps the only view from the field of modern psychological studies which has really achieved popular currency, and there it is often accepted as the kind of dogma Freud gave Jung the impression of wanting to make it. Yet, as Dr Storr continues, 'if our view is correct, the achievement of genital primacy and the becoming an adult member of one's sex is not the whole of development'. Even within a heterosexual pairing there is 'a stage of development in which being "in love" is superseded by loving, in which projection is replaced by relationship'.[6] What the poems and songs of romantic love inevitably tend to celebrate is a temporary condition of bliss which often makes it difficult for being 'in love' to be superseded by loving. For *that* to follow and develop different arts and other insights are needed, as the high proportion of laments for infidelity in the song-books and in life testify.

There are immense disadvantages in the fact that the single word 'love' in English now has to do duty for discussing such a very wide range of experiences because it thereby becomes easier to avoid confronting the kind of differences which are already suggested by the larger vocabulary of Latin or Greek for talking about this subject. Yet there are also great advantages in beginning with the notion of love as a basic undifferentiated drive, as St Augustine concludes in a discussion of the vocabulary of love which, like so much he has to say on this absorbing subject, deserves to be the basis of a juster reputation than he normally enjoys among those who never read him.[7] St Augustine is not, of course, so foolish as to think we could ever catch and identify love in this pure, undifferentiated state. At the moment when we detect its presence, the instant it spontaneously declares itself, it has already taken on the shapes of desire or fear, joy or sorrow, which determine its relation to its object. The experience of the positive or negative aspects of loving, in one form or another, is as unavoidable as breathing if one is to be alive at all, and naturally far more determining. We may leave aside for the moment the moral implications of this basic observation of fact and note with the St Augustine of the *Confessions* the closely-connected notion of the pathology of love which he there calls 'weight'. It does not much matter that modern physics has somewhat upset the notion that light things invariably rise and heavy things fall because of something inherent in their nature which leads them to their proper place. It still remains valid to say that there is an analogy between gravity as a force and the spontaneous push or pull of love. 'My weight is my love: wherever I go, it is love that draws me'.[8] It is in these ways that Augustine makes us see how important it is to discern clearly what has happened to us, before we take up an attitude towards it. There can be no properly moral problems for anyone in whom this vulnerability to love is not operative, and those in whom it is inhibited at its source often have to be helped to experience the nature of what they genuinely feel before they can begin to lead a morally human life at all.

It is indeed because the drive of love is so basic that, even when it exercises its power in hidden and unconscious ways, it is always at work. St Augustine was as explicitly aware as modern psychology has made us that even where love goes unrecognized because it takes on twisted and clinically pathological forms, it is never quiescent.

Love cannot be idle. What is it that moves absolutely any man, even to do evil, if it is not love? Show me a love that is idle and

70

doing nothing. Scandals, adulteries, crimes, murders, every kind of excess, are they not the work of love? Cleanse your love, then. Divert into the garden the water that was running down the drain. Am I telling you not to love anything? Far from it! If you do not love anything, you will be dolts, dead men, despicable creatures. Love, by all means, but take care what it is you love.[9]

Only a single phrase has been omitted from this admirably compact little passage, to the import of which it will be necessary later, with St Augustine's help, to return. Clarity requires us first to see the essential point St Augustine is making. It is also the awareness of the need to make this same point that underlies the vehement defence of the use of the word *eros* in relation to God and spiritual things which occurs in one of the important books of the mysterious, early sixth-century Greek writer known as Dionysius the Areopagite.[10] It has sometimes been maintained in a widely-ventilated controversy in modern times that these two pre-eminently representative authorities of the undivided Church are the channels whereby a conception of love alien to distinctively New Testament and scriptural thought enters into and contaminates the Christian theology of love. Anyone who can seriously persuade himself of the truth of this view would appear to have disposed of the claim of Christianity to be of any relevance to life at all. For if it is really the case that there is nothing valuable in all the teeming life of the universe to redeem or transform what, it may be asked, can Christianity claim to do for us? It is, in fact, precisely because these two great exponents of Christian thinking believe in the transforming power of a kind of love which has its source beyond created things and is related to the fulness of human liberty that they can bear to take into account the power of a love which, transformed or not, drives everything on towards some destiny or other. Those who think they can escape the power of love in one or other of its forms are the most deceived of all men. Christianity simply believes that this is an area in which we genuinely have, and need to make, some choices. Let this stand for a first consideration from the tradition of the Fathers.

The notion of *eros* as a universal force, evidently active in mankind, and the aptest of images for the forces buried, as it were, in the deepest and least conscious inclinations of all other things is not the only element in this tradition which deserves our renewed attention. When the awakening consciousness of personal values and personal experience begins to exhilarate the liveliest minds in the West in the early twelfth century, inevitably love begins to be discussed again. One of the things that strikes the most coherent and articulate group of writers on this subject as they bend with renewed fascination over the old books is the element in the tradition which draws attention to the varieties of human loving. Since all these writers are directly or indirectly connected with the rapidly expanding Cistercian monasteries, their thought is easier to trace than that of the more loosely-grouped and elusive troubadours whose theories, sometimes a half-conscious parody of Christian thinking, are still matter for dispute.[11] St Aelred of Rievaulx in England, the young Benedictine abbot, William of St Thierry and, above all, the great St Bernard of Clairvaux pass on, in what would strike most modern readers as rather fanciful imagery, an observation that is by no means fanciful at any period, namely that there are several different sorts of loving and that these different sorts of loving, equally validly so-called, make different demands and create different expectations. They like to compare them to the five senses, touch, taste, smell, hearing, and sight, beginning, appropriately enough, with parental love compared to touch, a sense dispersed all over the body.[12] There is an accurate intuition behind this comparison, as we now understand better when the vital and all-embracing importance of the child-parent relationship for relationships of every other kind is more clearly understood. We shall certainly want to amplify and refine this scheme of the varieties of loving in the light of living in another context than that of the monastic life. But we shall need to retain its healthy regard for the connection between bodily life and all kinds of loving and ultimately, like St Augustine, for the crude passions upon which even the most spiritualized kind of love must inevitably work if it is not to be a pure illusion. It is to our great loss that we have forgotten that for the child 'fretted by sallies of his mother's kisses', if he is fortunate enough to begin that way, more possibilities of entirely authentic loving open out than many modern books ever roundly discuss in any such terms. It is, indeed, the very richness of these possibilities of development that makes Gregory Nazianzen say on one occasion: 'It seems to me to be the art of arts and science of sciences to govern a man, that most chameleonic and complex of creatures'. The phrase 'art of arts' was much in the minds of twelfth-century writers and thinkers too, but in other than Christian connections. For a licentious poem on the art of loving by the Latin

72

poet Ovid was being widely discussed and circulated again at that period. It was in deliberate allusion to this poem that William of St Thierry, eventually to be the friend and biographer of St Bernard, began a short early work *On the nature of love*: 'Loving is the art of arts', he writes, 'and the masters of it are nature and God, the author of nature'.[13] Arguments on this subject do not change much, though they use different language at different periods and have different authors in mind. William's opening sally is a direct rebuff to the claims of Ovid, more than once repeated, to be a master in the art of loving when what he really offers is a programme of excuses for what amounts to mutual seduction. But to return to Ovid, or to anyone else who makes such a claim, the retort that authentic loving is itself a complete education is to oblige oneself to explain what one means by asserting this. This William, in honesty, at once begins to do in his very next sentence, where he says: 'For love itself, an innate inclination from the maker of nature, love, I say, is itself the teacher, though those it teaches are taught by God, unless love's natural ingenuousness is enmeshed in alien attractions'. This is already to say a lot in a little. Its note of confidence in the wholeness that results from following the lead that accords with the intentions of the hidden God as they reveal themselves in the patient discovery of the needs and the true shape of loving is entirely characteristic of William. His thought, a fusion of all he had learned from St Augustine and Gregory of Nyssa, has a quality of penetrating lucidity and consistency uncommon in any century. He is no mere theoretician. William always writes as one who passionately believes in learning by living, and it is therefore not just theological principle alone that convinces him that love's authentic ways have in practice often to be fought for as we free ourselves, in an exacting school, of the impediments which prevent us from following our deepest and truest instincts. If he makes St Augustine's conception of love as a weight his own and shares an old view about the varieties of loving, it is because these notions explain to him what he experiences and suggest what he needs in practice to probe. Yet it is probably most clearly in St Augustine himself that we shall trace the meaning of that deep division in all the varieties of loving which makes us often alien to our true selves.

There is no aspect of the human situation as we have examined it in an earlier chapter that affects St Augustine more intimately and obsessively than that situation as it is exemplified in the common human experience of love. 'I cared for nothing but to love and be loved', he says of himself in adolescence and, as one who had tasted many of its most turbulent joys and deceptions, yet kept it the central preoccupation of his mature thinking, no one has a better right to speak of that canker in the rose, whose discovery turns many another into a cynic such as he himself never became. The choice of channels into which the basic drive of love may flow, to which we have already seen him referring in a plea for doing something entirely positive with our love, is the choice that underlies the conception of the two cities in that great work of St Augustine's maturity, his *City of God*. The two loves that have built themselves two cities are to be found throughout his thinking and in the *City of God*, as elsewhere in his writing, the temptation to identify the cities with anything other than that radical opposition in the human motivation of loving which they exemplify must be resisted. St Augustine's normal words for these two kinds of loving are charity and cupidity, and they are at grips with each other in every human society, including the Church, and every human being, including the holiest, while life in this world lasts. They are the application to the case of love of the consequences of the doctrine of the Fall which experience verifies. It is when we begin to love that the tendencies to disintegration within us appear. What starts by looking like relationship becomes the source of the sharpest conflicts and the bitterest divisions both with others and within ourselves if cupidity conquers where charity should rule. Since St Augustine's day these two words have become so contaminated by other uses that they neither of them satisfactorily explain the contrast he wishes to draw. It is a contrast he is at pains to clarify both in his discussion of the vocabulary of love in the *City of God* and elsewhere in his writings. He notes that love is a neutral word, but that cupidity is normally taken in an unfavourable sense. For him cupidity is passion or *libido* not, he is careful to explain, understood simply in a narrowly sexual sense.[14] We have noted earlier how for him the great sex-substitute, the desire to dominate, is *libido* in by far its most terrifying form. In a way, it is this untransformed and perverted instinctual drive as it expresses itself in lust for power over others that reveals the true face of cupidity and displays its intimate connection with pride. It is the capacity of love which ought to relate us to others, to the world and to God, when it has become supremely self-regarding and self-referring. Charity, by contrast, has its centre outside the self, and indeed outside every created thing, in the

74

ultimate mystery of God, who is the source of a share in a kind of love which, if it is allowed to transform the divisive tendencies of naked instinct, relates us to everyone and everything in a way that puts everything, including sex, in its right place. 'He is a man of upright and holy life', says St Augustine in his work *On Christian Teaching*, 'who sees things as a whole. He it is who has an ordered love'.[15] It is possible to present St Augustine's elaborate argument about ends and means in this particular book in a light which gravely misrepresents his profound appreciation of the delicate mystery of truly Christian love. We see better his capacity to grapple with a mystery like this, without betraying it, in the following concentrated passage from a work *On the Trinity*, which he was writing slowly over a period of about twenty years. He is commenting on the familiar words 'God is love', in a way which brings out love's humbling and reorientating character:

Let no one say: I have never known what to love. Let him love his brother and he will love the same love. For he knows the love with which he loves better than the brother whom he loves. Thus he can know God better than he knows his brother; better because more certain. Embrace the love of God and by love embrace God. This is the very love which brings together in a common bond of holiness all good angels and every servant of God and joins us to them and to each other and all of us to himself. In proportion, then, as we are healed of the inflation of pride, we become more full of love: and with what is he full, who is full of love, save with God? But you will say: I can see love and, within my limits, conceive of it, and I believe Scripture when it says that 'God is love', and if a man lives a life of love, he enters into the life of God; but when I see that, I still do not see the Trinity in it. But you do see the Trinity, if you see charity. And I will help you to see that you see, if I can; only let charity be present that we may be moved to some good. Since, when we love charity, we love one who loves something, precisely on account of the fact that he loves it, what does charity love that it too may be loved? For that is not charity which loves nothing, But, if it loves itself, it must love something that it may love itself as love. What, then, does charity love except what we love by charity? But this, to begin with what is nearest to us, is our brother. Let us note, then, how highly John the Apostle recommends brotherly love. To love your brother, he says, is to live in the light; it is to live a life in

75

which there is nothing to make a man stumble. It is clear enough that he makes the perfection of uprightness consist in the love of our brother: for he is certainly perfect for whom there is no occasion to stumble. And yet he seems to have passed over the love of God in silence, a thing he would never have done, if he had not intended God to be understood in brotherly love itself. And so when we love our brother out of love, we love our brother out of God; nor is it possible that we should not love with a love of preference that love whereby we love our brother. And so we gather that the two commandments cannot exist the one without the other. For since God is love, he loves God who loves love. But he must needs love love, who loves his brother. And hence a little later he says: 'For if a man does not love his fellowman whom he has seen, he cannot possibly love God, whom he has not seen'. And so let us not worry ourselves any further about how much love we ought to spend on our neighbour and how much on God; incomparably more on God than on ourselves, and on our brother as much as ourselves. And the more we love God so much the more do we love ourselves. So, then, we love God and our neighbour out of one and the same love; but we love God for the sake of God and ourselves and our neighbours for God's sake.[16]

This final sentence sufficiently indicates that St Augustine, like every sound theologian, believes that there is a laudable kind of self-love which can never be eradicated, our need of God being written into our very nature. But it is by no means the same kind of self-love as that upon which cupidity is founded, since the one opens us out, while the other closes us in. St Augustine went on growing in his understanding of these things to the end of his days and in the incomplete review of his own books he was making when he died he reproaches himself for having been a little too timid in his estimate of the good things of this world, when writing his book *On the Trinity*. It is not, he would now wish to say, to be turned aside from God 'to love a beautiful face to the praise of the creator that rejoicing in that same creator everyone may be truly happy'.[17] Here was final reconciliation for a man who certainly knew all his life what a beautiful face was.

It is in the light of these convictions and of this growing experience that love in a fully Christian sense comes to be thought of, particularly in monastic circles, as a kind of school in which every aspect of our personality is trained and developed. It is true that there are signs of timidity here and there, but the great figures are unequivocal. Thus Diadochus of Photike, a deeply impressive Greek mystical writer, who must have died about thirty years later than St Augustine, will say:

> When one begins to feel the fulness of the love of God, then one begins to love one's neighbour in the spiritual sense. For this is the love of which the Scriptures speak. For friendship which is according to the flesh is dissolved too easily on the least pretext to be found, since it lacks a spiritual bond.[18]

Here Diadochus indicates the inseparable connection that develops between the doctrine of Christian love and the doctrine and practice of friendship, another subject which, like love in general, had been of intense interest to the late classical world. John Cassian, a monastic contemporary of Augustine among the Latin writers, devotes an entire conversation to the subject of friendship in his series on the theory of the spiritual life. He is quite clear about the entirely positive spiritual help that each of us can be to the other when the love that links us is strong and genuine. But noteworthy are the remarks of the gentle Abba Joseph about broken friendships which had a good beginning.

> Their relationship began on a good foundation, but they did not seem to be equally concerned to hold to their original intention. And so their affection was of the kind which lasts only for a time, since it was dependent not on an equal strength of character, but on the long-suffering of only one. It is inevitable that, however generously and tirelessly one party holds on, the thing must be broken by the mean-mindedness of the other.[19]

This notion that all real loving requires courage and the kind of persevering willingness to grow which is not for the 'small-souled' is as vital for marriage as for any relationship in which sexuality necessarily plays a rather different part. But before we consider the implications of these views across the spectrum of our contemporary concerns, it is necessary to notice a little book by a twelfth-century Cistercian disciple of St Augustine, St Aelred of Rievaulx, which is in fact the only complete treatise on the subject of friendship by a Christian in the tradition of the undivided Church.[20]

It is clear enough that St Aelred was led to the subject of friendship by a strong personal inclination of temperament and he writes

77

as one who feels, like the two disciples on the Emmaus road in St Luke's Gospel, that he and the young man with whom he is talking will be joined by Christ to make a third, a feeling natural enough in one who shows every sign of always having been enriched by a variety of relationships. Like Bernard who, as we must see in a later chapter, believes that all spiritual love must inevitably begin as in some sense carnal, Aelred who certainly had to fight hard to feel secure with the acceptance of this fact, has attained the serenity of believing that what he fundamentally always most desired is indeed part of what God intends for the lives of those who feel as he does. His doctrine in the treatise on spiritual friendship is by no means something for the 'small-souled' or merely sentimental. It starts, as a section of an early work of St Ambrose suggested it might, on the basis of a short dialogue on friendship written by Cicero, which in the twelfth century was enjoying a renewed vogue. 'Friendship is an accord in benevolence and charity on things human and divine', Cicero had written. As St Aelred understands it, this implies an affection that shows itself in action amid the concerns of a shared life. This, as anyone can appreciate, leaves no room for empty idealism or merely verbal professions of love. St Aelred is as clear-headed as Diadochus of Photike about the kind of friendship 'which is entered into without reflection, never submitted to sound judgement or ruled by reason, swept on through everything by the impulse of feeling', and hence dropped as easily as it was begun. Yet even though the kind of relationship he is discussing clearly requires courage, honesty, and effort if it is to develop, Aelred cannot persuade himself that the young should be discouraged by their awareness of their weaknesses and their mistakes. It is, he says, already a great thing to attempt great things, and adds that in true friendship one travels by making progress. Realism simply requires one to recognize that real friendship is only possible between those whose lives, habits, and interests are alike and whose intentions are genuinely for their mutual good. It is thus not possible to have for a friend someone who has no respect for his own integrity, since it is mere folly to commit oneself to the keeping of such a person, which is what friendship does. As Scripture says 'a faithful friend is the medicine of life', and thus any expressions of mutual love, whether by word or gesture, ought to be compatible with a genuine concern for the true good of the other. Fidelity to this principle naturally demands an often searching personal discipline which is nevertheless in no way incompatible with a true warmth and spontaneity. St Aelred has little sympathy with those whose lack of generosity makes them want merely to play safe.

> I would say [he writes] that they are not so much men as beasts who say that one should live without being a comfort to anyone, taking no delight in another's good, causing no trouble to others by one's faults, loving no one, and caring to be loved by no one. Yet heaven forbid I should allow them really to love who think friendship is a business affair, only professing to be friends with their lips when the hope of some worldly advantage smiles on them, or who try to make their friends the minister of some vile practice.[21]

St Aelred thus dismisses mercenary and what he calls 'puerile' friendships, which are all emotion and unregulated feeling and insists that 'that man has not yet learned what friendship is, who wants of it any other reward than itself'. He readily admits that perfectly sound friendships may equally well begin on the basis either of mutual attraction or of mutual esteem, but thinks that each needs time to prove what it really is and to show what it can hope to become. Fidelity of the kind the heart longs for is naturally hard to find, but it is well worth waiting for it and being true to it when at last it has been found. It makes a natural stepping-stone to that love of God which offers to the open heart a completeness of the shared life for which the long and patient practice of loving sharing has prepared it.

Now it need scarcely be pointed out that all this tradition about the 'art of arts' was worked out in a primarily masculine context. Indeed, it has already been suggested that it is probably only as we approach our own period in history that it has become socially possible to begin to think of the relationship between men and women in terms of anything like the classical view of friendship. Yet nothing is more necessary than that this should be possible. History amply shows that sexuality alone is no basis on which to secure happy and lastingly fulfilling relationships, and much contemporary emphasis on sexuality is more aggressively male-centred than were any of the more despised attitudes of the past. It is, on the other hand, probable that the serious scientific study of the role of sexuality in human life as a whole will vindicate the primary importance of the traditional notions of what friendship involves as the surest foundation for happiness in marriage. If people do not really like or share with each other in any but physical ways, the link between them passes with the physical attraction. The expression of this conviction is not an attempt to underestimate the significance of sexuality in human relationships but simply to urge that it should be allowed to fall into its naturally subordinate place, even within marriage. The shared delight of male and female pairing is much wider in its range and much more deeply creative than commercial glamour about it suggests. But this is a discovery that can scarcely be made if some purely arbitrary criterion of sexual success is regarded as the condition upon which everything else in the relationship hangs. Outside marriage the familiar formula, whose parentage in St Augustine's 'cupidity' needs no demonstration, is even more perilous, particularly for the woman, whose psychology in relation to the 'art of arts' works in a different way from that of the man and is more easily and more brutally damaged by serious mistakes.

As for relationships between people of the same sex, it must now be freely admitted that many people appear to remain permanently incapable of emotionally involving feelings for those of the opposite sex, and that to regard this as a moral failure is as grossly to misrepresent the facts as it would be to attach moral significance to any other involuntary personal characteristic. There is no reason to suggest that such people cannot make something very fruitful and satisfactory of the relationships of which they do feel capable. But it is something quite different to suppose that compassion requires them to think that any and every physical expression of their regard for each other is thereby made permissible or advisable. Even in a heterosexual pairing in which friendship, and all that that means for life as a whole, has become the true criterion of the relationship, decisions will often have to be mutually agreed upon in which sexual considerations are quite rightly not the primary ones. Why should not this also be the case in a relationship between people of the same sex? Holy Scripture does not condemn David and Jonathan for embracing and kissing, and for sharing a love 'passing the love of woman'. But in consistently condemning the attempt between two people of the same sex to counterfeit the heterosexual relationship, it only insists upon the spiritual gravity of refusing to recognize the God-given limitations which, in this case, are actually built into the very physical form of the body. It is surely evident enough that what is really at issue in friendship in all its possible forms, whether between people of the same or of opposite sexes,

and what gives it its spiritual importance, is its profoundly formative influence upon the attitude of each individual to the mystery
of life as a whole. It must not be overlooked that, just as we are
born alone, so we must die alone, in the sense that both these
experiences are incommunicable, and that a way of loving that
does not help us to bear with this difficult fact and its consequences
cannot rightly be called love or friendship at all. Can anyone really
be helped to face the inescapable solitude and uniqueness at the
heart of every human life by a code of behaviour which habitually
tries to evade what necessarily has to be faced in the end? True love
must necessarily help us to become what, at least potentially, we
already are. It is the art of arts to achieve this for ourselves and for
others, an art in which every authentic aspect of our life and being
is inevitably involved. This is the reason why, although loving
relationships are, apart from what they are in themselves, the most
complete and searching kind of training there is, there are other
subsidiary disciplines which now deserve our attention. For without
resort to those the stability and maturity which true friendship
fosters and demands is always likely to be at risk.

7

DOING AND SEEING

There is no need to make heavy weather of the fairly evident fact
that there are two opposite tendencies at work in determining the
attitude of each of us to ourselves, to each other, and to life in
general. It may well be for constitutional reasons but, whatever the
cause, it is clear that, in ways he cannot help, the introvert tends to
be concerned with his own thoughts, feelings, and reactions to life,
while the extrovert plunges into action and is readily responsive
to and appreciative of external stimulus of every kind. Naturally no
one is the complete introvert for, as Carl Jung says, 'when you call
somebody an introvert, you mean that he prefers an introverted
habit, but he has his extroverted side too. We all have both sides,
otherwise we could not adapt at all, we would have no influence,
we would be beside ourselves'.[1] These things need to be noted, as
an older tradition has found it necessary to note them, especially in
relation to an overall view of what it is possible and desirable to try
to achieve in the development of our given personality. It is, after
all, perfectly possible to go very wrong in the attempt to apply to
ourselves even a sound theory, starting out with the wrong presuppositions and in quite the wrong way. Thus as R. D. Laing
notes, under the heading 'Children should be seen and not heard',
'The amount of "room" to move a person feels that he has is
related both to *the room that he gives himself and the room he is
given by others*'.[2]

Now there is one New Testament passage in particular which
appears to involve something of universal human significance, and
yet which often gets used a little like 'Children should be seen and
not heard'. It may therefore be useful, like most of the Fathers, to
find our 'room' in relation to it. The incident runs thus:

In the course of their journey Jesus went into a village. A woman
called Martha welcomed him into her house. She had a sister

called Mary, and Mary sat at the Lord's feet and listened to his talk. Martha was so worried about getting a meal ready for them that she was quite distracted. 'Master', she came up and said, 'don't you care that my sister has left me to attend to everything alone. Tell her to give me a hand.' 'Martha, Martha,' the Lord answered, 'you are worried and harassed about putting on a meal with a whole lot of courses. One will do perfectly well. Mary has chosen the best dish, and it is not going to be taken away from her.'[3]

This is one possible translation of the text of the Greek as it has come down to us, and its variants probably reflect an element of hesitation about the meaning which is doubtless best resolved, as here and generally in the tradition, by inferring that there is an intentional play upon the notion that, however urgent their need for their dinner, human beings also need another kind of food. The natural sense of the event is, in any case, clear enough. Martha and Mary, the extrovert and the introvert, have fallen into their normal roles. Each is simply being herself. Jesus is not going to make a great issue out of a small occasion and he is not going to allow anyone else to do so either. Thus he is gently quizzing Martha about a side of her character which does need to be seen in relation to life as a whole, where great issues often reveal themselves in little events. It is, however, equally natural that this scene should so often in the tradition of the undivided Church have been made the occasion for discussing the relative importance of all those kinds of engagement, duty, and effort which may loosely be classified as 'action', and those spiritual activities of reading, reflection, and prayer which may be referred to under the heading of 'contemplation'. It may seem surprising, in view of developments in Western terminology and theory of more recent centuries, that the Fathers, even those who owe nothing to each other's influence, are unanimous in their belief that no one ought to try to identify themselves with the tendencies which Martha and Mary symbolize, since everyone needs elements in the characters of both, as the psychologists, for their part, would agree. Discussing the priestly vestment with its chains of gold in his *Life of Moses*, Gregory of Nyssa says: 'The fastenings by which these ornaments are fixed to the arms seem to me to teach that the perfect life requires a combination of practical conduct and the exercise of contemplation, the heart being the symbol of contemplation and the arms of works'.[4] This single sentence may be taken as representative of the considered views of the Fathers as a whole, whatever scriptural symbolism they happen to be using to discuss these matters.

St Gregory the Great, among the Latins, would add an apt word of caution to those who would at this point feel free to develop theories about the relative value of the two kinds of living in total disregard of the predominant tendencies of individual character.

> In these matters [he says with a customary psychological shrewdness] it is above all things necessary to realize that the disposition of souls is infinitely varied. For there are some people so inactive by temperament that, if the demands of work fall upon them, they collapse at the very outset, while others are so restless that if they once stop working, they have only to work all the harder, in the sense that, the more time they have to think, the worse are the tumults of mind to which they are subject. Hence the need of the quiet mind not to open itself wide to unreasonable involvement in activity, and for the restless mind not to confine itself to the pursuit of contemplation. For often those who might have contemplated God in peace have succumbed to the pressure of business; while those who might advantageously have lived occupied in the service of their fellow men are frequently killed by the sword of their quiescence.[5]

This manifestly sane little paragraph is a reminder that whatever formula is found for the combination of practical conduct and the exercise of contemplation of which Gregory of Nyssa and all the Fathers speak, it ought to be one which is guided by an honest estimate of personal temperament and circumstances. It would be patently absurd to suppose that what is temperamentally and circumstantially possible for one individual is necessarily possible, or even always desirable, for another. Even the same individual may have different needs at different phases of his life and under different circumstances. We shall not have forgotten how Gregory of Nyssa notes that in an authentically spiritual life 'the most paradoxical thing of all is that stability and mobility are the same thing'. All these factors are regularly taken into account in the way the Fathers tend to see what is involved in the choice of 'the best dish'.

Put in the simplest terms, the little incident with Martha and Mary would seem to be drawing our attention to an ultimate matter in all human existence. Even the necessary preparing of a meal loses its properly human dimensions if the spiritual fulfilment of

84

man, of which the sharing of a meal is a part, is allowed to disappear from view. There is a relationship between doing things and seeing their significance which cannot be overstrained if life is not to lose its point and become a burdensome and meaningless labour. This may be said without fear of contradiction, even if we leave out of account the quite uniquely fulfilling significance implied in the conversation between Mary and the one whom she regarded as her Lord. It would naturally be dishonest to make such an omission since the scene involves unmistakable echoes of the Old Testament words that 'man shall not live by bread alone'. But some people will need reassuring that the story of Martha and Mary does not simply dismiss the realities of ordinary life in this world and has never been understood by anyone of repute to do so.

Indeed, if it were not too complicated to be useful, it would be possible to sketch a history of St Augustine's shifts of emphasis in the course of a life-long struggle not to lose his true sense of perspective about so vital a matter. Though easier to trace than that of many others, his would not be an isolated history among those of the spiritual masters. He who, as a young man, had believed and hoped that it would be possible to devote a major part of his energies to considering and dwelling upon spiritual things, to prayer, and to meditation, found himself steadily overtaken by the necessities of Martha. Early in his great work *On the Trinity* he comments on the words *Mary has chosen the best part which shall not be taken away from her*: 'He did not say that the part Martha was doing was bad, but that Mary's was the best, which should not be taken away. For the part which consists in serving need will be taken away when need is no more'.[6] In other words Martha's activity, like the need to eat, is determined by the fact of life in this world. This is not to undervalue it. When it is genuinely a yielding to the demands of the immediate situation it has in view that fulfilment in a relationship with God, of which Mary's preoccupation is already, however inchoately, a beginning. But St Augustine is also honest enough to admit that it is, in our fallen condition, not just the fact of bodily existence that makes some kinds of activity 'necessary' and even inevitable. We have seen in an earlier chapter how for him the word 'necessity' is often loaded with the force of our disintegrating compulsions. There is nothing to be done about these drives except enlist them in positive and constructive tasks. Hence for St Augustine, as for the Fathers in general, the life of 'action' includes the development of just these qualities which inner and outer stresses and demands require of us, making us gradually humble and integrated. 'Of course', he remarks, 'a man could wish it were possible, without enduring any of the labour which must be accepted in acting and suffering, to come at once to the delights of lovely and perfect wisdom; but this cannot be in the land of the dying'.[7] If there is in the mature St Augustine a wistful note of regret for the infrequency of the times of leisure and vision, this is not just a self-indulgent melancholy for the passing of so much that hints at an ultimate satisfaction without being able to give it. Experience has simply made him aware how easy it is to lose all sense of direction even in doing what is, considered in the abstract, good and useful, and how even a taste for that which gives life its meaning can be lost if one is not careful.

> This is why a love of truth seeks a holy leisure; just as the impulse of love undertakes an upright occupation. If no one lays on us a burden of this kind, we ought to give ourselves up to the search for and the contemplation of truth. But if the burden is laid upon us, it ought to be accepted at the need of love. Yet, even then, we should never quite give up our delight in the truth, lest we lose our taste for it and our obligations overwhelm us.[8]

Anyone who tries to follow this advice will realize that he can never have a settled formula for living but must keep himself spiritually responsive enough to see where the claims of true love lie. Whether he acts or refrains, St Augustine is arguing, it ought to be an authentic love that moves him. And his only chance of keeping that love authentic is by cleaving in his heart with a love of preference to ultimate truth. This does indeed seem to be the Christian message, whatever other influences may be discerned at work in its formulation. It does not choose between extrovert and introvert, but merely insists that each will only be fulfilled in what is ultimate when it is an authentic love which governs what they do. Thus St Augustine has pointed out in the preceding sentences that there is such a thing as a leisure which is merely laziness and a preference for contemplation which is merely selfish. Similarly, there is a kind of activity which is cut off from the springs of the action of God. Thus, whatever our personal character and endowments, the mystery of what we are must continuously confront the mystery of God in the maintenance of the right relation between doing and seeing.

It would, however, be to court disaster and frustration for the

inexperienced to confine themselves to a largely theoretical knowledge of the justice of these broad perspectives. It is especially the
masters of the monastic schools who are perceptively insistent upon
this. They point out what anyone at any period and in any circumstances can verify for themselves. There are some truths it is impossible to grasp, or sometimes even suspect, until one's heart is
freed of its compulsions by a specific training appropriate to one's
potentialities. Even sound insights get lost in the counter-claims
of the daily involvement unless they are progressively followed up
by application in the concrete. Both St Augustine's personal history
and his developing theory bring this out, in passing, clearly enough.
But a sharper delineation of this aspect of the relation between
action and contemplation may be gleaned from John Cassian.

> Spiritual knowledge [he writes] is twofold. First, practical or
> active, which consists in the improvement of one's way of living
> and the purgation of one's vices; and second, reflective or con-
> templative, which consists in the contemplation of divine things
> and knowledge by holy insight. Therefore anyone who wishes to
> arrive at contemplative knowledge must first pursue active know-
> ledge with all his enthusiasm and energy. For this practical
> knowledge can be acquired without the contemplative, but the
> contemplative knowledge cannot possibly be gained without the
> practical.... In vain does a man strive for the vision of God if he
> does not turn aside from the contamination of his vices; for *the
> Spirit of God flees from what is not genuine and will not stay
> in a body enslaved to sin.*[9]

The slight shift of emphasis in the meaning of the word 'active'
which is involved in an exposition of the thought of a writer whose
primary interest is in contemplation will at once be appreciated.
But, although Cassian's first interest is in the qualities of spirit
which are favourable to an authentic life of prayer, this does not
alter the fact that he sees these qualities as being able to be developed in a number of different ways of living. He is quite specific
on this point. Nor would it be just to him to represent him as being
only interested in the service of his fellow men as giving him an
occasion to develop the virtues. While making no secret of his own
preferences, he does not attempt to denigrate alternative paths to
union with God. Indeed, he attaches a far greater importance to
stability of purpose in the pursuit of each individual's sense of
personal vocation.

This is why it is profitable and suitable for each of us to try with all his might and main rapidly to attain perfection in the work he has begun, according to the line he has chosen and the particular grace he has received; and while he praises and admires the virtues of others, not to swerve from his own line which he has once for all chosen.[10]

There is a good deal more wisdom in this than many people, especially while they are still young, recognize. For, as Cassian observes by way of general conclusion on this matter:

It is an impossibility for one and the same man to excel in all the virtues which have just been enumerated. Men tend towards God in many ways, and so each should complete that one upon which he has fixed, never changing the course of his purpose, so that he may be perfect in whatever line of life his may be.[11]

Thus it is possible to see that in whatever way Mary's priority over Martha is understood in the accredited Christian tradition, it is never seen as a priority of one type of personality over another or of one way of life over another. All the masters insist, as the gospel story itself clearly does, that the really vital problem in the concrete is to get one's priorities right, and to keep them in view. Nothing else is spiritually maturing. To suppose that one has chosen 'the best dish', when one has only turned one's back on those indications of the call of God which come from one's own personality and circumstances, is the purest illusion. All agree that an authentic response to the demand for virtue which arises out of the situation in which one has by choice placed oneself is a precondition of the life of contemplation. For nothing else brings each of us the peace of heart which false claims can neither challenge nor threaten. It is in this sense, and only in this sense, that action comes *first*. It is, of course, hardly likely to do so unless some sort of insight already accompanies whatever effort we are making.

But this naturally leaves us with a very adult difficulty. Once freed of the romance in which we cast ourselves for a role we cannot play, and determined on the acceptance of the only one which would be really maturing for us, we are faced with the snares of settled habit and the solid difficulty of the limitations of the fixed path. It can only be said that the right relation between doing and seeing, action and contemplation, effort and repose, must be rediscovered every day and that this rediscovery is normally incompatible with the death of doubt about where the claim of the one thing necessary calls us. St Bernard, referring to the case of Job, says on one occasion:

> You see how even a holy man feels a grave uncertainty between the claims of fruitful work and the repose of contemplation and, although he is always occupied about good things, still he feels something like a sense of guilt, and seeks with sighs from moment to moment to know the will of God. The only remedy or refuge in such a case is prayer.[12]

Thus Martha, if she keeps herself sensitive enough, gets driven back to Mary's position.

The matter, as St Augustine saw, is no easy one, and anyone who puts it to the test will discover all its honest yet formative difficulty. Habits of mind and ways of living that are really appropriate to our particular case go a long way towards its resolution. But only on condition that here and there we take time to pause and consider alternatives whose attractions we know how to resist for the right reasons. Robert Frost's rider stops by woods on a snowy evening, saying to himself:

> The woods are lovely, dark, and deep,
> But I have promises to keep,
> And miles to go before I sleep,
> And miles to go before I sleep.[13]

8

WORK

Anyone who has, in a modern city, to try to live with the aware-
nesses which this book has so far been discussing may understandably be tempted to feel that a man who can stop by woods on a
snowy evening, even to decide to go on, is already in an unusual
and privileged position, and must carry away in his heart something
that it is harder to derive from dark openings in factory yards or
even dusk in public parks. Yet all that appeals to a merely shallow
and romantic sentimentality in such a reflection must be firmly
resisted if the problem it rightly poses is to be seen in all its seriousness. Ronald Blythe's *Akenfield: portrait of an English village*
(1969) is a recent and admirably documented antidote to the common supposition of some reluctant townsmen that country life is
inevitably shot through with intuitions of vision and meaning just
as, in its rather different way and for an earlier period, is Flora
Thompson's trilogy *Lark Rise to Candleford* (1954). Indeed, many
townsmen are infinitely more favourably placed to develop the kind
of sensibility which distinguishes the unusual writing of Flora
Thompson, who was born and bred with what she later described
as the 'terrible handicap' of country poverty in the seventies of the
last century. Her only biographer has said of her that 'what made
her different from the other children who shared her experiences,
but who found in them nothing significant or remarkable, was her
marvellously deep focus of observation'.[1] It is with the problem of
the development of such a 'deep focus' that this book is concerned,
and the background to that problem is inescapably another problem:
the problem of work.

It would naturally be an exaggeration to say that only comparatively recently in human history has work become a *problem.*
It has always been more or less articulately realized that if working,
like eating, is to be a human and hence a morally significant activity,
it must be seen as a factor—and very often a particularly large factor

—in the whole of life. At the very least, the moral effects of not working at all, or of working too much, or of working in the wrong way, have long been manifest in their human consequences and have been the subject of a fairly constant stream of incidental comment from preachers and spiritual masters over the centuries. But with the steady disappearance of the craftsmen and master workmen of whom the book of Ecclesiasticus speaks with such respect, as of those who make city life possible, work and its consequences have progressively taken on the character of a quite new and major human dilemma. The developing situation is brilliantly analysed from a Marxist standpoint in an essay by the veteran Austrian philosophical and literary writer, Ernst Fischer, whose outspoken condemnation of the invasion of Czechoslovakia has earned him, since its publication, expulsion from the Communist party. Starting from the words of Leonardo da Vinci that 'the works of men will lead them to their own destruction', Fischer observes that what Leonardo da Vinci prophesied became at the time of the Industrial Revolution a nightmare that could no longer be banished. Industry produced not only goods but crises, not only wealth but want. Their works overtook their makers. The way to freedom was barred by things. The world had become alien, and man a stranger to others and to himself. This alienation was the fundamental experience of the Romantics and Fischer quotes Shelley and Schiller, among others, in their expression of this sense of loss. The alienation of man from himself, Fischer continues, his alienation through the State and various institutions, cannot be treated in isolation. They have an inseparable connection with the problem of work. Hegel had appreciated the immense significance work acquires. Marx saw in it the distinctive mark of mankind. He can be quoted as saying: 'An animal is one with its activity. A human being actually makes his activity the object of his will and knowledge. Conscious activity distinguishes man completely from animal activity'. It is thus

> through his work, through his conscious deed, that man makes his own the raw material of nature and gives it the form he needs for his own life. As by this activity he works upon nature outside himself, and transforms it, so at the same time he transforms his own nature. He develops its dormant possibilities and brings the play of its forces under his control.[2]

Up to this point this analysis must command not only respect but a large measure of explicit agreement from an older tradition in regard to these things. This may possibly surprise those who have been brought up to suppose that Christianity is committed simply to a penal conception of work. Two general considerations from this Christian theological tradition deserve immediately to be urged. In the first place, it is necessary to notice that, according to the teaching of the Bible, work, in *some* sense, was from the very first an expression of a law of man's nature. It is before the Fall has occurred that we are told in the book of Genesis that 'the Lord took the man and put him in the garden of Eden to till it and keep it'.[3] St Thomas Aquinas follows the suggestion of St Augustine, made in the longest of his commentaries on Genesis, that the tilling and keeping of the garden was 'not toilsome, as it became after the Fall, but joyful *on account of the experience of the powers of nature*'.[4] The intriguing reference to the importance of *experience* in the delights of husbandry in Eden is original to St Thomas Aquinas. There is no way of determining from his Latin whether St Thomas has in mind the experience of man's own powers or those of nature in general, but it is certainly legitimate and consonant with the rest of his thought to regard him as referring to both. In any case, it will be clear from what has already been said in this book that in the view of traditional Christianity the powers of man, although impaired by the Fall, have not been destroyed by it and that, although the material things, upon which man must sometimes labour to subdue them to his ends, are often stubbornly resistant, *still* both the one and the other contain springs of joy which the creator has put there in the beginning, springs which have only become less accessible through the disintegration of sin. That there is, even after the Fall, a real, though hidden, possibility of joy in effort and work is a notion which will need to be retained in any sound view of what work involves.

This joy in the experience of the powers of nature is not unconnected with the fact that, as St Thomas says elsewhere, man is subject to divine providence in a more excellent way than any other creature. For he has his own quite real and vital share in the government of the world, that government which, in God, we call providence. Hence, in virtue of his rational nature, man may be said to be 'a sharer in providence', since he foresees his needs and provides for them, both for himself and for others.[5] This too, which is certainly implicit in the command to dress and keep the garden, is a part of man's natural endowment which is not destroyed by the Fall. It is, we may even say, pre-eminently in well-planned and well-conducted work that man exercises his own special kind of providence. If his developing techniques enable him to extend the range of the area over which this providence may be exercised, while doing less 'work' in the narrowly laborious sense of that word, this still seems to be within the authentic perspective of man's God-given nature. Yet it must also be noted that there is an important implication in saying this. Whatever extends the area of man's potential providence over things also, inevitably, extends the area of his moral responsibility. Our knowledge makes us answerable to our fellow human beings and to God in a more searching way. It is in this situation that the influences of original and personal sin become evident. For it does not follow that it is wise for a man actually to do everything he knows *how* to do. The dignity of being 'a sharer in providence' imperiously requires a growth in true wisdom proportionate to the complexity of the judgements that have to be made and the extent of their effects. It is in no vague or merely intellectual sense that the concept of wisdom is invoked in this context. The wisdom here referred to is not 'know-how'. It is that kind of knowledge about things which is penetrated with love and is a spiritual gift that must be sought in prayer, for it is under the influence of a living affinity with what is ultimate that genuine wisdom makes its judgements. This may sound like something too rare and exalted to have much bearing on most ordinary human enterprises. Yet a common mark of those who are profoundly and effectively responsible for the extension of our understanding of and our capacity to intervene in the processes of nature must be recognized. Such people are compelled to develop the human virtues which enable them to appreciate the limitations of what they know. Above all they tend to achieve an humility before facts not of their own devising, which is less often found in those whose knowledge is merely derived from that of others. These are already qualities not far from those of heavenly wisdom, as the Second Vatican Council acknowledged when it said that 'he who with humble and unwearied mind tries to penetrate the mystery of things is, as it were, without knowing it, led by the hand of God who, upholding all things, makes things to be just what they are'.[6] It is, however, so easy and so common for the far-reaching discoveries of a few to be put to dangerous and destructive uses by men of a rather different quality. The reason for this is closely connected with the situation which makes it hard even for those who are persuaded by a theory of work as a potentially ennobling activity to apply this theory in the context of the kind of work they find themselves having to do in order to earn their living. In an increasingly complex society, where defined and limited tasks fall into place in a structure, the blue-print of which fewer and fewer are in a position to grasp and determine, not only has the architectonic influence of the master craftsman almost disappeared, but the level of personal discretion required of the individual worker has often fallen below what is tolerable for an intelligent human being.

This is the apparent weakness of the older theories of work, including that of Marx, if they are understood to be directly applicable to any and every kind of work in the world as we now have to live in it. Ernst Fischer writes:

> If Marx says that it is work which makes man a man, it is not just manual work as distinct and reduced to an independent entity that is meant, but work as an overall process, creative activity, in which hand and head, speech, imagination, and knowledge combine, in which man anticipates the result of what he does and thus his own future, approaches himself from the starting-point of his project, finds himself in his work, discovers his capacity, develops and moulds his own being.[7]

This is splendid as a description of what perhaps often happened in the building of a medieval cathedral and what *could* happen under any conditions in which the participants were in a position to gain a view of their part in the whole. But how often does it, or even *can* it, happen on the assembly line in a great modern factory or in the offices of a great modern combine? It is in relation to this question that Professor Galbraith has poured scorn on what he describes as 'one of the oldest and most effective objuscations in the field of social science'.

> The identity of all classes of labour is one thing on which capitalist and communist doctrine wholly agree. The president of the corporation is pleased to think that his handsomely appointed office is the scene of the same kind of toil as the assembly line and that only greater demands in talent and intensity justify his wage differential. The communist office-holder cannot afford to have it supposed that his labour differs in any significant respect from that of the comrade at the lathe or on the collective farm with whom he is ideologically one. In both

societies it serves the democratic conscience of the more favoured groups to identify themselves with those who do hard physical labour. In fact the differences in what labour means to different people could not be greater. For some, and probably a majority, it remains a stint to be performed.... The reward rests not in the task but in the pay.[8]

This, as an observation about a situation of fact, would be likely to be confirmed by any representative collection of personal accounts of what their work meant to a large number of wage-earners.[9] Their mood is caught in a parody of a song of Marlowe by Cecil Day-Lewis, which dates itself as having been written between the two world wars:

> Come, live with me and be my love,
> And we will all the pleasures prove
> Of peace and plenty, bed and board,
> That chance employment may afford.[10]

The folk poets of more recent date still retain literary allusions to a vanished and more lyrical past, while embodying a more robust acceptance of urban life as their natural setting, even though it is a setting in which work, in the sense of employment for pay, remains an unresolved problem for so many. It is an encouraging sign that there are a few who see that the cure for the depersonalization and frustration which results from technological change is not necessarily an unlikely and impracticable return to rural conditions, where the same symptoms often resulted in the past from other causes. These insights are matched by warnings from specialists in various fields that we are passing rapidly through a period in which certain vital human choices *could* be made, and could equally well be allowed to slip through our fingers with gloomily predictable results in the onset of consequences it would be beyond our power to reverse. A recent and balanced account of computerization, its nature and the choices it poses, has this to say in its first chapters:

Computer technology, like any technology, nuclear included, is itself neutral, capable of both legitimate and improper methods of exploitation. The computer is not an electronic brain: but it can certainly be used by the unscrupulous to spy, control and manipulate.... Ordinary individuals are quite capable of blocking the improper uses of the computer. On the other hand we shall not reap the full economic benefit from the machine's valid uses without a good deal of ingenuity and hard work. And the first bit of hard work for most of us is to arrive at a broad appreciation of what the machine can and cannot do, has and has not done.[11]

Whatever Professor Galbraith may pertinently say, the use of the phrase 'hard work' in this passage would seem to be quite legitimate when seen in relation to any defensible expression of the human significance of work as drawing out and developing the capacities of man through his discretionary skill. Nor does the necessary sophistication of skill in this particular context put its satisfaction in a completely different category from those of the modern farmer or deep-sea fisherman, both of whom have to use physical exertion as well. That satisfaction for more than a privileged and controlling few is both desirable and possible in the world of the computer is firmly asserted in the concluding reflections of a book that goes far to explain to the lay reader where the areas of choice lie in what may appear to his inflamed imagination to be a vast man-eating trap.

> Why should routine duties not be leavened by more creative work, in planning or research for example? Why should there not be suitable personnel training and development programmes to equip junior and middle ranks for higher responsibility? The structure of responsibilities and positions which could emerge, far from being rigid and narrow, would offer the individual much more variety, interest and scope for self-development than he has at present. Rather than conflicting with the notional technically 'one-best-way' of the computer system it might substantially improve on it.[12]

All this is said with the frankest admission of the dangers with which our present situation is fraught.

> The main human risks of advanced computerization stem less from possible internal effects on staff structure and work organization than from their more general implications for the location and nature of major decision-making. Put at its simplest, a centralized computer system necessarily enhances the power of the central controlling group since it creates a monopoly of comprehensive information about actualities. In private business

this concentration of intelligence gives enough potential cause for concern. In government it is still more alarming.[13]

It would be absurd to pretend that one can ask the Fathers or the older Christian tradition direct questions on subjects like these. But it would be equally dishonest to maintain that a statement of the positive human value and significance of work can indeed be legitimately derived from this tradition if one is unwilling to admit that bold and even magnificent enterprises in human endeavour are not necessarily bad in themselves. To face what these enterprises in our own period involve is only to fill out in its vivid actuality the point made on an earlier page that whatever extends the area of man's potential providence over things inevitably extends the area of his moral responsibility. In their own terms, most serious writers on this subject concede this point and those cited here rightly insist on it. Further, Freud, who believed that most people hate working, and certainly held no brief for any Christian theories on this subject, was nevertheless convinced that men really *need* to work, even if not for a living. In *Civilization and its discontents* he wrote:

Laying stress upon the importance of work has a greater effect than any other technique of living in the direction of binding the individual more closely to reality; in his work, he is at least attached to a part of reality, the human community. Work is no less valuable for the opportunity it and the human relations connected with it provide for a very considerable discharge of libidinal component impulses, narcissistic, aggressive and even erotic.

Michael Harrington, who quotes this passage in his book *The Accidental Century*, has this useful comment to make on it:

Freud's really profound point here is that such activity would still be necessary, even if not for subsistence. Work, he says, does not merely discharge narcissistic and aggressive impulses; it can, when freely chosen, even be erotic, a 'path to happiness'. There is, Freud would say with scientific rigour, a labour of love. In it, man is united with reality and his fellow man, thus discovering some of his deepest satisfactions. And conversely, a man without any work at all would be shallow and sick and his narcissism, aggressiveness, and erotic energy could express themselves in subhuman and antisocial form. In this psycho-

97

logical analysis of the meaning of work, one glimpses the extraordinary ambiguity of the present moment. Abundance could be the prelude to bread and circuses. A degrading leisure would be society's substitute for a degrading work. On the other hand, there could be a new kind of leisure and a new kind of work, or more precisely, a range of activities that would partake of the nature of both leisure and work. This latter development will not simply happen.[14]

Everyone will be likely to feel a different sense of vocation with regard to what it is appropriate to do about this state of affairs and, in any case, will see before them different possibilities of involvement. But it is impossible to see how a Christian can exempt himself from helping to create the climate of thought in which the right decisions are made about matters which must in the end determine the quality of the life of the spirit of man and even his continued existence at all. What his broader perspectives could profitably be has already been suggested along lines with which much contemporary thought is clearly consonant. In those areas where he is still free to exercise a choice he may look more directly to an older tradition to suggest what his attitude for himself should be. He could well begin with the attitude implicit in the striking directive of St Benedict to the cellarer, or bursar, of his monastery, which tells him what kind of man he ought to be. 'Let him look upon all the utensils of the monastery and its whole property as upon the dedicated vessels of the altar. Let him not think that anything can be neglected'.[15] In a life which is lived with and for God and one's fellow men in a spirit of love, Benedict seems to be urging, nothing can safely be thought of as merely profane. The notion is as valid outside a monastery as inside one, wherever any properly human dimension of work is recognized. Moreover, if one is looking for a doctrine of self-discipline in relation to one's work and one's way of doing it, this very positive attitude is likely to prove more searching and more valuable than any rougher and more negative one. Human experience tends to show that an intelligent attention to detail, even in matters which appear to be trivial, develops and strengthens all kinds of qualities which may seem at first brush to have no connection with little things. A respect for the tools of living is a part of sound living itself.

Yet the reader will remember the question of the curse which God placed on the earth after the Fall, whereby the earth brings forth thorns and thistles and man must eat his bread in the sweat of his brow. It is indeed true that there is a condition upon which work can become a blessing rather than a curse. It must be undertaken in the belief that the attempt to conform to the original intentions of God for man will be one of the means of applying to ourselves the benefits of that reintegration which the voluntary suffering of Christ made and still makes possible, though never without some degree of suffering. Even technology does not dispense with the need for human effort and, though it may not always be physical in kind, it is not necessarily any the easier for that. Indeed, St Ambrose is explicit in bringing mental toil into relation with the curse after the Fall when, in the prologue to his commentary on the Gospel of St Luke, he writes:

That which was said to no other living thing was not said to man in any idle manner 'In the sweat of your brow you shall eat your bread'. For the animals that are irrational by nature the earth is ordered by the command of God to yield their food, but to man alone *that he might exercise his gift of reason* a life of work is prescribed.[16]

Undoubtedly the acceptance of the burden of work ought to go deeper than a mere readiness to endure what is physically hard and heavy, when necessary. A truly religious ideal of work must involve that degree of engagement of mind and heart which makes it genuinely human. This is not normally possible without both training and toil.

All these notions are connected with the struggle to return under our present conditions to God's original intentions for man, and so worthy of man's distinctive dignity. They are also, as Freud in his own way observed, a means of pacifying the desires and appetites which might otherwise pull us and others to pieces. This progressive pacification normally only results, among other sorts of effort, from work done with intelligence and insight, and so work which is fit to be one of the forms of our love. Work is not just something we have an inner need to do, in spite of our reluctance, and a social need to do, within limits. It is an essential part of our response to our own making in a world in which we can gradually discover that work and rest ultimately converge upon a point beyond our comprehension.

9

HOLY WARFARE

An honest appraisal of the problems raised by modern work, its methods, its setting, and its products, in the light of all that is most balanced and positive in the Christian tradition of earlier times may lead us to the admission of the previous chapter that an opposition between technology and the deepest needs of man is not, in itself, inevitable. But so far-reaching are the predictable consequences of unsound and inhuman decisions at a level over which there appears to be no adequate social control, and so insidious are the results already being felt physically and psychologically in a world in which the field of personal choices is daily narrowing, that it is difficult not to experience a profound sense of shock at the spiritual prospect before us. As all except the very rich and influential awaken to the realization that there are virtually no more deserts to flee to, and that the small trader and the self-employed workman at his bench offering a personal service of integrity find economic survival almost impossible, a numbness overtakes the heart like that which follows the death of a dear friend.

> And ghastly through the drizzling rain
> On the bald street breaks the blank day.[1]

Yet, whether it is for oneself or one's fellow human-beings that these frightening apprehensions overtake one, one slowly discovers that it is the intrepid courage and insight of the great Fathers of the past which has most to say to one's condition, a condition so like theirs in ways which the intervening years of change in language and social organization at first conceal. We must urgently recognize that a war is on and that it is not a war which can be fought with political and military weapons. Our only hope of human and spiritual survival lies in a victory which must take place first in our own hearts and then extend its influence to those of others. In this war, as St Teresa of Avila tells her pioneering group of nuns:

> It is most important—all-important, indeed—that we should begin well by making an earnest and most determined resolve not to halt until we reach our goal, whatever may come, whatever may happen to us, however hard we may have to labour, whoever may complain of us, whether we reach our goal or die on the road or have no heart to confront the trials which we meet, whether the very world dissolves before us.[2]

If one is going to die it is, after all, better to die to some purpose!

There is, it may be noted, one initial obstacle to be overcome in our thoughts if this desirable state of mind is to be achieved and maintained. We must resist the folly of supposing that the claims of the point of view represented by Martha in the Gospels can be answered on its own terms. It cannot. She can always find us more important and more urgent jobs to do. But let her once take complete charge of the situation and she will kill both herself and us, for she always knows all the answers. She is, in fact, unanswerable *unless* our Lord Jesus Christ and the tradition of the Fathers, into which St Teresa of Avila had entered, had justice on their side, and man is made for a relationship with God which is so necessary to us that, when need be, every other necessity must be put off that this one necessity may be satisfied. The sad thing about Martha in her kitchen is not, in itself, that she is there but that, being there, she has lost her sense of perspective. Instead of her work bringing her closer to God, which theoretically it *could*, it only makes her angry with and envious of Mary. If and when this happens, Martha has lost the sense of the meaning of work, lost the sense of what it is all for, and this sense must be fought for at all costs. It is for *her* sake that our Lord returns to her the reply he does. She can no longer let the Mary in her *be* Mary. Jesus is, in other words, insisting that it is not the Mary sitting at his feet for whom she has no time. It is herself. She must always feel justified by tangible results in what she does. She cannot understand the fact that love is enough, whatever form it takes. It is essentially Martha's voice which speaks in the person of the disciples who, seeing the woman pouring the very expensive ointment on our Lord's head in the house of Simon the Leper, say: 'What is the point of this waste? This could have been sold for a large sum of money, and the proceeds could have been used to help the poor'.[3] Our Lord does not deny this. He simply points to the time and the circumstances, and this is what the tradition we have been studying consistently does. It refuses to make an absolute choice between doing and seeing, between Martha and Mary, for such a choice is not possible in this world. Jesus does not make it, and we must not do so either. But, in order to help us make the concrete choices we have to make, the tradition asks us to look at these two aspects of our life in a theoretical manner so that we may get our sense of values right and then give this sense of values a practical recognition in the vastly differing circumstances of our individual lives.

It is clear that in these circumstances and in what we make of them both temperament and need have their part to play. But we must from the beginning, assert that the overall picture is a mystery, that it is, indeed, what the Cistercian, William of St Thierry, called 'the mystery of all the mysteries'.[4] It is hidden in that mystery of the destiny of all things of which St Paul is speaking in the opening phrases of his letter to the Ephesians. 'This purpose is finally to bring to their conclusion all the events of history, and to make of all things, things in heaven and things on earth, one perfect whole in Christ.[5] Our personal part in this mystery, into which we are moving, is different for each one of us. For it consists in what God has done and is doing, not only in the world as it affects us from without, but also in the world of thoughts, impressions, and feelings affecting us from within. In its totality it consists both in what we have reason to believe God directly wills and in what he merely permits. The latter is a very large area in those whose freedom permits them to make the gift of love or to withhold it at any and every level of their lives.

Before it is possible to talk about that level of living at which prayer is possible and, in a certain sense, as natural as breathing, it is necessary to become aware of one or two fundamental facts in addition to those we have already been considering. As our Lord Jesus Christ says, in the context in which he is talking about the taking up of each one's personal cross: 'What good will it do to a man to gain the whole world, if in so doing, he forfeits his own life? For what could a man give that would be an equal exchange for his life?'[6] This 'salvation', or saving of ourselves, which is what life is about, consists in a kind of losing. It consists in the taking up of the cross in so far as this means the denial of our egotistical selves by submitting to what really and positively *is*. This is always a kind of continuous death. It is a death to our own perceptions, to our own understanding of things, to our own merely private point of view, and it is a death we desperately need to die in order to live. But it is one to which we can only wisely and properly submit if we understand that the work of our saving is primarily God's work, and that in that work he will not fail us unless we insist upon making it impossible for him to succeed. It is precisely for this freedom of God's action in our lives that we have to struggle and pray every day.

This point suggests one way of defining the two factors which are operative in our lives. There is, one may say, a kind of growth and development about which we have nothing to do but let it happen. Whether in those special mysteries called 'sacraments' in the formal sense or in those uncovenanted mysteries with which every event and everything in the world confront us, God wishes to save us and nothing can prevent this, unless we do. Even the sins he permits us to commit cannot hinder this work and can sometimes unexpectedly further it, provided we are genuinely sorry for the evil we do, and ready to learn by it. Consequently we need to receive the mysteries in which God acts, of whatever kind they be, as humanly as we can. For, being by nature human, unless we act and live humanly in the light of our understanding of the divine likeness in us which we have earlier been considering, we shall deny the sources of our true life with every breath we draw. In other words, the basic forces of our life, as it wells up from our wounded centre, must be converted or turned into the paths which reintegrate us. This turning is both God's work and ours. It is God's in so far as, through sacraments and events, he wishes to heal us. It is ours, in so far as, in order to be healed, we shall have to respond according to our God-guided capacities, and in order to respond as we should we shall often have to struggle. Speaking in the most broad and general terms, the two basic forces in connection with which our life manifests itself are those of love and aggression. One way of discovering just where we are at any given moment is by taking an honest look at what our love and aggression are doing. Are they drawing us together, or are they pulling us apart? Even where we find that our love is genuinely engaged by and involved in worthy objects, is it a weak and inconstant love? And if it is weak, does this mean that our aggression is being dissipated, draining away in a merely negative anger against others or against ourselves, instead of being enlisted in the service of love, in the form of courage, patience, perseverance and fortitude, in a word, in those transformations of aggression that give true strength? The study of the ascetic life, is from one point of view the object of this book; the aim of the ascetic life is to release our basic forces from their frustrations and limitations and engage them in the wholly positive task of our fuller human development through the following of Christ who, as we have seen the Fathers saying, 'became human that we might become divine'. Our capacities for love and aggression ought to be coming to our aid in this transformation. But are they?

Let us face it: love, whether human or divine, if it is to be worthy of the name, demands courage. That the transformation of our capacity to love should be maintained and deepened is not really possible unless our spirit is growing in its ability to surmount the spiritual obstacles it meets, both within itself and in the world at large, and to face all its hardships with courage. This growth will normally progressively transform our aggression by the development of the virtues demanded in that struggle with the forces of evil which are always at work in the world, though our victory over them is already assured by the redeeming work of Christ. The concluding admonition of the letter to the Ephesians must sound strange in the ears of many modern people who have little or no real experience of themselves and have persuaded themselves that the devil is only a myth. Paul says:

Finally your union with the Lord and with his mighty power must give you a dynamic strength. Put on the complete armour which God can give you, and then you will be able to resist the stratagems of the devil. For our struggle is not against any human foe; it is against demonic rulers and authorities, against the cosmic powers of this dark world, against spiritual forces of evil in the heavens.[7]

It is only those who seriously take up the struggle with evil within their own hearts who also begin to find that, after all, they do not need to go on thinking every thought that comes, or yield to the suggestions of every emotion, and that this exercise of choice about their own inner life does not ruin their health but, on the contrary, releases their energies for different and more constructive purposes. They become aware, further, of how much the world is run by forces of which few are conscious, since they are often involved with those forces by yielding to their effects on beings who are continuously subject to the experience of physical and psychological change. It is not necessary to have any fanciful picture of what these cosmic forces of evil are, or how exactly they operate, to perceive that there are many morally evil effects in the world which betray an intelligent planning. These effects go well beyond anything which even the most evil of men could devise in their scope, though it is true the effects may escalate through that fatal mastery over the minds and hearts of men which is so much easier to obtain when people do not understand themselves. There is, in brief, no evidence which requires us to suppose that St Paul's description of the two inter-related factors of human and cosmic evil is outmoded by anything we now know of the complexities of human behaviour. There is, on the contrary, everything to persuade us that there is no crime we could not personally commit, given the right circumstances, though there may be some to which we are individually more inclined all the time. Nothing could be more dangerous than to forget that it is in our own hearts that the decisions about these things are made—unless it be the still greater danger of allowing ourselves to slip into an unconscious ritual identification with righteousness such as that which may be thought to characterize the warrior of Old Testament times. Be the illusion established how it will, it must be a peculiar satisfaction to the non-human forces of evil in the world either to get themselves dismissed as pure chemistry or as the easily identifiable enemies of those who never themselves have a doubt that they are on the side of the good. Whether he is speaking of the Christian as the athlete who 'disciplines himself' or as the soldier who puts on his armour, it is always of the mastery of the forces within himself by grace and ascetic effort that St Paul is speaking as the necessary condition for engaging in the heavenly warfare and 'keeping the rules of the game' that wins the victor's laurels. The man whose heart is not pure enough to 'discern the spirits' which speak to him, whether they come from his own powers or powers higher than his own will, will often be deceived when the devil appears as an angel of light, and he will be caught with his armour off.[8] Need it be said that the purity of heart which is here referred to is not sexual purity, but that purity which is true detachment from every corrupting and perverting influence? That all these are constant New Testament preoccupations requires no more substantial demonstration and, puzzling though some modern men may find them, they evidently have something to say about the subtleties of human experience which only a shallow mind could dismiss as meaningless. Some understanding of them is also necessary to see the direct continuity with them of the teaching of the Fathers of the desert and the spiritual masters of later times.

The desert wanderings of the people of Israel recounted in the Old Testament are already explicitly seen in the New Testament letter to the Hebrews as a symbol of the kind of setting in which the true inclinations of the heart are tested and decisive human choices made. This letter believes that only with the coming of Christ does true entry into the promised land become a possibility, and this land, like the desert of testing which leads into it, is not a physical but a spiritual reality. Now it was the devout third-century biblical scholar, Origen, who first fully elaborated this notion of the desert wanderings of the Jews as symbolic of the entire inner life of the spirit in his wonderful commentaries on the books of Joshua and Numbers. These commentaries are positive storehouses and sources of later monastic and ascetic teaching, and understandably they never ceased to exert their influence even when Origen's doctrine in other matters came to be treated with reserve and even disapproval. It is still possible to understand how Origen moved his hearers and fired the enthusiasm of his disciples. Near the beginning of his twelfth homily on Joshua, he says:

> We shall not fight, as the men of former times fought, nor will our battles be against men on earth, but against principalities and authorities, against the cosmic powers of this dark world. So now you know where you have to fight battles like this.[9]

The battleground, as Origen says in more than one place in the course of these homilies, is in the heart.

> When the Israel after the flesh read these identical Scriptures before the coming of our Lord Jesus Christ, they saw nothing in them but wars and the shedding of blood.... But later, when the presence of my Lord Jesus Christ had shed the peaceful light of knowledge in human hearts—for, according to the apostle, *he is our peace*—he taught us peace even in reading about wars. For peace comes to the soul if the enemies of its sins and vices are thrown out of it. Therefore, according to the teaching of our Lord Jesus Christ, when we read about these things, we also arm ourselves and bestir ourselves to do battle, but against those enemies which come forth from our own hearts, evil thoughts, thefts, lies about other people, blasphemies, and all the other

enemies of our soul that are like them. We try, as the Scripture relates, not to leave a single one of them alive if possible, or capable of reviving. For if we prevail against these enemies. we shall lay hold on the spiritual forces well enough and throw them out of that kingdom which they have set up within us upon the basis of our vices.[10]

Again he writes:

The battle you are to fight is within you; within you is that wicked city that must be overthrown; your enemy comes out of your own heart. It is not I who say it, but Christ.[11]

This may be an unfamiliar way of reading the Bible but it is one which the New Testament does not hesitate to use and it is entirely consonant with its spirit and meaning. It seems almost incredible that teaching as clear and forthright as this of Origen should of more recent centuries have been allowed to lie so long forgotten and unused. It burns with spiritual life and enthusiasm, yet there is nothing unbalanced about it. There is no question in this teaching of attempting to exterminate man's natural powers in this holy warfare. Consistently with the tradition we have been examining, it is rather a question of transforming those powers. Origen is quite explicit on this. He says:

We are not commanded to overthrow or exterminate the natural movements of the soul, but to purge them, that is to say to purge the stains and impurities which have come to them through our negligence and drive them out, so that the natural vigour which is proper to the soul and its native wholeness may shine out.[12]

Indeed, as he insists elsewhere,

Just as that one well which is the word of God becomes wells and fountains and countless rivers, so the soul of man which is made to the image of God is capable of containing and producing wells and fountains and rivers. However, in point of fact, the wells that are in our souls need someone to dig them out. They have to be cleansed and everything earthly taken away from them that those springs of spiritual sensibility which God has put there may produce pure and wholesome waters.[13]

Reduced to practical terms, what Origen is saying in these

passages is that the process of the soul's purification takes place in the course of that struggle in which the ordinary business of living necessarily involves us—provided, naturally, that we respond to the true demands of the occasion, and so let the transforming virtues take over and develop. In common with the great spiritual masters of all times, and also with the whole tenor of holy Scripture, Origen teaches that nothing, and one must insist *nothing*, in the providential government of the world is, as such, an obstacle to spiritual progress.

Meanwhile, we say that by a certain arrangement of the wisdom of God everything in this world is so disposed that nothing whatsoever is without its purpose with God, whether it be evil or whether it be good. But we shall explain more fully what we are saying. God does not cause malice. However, though he could prevent it when others do cause it, he does not. Rather, he uses the malicious for necessary purposes. For through those in whom there is malice he makes those who are moving towards the brightness of the virtues illustrious and seasoned. Unproven and untried virtue is not virtue at all.[14]

The whole story is, in fact, the story of a long journey, with many halts on the route.

For, before the soul comes to perfection, it dwells in the desert, where it can be exercised in the commandments of the Lord, and where its faith may be tried by temptations. Thus, when it overcomes one temptation and its faith has been tried in that, it comes to another. And so it passes as if from one stopping-place to another, and when it has gone through what happens there and borne it faithfully, it goes on to yet another. And thus by passing through all the trials of life and faith, it is said to have stopping-places, in which the growth in the virtues is every time the real issue, and there is fulfilled in them the saving of scripture; *they shall go from strength to strength*, until they come to the last, even to the highest stage of the virtues, and they cross the river of God, and receive the promised inheritance.[15]

As Origen goes on to point out, God attaches such importance to the idea of these stopping-places that they are actually listed by name twice over in the Bible. On the first stage out, the soul learns that it is going to have to live in a tent like a traveller, so that it may be ready to escape the ambushes on the road. Its virtues grow in its continual struggles with the forces of evil. It may require great courage and constancy to keep going:

> We cannot get through to the promised land, unless we go through bitterness.... The physician of our souls wishes us to endure the bitterness of this life in various trials, knowing that the result of this bitterness will gain us the sweetness of our soul's saving.... Do you, then, who begin on the way of virtue, not refuse to draw near to bitterness. For by it you will make progress, like the people of Israel. These are the labours by which the soul is healed.[16]

However strange and imaginatively exacting this classical way of talking about the development of man's spiritual capacities may seem, it well deserves a careful pondering by anyone who takes the most valuable human qualities seriously. For as John Cassian, writing in the early fifth century, makes one of his desert Fathers say, when talking about these general perspectives,

> a man who is travelling in the wrong direction has all the trouble and gets none of the good of his journey. It is true that the purpose of our profession is the kingdom of God or the kingdom of heaven; but the immediate goal or aim is purity of heart, without which no one can gain that end.[17]

It would clearly be absurd to maintain that these are thoughts which are appropriate only for monks. Everyone can profit by them. All the early ascetic masters are, in effect, speaking about thoughts as the patterns which suggest what we should do and become, and they all point out that it is not just thoughts which are obviously evil that make obstacles to progress in spiritual things. The greatest potential obstacles to prayer are often those thoughts of whose importance we are so egotistically convinced that they actually imprison and limit us, preventing the bigger world of reality from breaking in. If the devil is a great deceiver it is because in traditional theology he is seen as the one who is supremely deceived. His trust in what *he* sees with his powerful intelligence is so absolute and unreserved that it is the cause of his fall. Even the true thought of anyone, man or angel, who does not recognize the limitations of being only a creature and consequently, in the wider vision of the creator, the possibility of being deceived, is in potential danger and caught in a cause of stumbling. The more spiritual the thought the greater the possible fall. This is a critical dilemma in which anyone with any vision, in any walk of life, can be placed and to suggest that this notion is faithful to the thought of the Fathers is not to impose upon them something alien to their supposedly exclusively monastic categories of thought. There is at least one of the *Sayings of the Fathers* which is quite explicit on this point, and its opening words have already been alluded to earlier in this book:

> A brother asked an old man: 'What thing is so good that I may do it and live by it?' And the old man said: 'God alone knows what is good. Yet I have heard that one of the Fathers asked the great Abba Nesteros, who was a friend of Abba Anthony and said to him "what good work shall I do?". And Anthony replied "Cannot all works please God equally? Scripture says, Abraham was hospitable and God was with him. And Elijah loved quiet, and God was with him. And David was humble and God was with him. So whatever you find your soul wills in following God's will, do it, and keep your heart" '.[18]

The last, apparently innocent-looking, words are the really operative ones, and the man to whom they are attributed is one of those key figures in the development of Christian understanding who can never be faced in the honest realities of what we know about him without disturbing our minds with new insights. It is fascinating to notice how the latest explorer of the sites of those desert monasteries, of which in a very real sense Anthony was the founder, starts out with all the presuppositions of the most ordinary twentieth-century man and indeed retains them to the end, yet is won over with respect and praise for what emerges from the records about this remarkable man. He opens the estimate of what we can know about Anthony with the following apposite words:

> In this kind of world, run by greedy politicians, ambitious generals, avaricious tax-gatherers, and brutal thugs, Anthony stood out as a symbol of peace and stability, and even more, as the hope of virtue and sanity in an otherwise vicious and mad system. Where every other member of society, from the self-proclaimed emperors to the local administrators, was grabbing what he could at the expense of his fellow-men, Anthony took nothing and gave everything he had away. While most men must have dreaded the distant if not the immediate future so that

their lives were a series of compromises, Anthony feared nobody and compromised not at all.[19]

Anthony was, in fact and in symbol, a more important figure than even these and subsequent admiring words suggest. In point of time he occurs at that crucial period, spanning in a long life the second half of the third and the first half of the fourth centuries, when Christianity was slowly and unsteadily moving out of the days of political persecution into the rather different and perhaps more dangerous days of establishment. In his person he exemplifies an apparent contradiction which must always lie at the heart of an authentically Christian asceticism. This tradition appears to teach two diametrically opposed views of what the Christian life involves. On the one hand there is the view expressed by the great fourth-century theologian, Gregory of Nyssa, in the single phrase: 'The man who is informed about the divine mysteries cannot possibly be ignorant of the fact that the life which bears a likeness to the divine is completely in accord with human nature'.[20] On the other hand there is the clear teaching of the Gospels that the following of Christ involves the taking up of the cross, an imitation of Christ literally exemplified in the case of the first Christians to be venerated as saints, namely those who shed their blood in the witness of martyrdom. Anthony the Great had known and been in touch with the last generation of those whose faith had involved this form of witness and had, as Athanasius tells us in his unforgettable life of Anthony, deliberately exposed himself, like those whose courage and fidelity he so much admired, to the possibility of arrest and execution. His was to be the almost more exacting path of discovering how to be an authentic Christian in a less dramatic way. For, as Athanasius informs us in a telling and instructive phrase, 'when the persecution finally ceased, Anthony went back to his solitary cell; and there he was a *daily martyr to his conscience*, ever fighting the battles of the faith'.[21] The practical reality of this experience of fighting the battles that have to be waged in the heart was very different: both in its course, from that depicted in paintings from Bosch to the Surrealists, and in its consequences, from those imagined by anyone unacquainted with what those who knew Anthony observed about him. There is no more memorable statement of the result of the pursuit of human harmony through the daily martyrdom to one's conscience than that which Athanasius gives when he describes Anthony as he appeared when he emerged from the disused Roman fort where he had lived for so long:

> So he spent nearly twenty years practising the ascetic life by himself, never going out and but seldom seen by others. After this, as there were many who longed to imitate his holy life, some of his friends came and forcefully broke down the door and removed it. Anthony came forth as out of a shrine, as one initiated into the sacred mysteries and filled with the spirit of God. It was the first time he showed himself outside the fort to those who came to him. When they saw him, they were astonished to see his body had kept its former appearance, that it was neither obese from want of exercise, nor emaciated from his fastings and struggles with the demons; he was the same man they had known before his retirement. Again the state of his soul was pure, for it was neither contracted by grief nor dissipated by pleasure. It was not pervaded by jollity or dejection. He was not embarrassed when he saw the crowd, nor was he elated at seeing so many to receive him. No, he had himself completely under control—a man guided by reason and stable in his character.[22]

Gregory Nazianzen is clearly correct when he says in his discourse in praise of Athanasius that Athanasius is here describing 'the ideal of the solitary life in the form of a story'.[23] But this is in no way to discredit the account of a man who had known Anthony personally and whose witness is thoroughly corroborated by independent evidence on the matter. Athanasius certainly had a solidly-based case to make, and, as the inheritor of Anthony's sheepskin and cloak, he was also the inheritor of his ascetic convictions. Athanasius is surely helping us to see that here was a man following an admittedly most unusual path, and one quite different from the very busy and active road he had himself followed. Yet precisely because this particular path was right for Anthony—an authentic vocation—it produced the result which any genuine calling faithfully followed tends to produce. The road of true asceticism, the road of discipline appropriate to this man personally, the road of being 'a daily martyr to his conscience', leads Anthony back to his human wholeness. Although Anthony was pursuing a way of life which is meaningless outside the context of faith, he was obviously thereby becoming and remaining the kind of man whom anyone could recognize as entirely sane and normal, 'a man guided by reason and stable in his character'. Manifestly, not only was Anthony's vocation a quite special one, but so was the unusual quality of the result of following it. Yet it remains true that there will always be grounds for wondering whether a chosen vocation is genuine, or at least is being correctly understood and pursued, if it does not *in the long run* tend to produce a result like this. Nor would it be correct to assume that such results are normally achieved by accident. The secret, according to the unanimous words of the Fathers, lies in 'discretion', that is to say, in a balance of the elements from a tradition of doctrine weighed anew every day in a tireless personal assessment. It is the purpose of this book to suggest to the reader what the often forgotten elements in this tradition are. He alone can discover by reflection and prayer how they apply to himself.

It would, however, be a mistake to leave the question of the vocation of Anthony the Great with this general observation of fundamental principle. The entire tradition at all periods has recognized that Anthony's calling was an exceptional one. But this does not mean that anyone can afford to ignore certain important truths applicable to any life, to which it bears witness, and which are often not appreciated with sufficient explicitness. They may perhaps be reduced to four closely interrelated notions. There is, first, a profound truth in the conviction, which the hermit asserts in an extreme form, that there must be a separation between the Christian life and the life of what the New Testament calls 'the world', its ways of thinking, judging, and acting. 'The world' which is thus referred to is not the physical creation as such, but everything about the creation which results in it from the Fall, whether of angels or of men. It is all that is alive in moral separation from the kind of life and purposes for which it was properly designed. This perversion of life which is alienation from God leads to the state of affairs to which St John refers in the prologue to his Gospel, when he says of Jesus as Word of God: 'He was in the world and, although it was through him that the world came into being, the world failed to recognize him'. It is to this 'world' that Jesus, when he is standing before Pilate, says that neither he nor his disciples belong. 'Do you not know that friendship with the world means enmity to God?' St James asks the Christians to whom he writes.[24] Whether some physical expression is given to this sense of separation or not, it must always be there in the heart as an inescapable fact. With evil itself there can be no compromise, even though the disciples of Jesus may express their compassion with, and love for, those who may do evil, as they also do it themselves. It is, indeed, because 'the world' is inevitably also going to be at work in their own hearts that the Christians who decide to make a physical separation from the world will be in great danger of self-deception if they imagine that the spiritual separation with the world required of a Christian can be brought about so easily. When this sense of separation is genuinely present as a result of fighting the battles that have to be fought in the heart, it does not have to be explicitly asserted to be felt. Jesus got himself hated for what he clearly was, even when he was silent.

Secondly, and consequently, a Christian must be prepared to be an athlete and a soldier, fighting with the devil and evil in every form, not only in its external manifestations, but also in the secret places of the heart where, if evil holds sway, all bad actions have their origin. Now it is true that those leading a more active life than a desert solitary will be gradually purified and made true by developing the virtues that their life of activity requires of them. But they would be misled to assume that they can safely ignore the way of self-knowledge along which those leading a less externally exacting life ought to be walking. An authentically Christian life imperiously requires an alternation between doing and seeing, action and contemplation. It may further be remarked that those who burn up all the energies of their youth in pursuit of the active virtues are inevitably left without inner resource in their later years, when it will be too late to form new habits of thought and action. 'It is by faith that we have to live, not by what we actually see'. St Paul insists.[25] It will be impossible to keep an authentic separation from 'the world' if we make our own its tendency to judge everything by what it sees.

As a third point, and an implication of what goes before, it must be noted that the solitary life bears witness to the fact that a Christian life lived out in any form should be a steady return to that simple and intimate relationship with our maker which was once Adam's in paradise. Everyone needs to realize, in his own way, not simply in theory but also by experience, that the human heart cannot be satisfied with any created thing unless it has achieved its peace by resting in that which is beyond every conceivable hope and aspiration. This is, of course, to move still deeper into the mystery of the soul's hidden life with God, when that link with God, which is known only to faith, becomes the living centre of our lives. Yet it is a link which has been wont often to manifest itself in a harmony which extends beyond what is interior, as many old, and some fairly new, stories of beasts and saints declare. Such stories and experiences, confirming that the world is a happier and a more harmonious place where God's holy ones have walked are only reminders that the works of grace are never merely private but, like God's own generous and abounding life, freely shared with everyone. Gregory of Nyssa, talking on one occasion of the dances of King David after his victories, develops his thought in a striking image when he says:

> For a similar reason every victory over the enemy won with sweat and labour should be received with joy and dancing, since every rational creature shares in and sympathizes with the victors as in a ballet. There was a time when rational creatures made one corps de ballet, looking to one leader, fanning out from and whirling back to him.[26]

Finally, and also for everyone, there is the witness that the solitary life bears to the fact that God alone suffices. A good deal of frustration in human relationships results from a failure to recognize that there is an inescapable element of solitude in every human life, which not even marriage or the most intimate of friendships can invade. This is, indeed, something which each person must respect in themselves and in others as the most precious thing of all about them. It is something that cannot be given away, for in its ultimate depths there must be an aspect of every human soul which is virginal towards God. Most of the more terrible kinds of human unhappiness arise from a refusal to recognize this fact or the desire to evade it. It is the real root of each man's individual dignity, however, and the true source from which his greatest joy will flow, when the love of this unique love becomes fruitful at the level of his being which is accessible only to God. The Virgin Mother of God is thus seen as the type and the ideal of what each soul is meant to be, and not just those who are formally consecrated to virginity. This the Fathers clearly saw and explicitly taught. Thus, St John Chrysostom, commenting on the passage where St Paul says:

> *It was I who arranged your engagement to Christ as a chaste virgin bride to her one husband*, interprets him quite correctly when he says that in the context *all* Christians are being ad-

dressed for 'this belongs to all who are virgins in soul. For the incorrupt soul is virgin, though she have a husband'.[27]

The point is an important one since this virginity, like that of Mary, is meant to be fruitful. As Gregory of Nyssa says:

What happened in the stainless Mary in a bodily fashion when the fullness of the Godhead that was in Christ shone through her virginity, happens in every soul that is virginal. We know Christ no longer according to the flesh, but spiritually he dwells in us and brings his Father with him, as the Gospel says.[28]

St Simeon the New Theologian, at the end of the tenth century, will explain in a lovely passage:

The ineffable birth of the Word of God in the flesh from his mother is one thing, his spiritual birth in us another. For the first, in giving birth to the Son and Word of God, gave birth to the mystery of the re-forming of the human race and the salvation of the whole world—Jesus Christ, our Lord and God, who reunited to him what had been separated and took away the sin of the world; while the second, in giving birth in the Holy Spirit to the word of the knowledge of God, continually accomplishes in our hearts the mystery of the renewal of human souls.[29]

Thus, in summary, anyone married or unmarried, who lives with integrity towards God in the deepest level of their being may not, like Mary, bear the son of God in the flesh, but they can and do become, like her, both virgin and mother, and will be God bearers to mankind.

10

HOLY READING

It is a matter of no small moment that people who have followed the argument of this book up to this point should not be too dazzled by their prospects. They may have begun at last to see how the elements of the tradition of the undivided Church fit together to give at least one possible account of human experience and culminate in a vision of the development of man's spiritual potentialities which may suddenly seem to be new and exciting. But there is a long stretch of country to be travelled between the vision and the achievement. There are some who will see this at once and feel dangerously downcast. A few will feel healthily braced. Yet others will feel puzzled, trapped and frightened, or even deeply rebellious. One and the same person may at different times and in different moods feel each and all of these things and, indeed, normally will. This is therefore the stage at which to reassert a point upon which our reflections have, for practical and theoretical reasons, insisted from the beginning. Our personal dilemma, our particular involvement in the human situation is unique with a uniqueness that begins with our individual endowments of body and spirit. Consequently there should be nothing to dismay us about the fact that our personal salvation will have to be worked out in a unique way. In the midst of the common life of the children of God we come closer to each other and to God by the humble acceptance of that uniqueness which any real community of persons must *presuppose* before it can become fruitful and happy. An unrealistic optimism needs to recognize that it is not possible to have a relationship with someone or something with which one is completely emotionally identified. The very idea of relationship implies that one is not the other. Many a lovers' tiff turns upon the failure to acknowledge this elementary fact. The danger of moments of vision is that one may suppose that one has already arrived at the point to which one is only getting ready to set out. When the vision passes, one is left simply with the vast distance between two points, feeling utterly betrayed by what one saw, as though it were only an insubstantial dream. This chapter is concerned with what the tradition of the Fathers has to say about the business of measuring the distance between the dream and the reality.

For no sense of perspective, however true and persuasive, ever grips us with the force needed to hold us through every event and circumstance unless it is constantly renewed within us. If the tradition of Scripture and the Fathers persuades us of its substantial truth, we are still left with the task of finding our personal relationship to it. No one can relieve us of our personal responsibility for deciding to which of its voices we need most urgently to listen at any given moment. But, that we may be able to shoulder this responsibility, we need to to be able to hear those voices and attend to them when it is the right time. It is often assumed that there must be some secret about the life of the spirit which could be finally formulated and once for all learned. None of the great spiritual masters believes this, nor does the Church, in spite of the rare dogmatic formulations which enter into her creeds. Indeed, the creeds are meant to help us to keep intact in our minds the frontiers of the mysteries to whose living reality we must constantly return. It is for this reason that the creeds have never been regarded as a substitute for that picture of the total mystery of salvation which the Scriptures more obscurely and more diversely embody, and their place in the Church's liturgy and the teaching of her great masters has never been supplanted or fundamentally challenged. The instinct of the orthodox Christian can only assent to the truth expressed by a modern protagonist of the power of the primitive story when he says 'the word or dogma that claims sovereignty over the whole of the image and does not often and humbly present itself before the image for renewal, in the end imprisons us'.[1]

The traditional name for the ascetic practice of 'often and humbly presenting oneself before the image for renewal' is *lectio divina*, 'holy reading', in which the stories and images of holy Scripture inevitably hold an altogether privileged place. The mark of this position of privilege is that a fairly large library of books, often very different in style and purpose, which make up the Old and New Testaments, has come to be called in modern languages by the single name of *the* book, or the Bible. The original Greek word from which this title derives was a plural form suggesting the composite character of this book, just as the continued use of the plural form 'Scriptures' does. It nevertheless remains true that this library of books, seen and taken as a whole, is *the* book among books for the Christian and the man of prayer, since it embodies a vast range of variations on a central theme. Although we have often been referring to notions in that book and quoting passages from it, it has been useful to postpone an explicit consideration of our relationship to it since it is necessary to approach it in the right frame of mind if one is not to read it in the wrong way. This approach has already been implicit in what has been said so far. It must now be examined more directly.

This present book has been an attempt to bring to contemporary consciousness a sense of a living tradition and a living community of those who seek God from the depths of their being. If we have to use books in order to uncover that tradition and the sources of its life, it is necessary not to forget that those books, including the quite exceptional case of the Bible, are themselves, from one point of view, witnesses to the existence of a tradition and a community. Even the decision as to what books had a claim to be included in the special library which we now know as the Bible was ultimately a decision of the Church as a body, just as the books of the New Testament are, on their human side, the products of the life of the primitive Church and completely inconceivable without it. Only a deliberate perversity of mind can dismiss this point as trivial. The Church's belief that she was 'the new Israel'—an idea without which a good deal of the New Testament cannot really be understood at all—explains, in part, her interest in the sacred Scriptures of the community which was her spiritual parent. But, deeper than that, is the Church's belief, clearly enunciated more than once in the New Testament, that it is the same God who speaks through holy Scripture and who acts and intervenes now, as he is shown acting and intervening in the life of the old Israel. To say this is not to deny that there are even people who claim to be Christians who feel free to examine the Bible as though it were simply a book like any other. It is possible to admit that there are aspects of studies like these which may be profitable to the believer, while at the same time insisting that the attempt to study the Bible as though it existed, or ever had existed, in a vacuum apart from the living community of the Church is necessarily vitiated from the start. This conviction is firmly and moderately expressed by the Second Vatican Council when it says:

> Holy Tradition and holy Scripture constitute one holy reserve of the Word of God committed to the Church. To it the entire holy people, at one with their pastors in the teaching and communion of the apostles, cleaves, as it always continues in the breaking of bread and in prayers.[2]

One may, in other words, say that if the scriptural themes and images seem to live again in the teaching of the Fathers and spiritual masters of the Church it is because in them, as in all God's holy ones, what the Scriptures are really *about*, at the level of life, lives on. It is a very real insight into the meaning of this vital tradition of Christian living that makes a twelfth-century theologian like Hugh of St Victor normally include the writings of the Fathers in the New Testament. Not that he fails to distinguish between their writings and those of the Bible itself. For, as he says, the writings of the Fathers are not counted as part of the New Testament text 'since they do not add something further, but rather draw out the same things that are contained in the aforementioned books, explaining and treating of them more extendedly and openly'.[3] One has only to read Hugh's own writings, father and master as he was of a school of mystics and men of prayer, to realize that he sees himself and those he is teaching as living in the world of Scripture, since there is, after all, no other world to live in as far as the Christian is concerned, living, as he does, 'in the age to which all the ages have been leading up'.[4] It is in this and like phrases, that St Paul expresses the Christian conviction that the last age of Scripture is already working itself out in faith. Thus the Scriptures open upon the ultimate and the God of Scripture is not time-bound.

Thus, too, it is that the genuine Christian life is always a rediscovery of everything about which the Scriptures speak and a discovery of it, not as something written in a book, but as a living reality. Into something of this reality we have already been trying to find an entrance in this book, and for this reason the special role that the reading of the Scriptures has always played in the rejuvenation of the Christian life must be correctly appreciated. The context in which the Bible can alone be profitably read is in the living understanding of God's holy ones, so that a wider conception of what Scripture involves, such as a representative theologian like

Hugh of St Victor had, remains essential for us. In this connection it is not irrelevant to note that the primary sense of 'holy reading' for the Fathers was not that silent scanning of the pages in some quiet corner which the words suggest today, but their public proclamation.[5] There can, in fact, be little doubt that it is the loss of the sense of the unique power of the public liturgical reading of the word of God which has been a notable factor in the split between the religion of tradition and the religion of the book. The older tradition thought of the solemn readings as literally *breaking in upon* a man's private reflections and thoughts to speak to him and give him light. It is no accident of history that it was in church, during the public reading, that Anthony the Great heard the words which gave him his special vocation, as St Athanasius tells us. Anthony had, apparently, been reflecting nostalgically upon the simple communal life of the early Christians, as described in the Acts of the Apostles, and it was upon these thoughts that the Gospel being read seemed suddenly to make a direct comment. 'As though God had put him in mind of the saints and as though the reading had been directed specially to him, Anthony immediately left the church and gave to the townsfolk the property he had from his forebears'.[6] It is God, then, who suggests the thought taken, we must not fail to note, from Anthony's previous knowledge of the Scriptures, and upon this thought the liturgical reading makes an observation in which Anthony believes that God is addressing him personally. It is, no Christian can doubt, the fact that it is God who, in a very special sense, speaks in the Scriptures that enables them to address us directly in a way that no other books can, when our minds and hearts are properly attuned.

> So [Augustine advises his congregation] let us listen to the Gospel as though the Lord himself were present. And do not let us say: 'How fortunate were those who could see him!' For many of those who saw him also killed him, while many of us who have not seen him have also believed in him. The precious things that came from the mouth of the Lord were written down for us and kept for us and read aloud for us, and will be read by our children too, until the end of the world. The Lord is above, but the Lord of truth is here. The Lord's body in which he rose from the dead can be in one place only; but his truth is everywhere.[7]

There is implied in this passage a sense of the presence of God in the words of holy Scripture which runs through the thought of the Fathers and continues at least into the early Middle Ages. If this kind of presence was gradually obscured by a special awareness of the rather different kind of presence of Christ in the sacrament of the altar, it is enough to read some of the things the earlier writers have to say to see that these two kinds of presence were by no means mutually exclusive, but rather intimately interconnected in their minds. Origen is explicit on this in the third century. Trying to encourage a habit of attention to the smallest details in the sacred text, he says:

> You who are accustomed to be present at the divine mysteries know how you receive the Lord's body with every care and reverence, lest the smallest crumb of the consecrated gift should be dropped. You would think, and think rightly, that you were culpable if something fell to the ground through your negligence. If you use, and rightly use, such care about his body, why do you think it less of a crime to be negligent about his word than his body?[8]

Rupert of Deutz, an early twelfth-century abbot, clearly still moves in the same climate of thought when he says:

> As often as the Holy Spirit opens the mouths of apostles and prophets and even doctors, to preach the word of salvation, to unveil the mystery of the scriptures, the Lord opens the gates of heaven to rain down manna for us to eat. As long as we are going through the desert of this world, as long as we are walking by faith and not by sight, we need these goods desperately. We are fed in our minds by reading and hearing the word of God, we are fed in our mouths by eating the bread of eternal life from the table of the Lord, and drinking the chalice of eternal salvation. But when we come to the land of the living, to the blessed Sion, where the God of gods is seen face to face, we shall not need the word of doctrine, nor shall we eat the bread of angels under the appearances of bread and wine, but in its own proper substance.[9]

There at last all the mysteries are transcended in vision.

But, 'as long as we are going through the desert of this world', all the Fathers believe that we need these two mysteries of word and sacrament. The comparison between our situation and that of the old Israel is, as we have seen in an earlier chapter, rooted in the

New Testament conviction that the new Israel passes through the same saving experience as the old, to reach fulfilment in and through Christ. It would not be right to regard this as a poetic fancy. God does not change in the way he works. People at an Old Testament stage of development are apt to have to go through a very Old Testament kind of experience of God, and there are some ways in which each generation of Christians finds itself having to relive the entire experience of God's saving work as it is portrayed in holy Scripture, since Scripture is pre-eminently the place where God speaks to man about himself. The Fathers, in their virility, would remind us that if we only want the Bible for a bedside book and its God for a comfort, we shall never know the true comfort of the God who leads us through the rough and dry places of the desert and brings, if necessary, water out of the rock. Nor shall we understand man's need to pray and be silent before God, to suffer with Christ, and to follow him, unless we can bear to look at the picture of what man is and does as holy Scripture knows him. It is of the utmost importance that the Bible is an uncensored book. There is no blasphemy or impurity that does not find its place there, since we have to be able to see the human situation reflected there in its completeness.

> Holy Scripture [says St Gregory the Great] is set before our minds like a mirror, that we may see our inward face in it. It is there that we come to know our ugliness and our beauty. There we realize what progress we are making, how far we are from improvement. It tells of the doings of the holy ones, and stimulates the hearts of those who are weak to emulate them. For as it records their successes, it strengthens our frailty in our struggles against the vices. Its words have the effect that our mind is less afraid in its conflicts for seeing the victories of so many brave men set before it. Sometimes, however, it not only tells us of their virtues, but also reveals their falls. In the successes of the strong we see what we ought to aim at imitating; in their falls what we should fear. Thus Job is described as raised up by temptation, but David brought to the ground by it.[10]

There is, indeed, nothing more mysterious than the contrast on which Gregory is here pondering, that experiences apparently so similar should produce so often in different lives such very different results.

Certainly, part of the explanation lies in the kind of food with which the heart has been habitually fed. Abba Moses, in the first of John Cassian's *Conferences*, remarks:

> The movement of the heart may not unsuitably be compared to a mill worked by water-power. It can never stop working as long as the flow of water drives it round. But the man in charge can decide whether he would rather grind wheat or barley or darnel. It will undoubtedly grind whatever the man who is working it puts into it. Just so, the mind cannot be free of the trouble of thoughts when it is being driven on by the events of life and the streams of trials that pour in upon it. But which thoughts it should admit or provide for itself, must be its own attention and care to arrange. If, as we have said, we always return to our reflections on holy Scripture and go back to the memory of spiritual things, the desire for what is perfect and the hope of future happiness, it will be inevitable that this will give rise to spiritual thoughts which will keep our mind occupied with what we have been thinking. According to the word of the Lord, wherever the treasure of our occupations and interests lies, there too our heart will necessarily remain.[11]

This is clearly no casual or passive attitude to what occupies the central concerns of the human spirit, such as so many of the modern media of information and entertainment encourage. Never has the advice of a man like William of St Thierry been more necessary or more apposite than in an age like ours:

> Further, you should spend certain periods of time in specific sorts of reading. For if you read now here, now there, the various things that chance and circumstance send, this does not consolidate you, but makes your spirit unstable. For it is easy to take such reading in and easier still to forget it. You ought rather to delay with certain minds and grow used to them. For the Scriptures need to be read in the same spirit in which they were written, and only in that spirit are they to be understood. You will never reach an understanding of Paul until, by close attention to reading him and the application of continual reflection, you imbibe his spirit. You will never arrive at understanding David until by the actual experience you realize what the psalms are about. And so it is with the rest. In every piece of Scripture, real attention is as different from mere reading as friendship is from entertainment, or the love of a friend from a casual greeting.[12]

Taken seriously, how devastating a criticism such a passage is of many of our modern habits of reading, and even of much that passes for study, with its clattering and noisy apparatus and comparative indifference to real content. If, in our own day, we are to do 'holy reading' in the traditional sense of that phrase, nothing but conscious choice and the development of conscious habits of attention will be likely to cure us of a dissipation of mind that so much that we see and hear is designed to foster. As William of St Thierry goes on to point out, it is less what one reads than *how* one reads it that counts. It is an attitude of mind that is at issue. 'If he who reads genuinely seeks God in his reading, anything he reads will promote his good, and his mind will grasp and submit the meaning of his reading to the service of Christ.'[13]

It will be appreciated that the central concern of this chapter has been our approach to the reading of the Scripture.[14] But, as we see, by implication this approach must be able to be extended to any reading which deserves to be classified in a closely related category. Already, in the early eighteenth century the great Jesuit Jean-Pierre de Caussade, was having to say to a correspondent to whom he was sending a promised book suitable for 'holy reading':

> If you are to get from it all the good I anticipate, you must not throw yourself greedily upon it or let yourself be drawn on by curiosity as to what comes next. Fix your attention upon what you are reading without thinking about what follows. I recommend you primarily to enter into the helpful and sure truths you will find in this book, by cultivating a taste for them rather than speculating about them. Pause briefly, from time to time, to let these pleasant truths sink deeper into your soul, and allow the Holy Spirit time to work. During these peaceful pauses and quiet waiting, he will engrave these heavenly truths upon your heart. Do it all without stifling your interests or making any violent efforts to avoid reflections. Simply let the truths sink into your heart rather than into your mind.[15]

As early as October 1928, D. H. Lawrence, writing in an evening newspaper about the influence of *Hymns in a man's life*, was noting how the way we are now brought up tends to produce effects exactly contrary to those which the tradition of 'holy reading' seeks to produce, and which the foregoing letter memorably suggests. Although he was certainly unconscious of it, Lawrence's insistence upon the primacy of experience is authentically akin to what we have seen

William of St Thierry saying in the twelfth century. Lawrence writes:

> Now the great and fatal fruit of our civilisation, which is a civilisation based on knowledge, and hostile to experience, is boredom. All our wonderful education and learning is producing a grand sum total of boredom. They are bored because they experience nothing. And they experience nothing because the wonder has gone out of them. And when the wonder has gone out of a man he is dead. He is henceforth only an insect. When all comes to all, the most precious element in life is wonder. Love is a great emotion, and power is power. But both love and power are based on wonder. Love without wonder is a sensational affair and power without wonder is mere force and compulsion.[16]

Is it to be marvelled at that, in such a world, the expedition of the Kon Tiki and the exploits of various lone sailors have been followed by the avid and often envious eyes of those who no longer go down to the sea in ships or see the wonders of the Lord in the deep? For a moment, at least, such adventures awaken in everyone a capacity that each could and should realize as and how he can.

For it is not enough that we should have our experience only vicariously. Our sense of wonder, our God-given imagination, must in modern city life be consciously cultivated by whatever means are possible and authentic. Further, a poem or a novel will often be more likely to lead us back to the world of the Bible than many consciously 'spiritual' books, for the Scriptures themselves are poems and songs and war-cries and never desiccated theology. If, as William of St Thierry voicing the tradition insists, we are really to enter into what the Scriptures are about, then we must do anything we can to develop an affinity of mind with them, and consciously avoid all that deadens our awareness of reality. This, it need scarcely be said, we shall never succeed in doing if we go to our 'holy reading' merely as fine literature, splendid though the Bible and other great spiritual writings often are. It is *for* life that we need 'holy reading' and *from* life, even warped and alienated life, that we come to it. But it only begins to live in us when we take it back into life. If we start by trusting our imagination, we must go on to trust that to which, in images and metaphors, it leads us. St Bernard, in an Advent sermon, on one occasion says all this with typical and unforgettable succinctness, starting out from a sentence in the psalms which declares: *I have laid up your words in my heart: that I may not sin against you.*

But how are they to be kept in our heart? Is it enough simply to preserve them in our memory? To those who only do this the apostle says: *Knowledge puffs up.* And, further, forgetfulness easily obliterates a memory. You must keep the word of God in the same way as it is best to keep your bodily food. For this is living bread and the food of the spirit. While earthly bread is in the cupboard it can be stolen by a thief, gnawed by a mouse, or simply go bad from being kept too long. But if you eat it, what have you to fear? Keep the word of God in this way: for blessed are those who keep it. So let it be taken into the stomach of your mind and pass into the things you care for and the things you do. Eat what is good and your soul will enjoy prosperity. Don't forget to eat your bread, lest your heart should dry up. If you keep the word of God like this, there is no doubt that it will keep you.[17]

11

SILENCE

It slowly becomes apparent from asking the Fathers the kind of
questions which have a vital bearing on human living that their
views are neither so inflexible as they are sometimes reported to
have been, nor do they ever confront us with the kind of false
dilemmas in which Christians of lesser stature sometimes appear
to place us. Theirs is neither a holy naturalism, nor an empty-
headed supernaturalism. If anyone doubts this book's fidelity to the
spirit of the teaching of the Fathers when it cites their views beside
those of a writer like D. H. Lawrence, where they seem to echo
a common human truth, they would do well to consider the case
of two of the greatest of the Greek Fathers of the fourth century,
St Basil and St Gregory Nazianzen, who had taken up a quite
conscious position on this matter of principle. As young men they
had shared the advantages of all that a mixture of pagan and
Christian teachers in the contemporary university of Athens had
to offer. Nor did their subsequent definitive conversion to explicitly
Christian ideals lead them to a repudiation of all they owed to
secular learning. Not only did Basil later write a short work for his
nephews *On how to draw profit from the study of Greek literature*,
but Gregory Nazianzen, in a forthright passage in his memorial
discourse on Basil, voices the common convictions of them both in
their period of maturity and productivity.

> I take it that all sensible people agree that among human advan-
> tages education holds the first place. I mean not simply that
> nobler formation of ours which avoids ingenuity and show in
> speech and concentrates only on salvation and the beauty of the
> spiritual. But I mean that secular culture which the common run
> of Christians mistakenly despise as being a snare and a danger
> that turns us away from God. We ought not to dishonour educa-
> tion because people like this take such a view of it. But we should

regard those who think like this as uncouth and unformed people who want everyone to be like themselves so that their own deficiencies may be hidden in the common condition and their ignorance pass without notice.[1]

That Gregory's point needs often to be reaffirmed the consequences of its neglect have always convincingly shown. It would be as entirely unrealistic for a Christian in the twentieth century to suppose that he could safely dispense with the works of the creative imagination or the more exacting kinds of study appropriate to his mental capacities, as it would be to suppose that it will suffice if he merely prays for his neighbour without attempting actually to love him. Our examination of the tradition of the Fathers ought by now to have made it sufficiently clear that this tradition is quite unable to believe in a life of the spirit or a life of prayer that does not presuppose an authentic life of the virtues or disciplines which a full human life demands. The secret of a genuine spiritual life in this world, the young St Augustine will say in a fascinating work, *On Music*, lies in learning how to perform the rhythms of one's life without getting entangled in them. If someone has learned to do this, 'Would you not call him a great man and humane in the truest sense of the word?' he asks.[2] Similarly St Thomas Aquinas, in his concern with the life of reflection and contemplation, declares his belief in an authentic virtue connected with play, which gives the right place to 'that rest of the spirit which is delight'.[3] All these notions make sense in a context in which one has the humility to regard man's embodied condition as the expression of God's intentions for him, and they involve, like 'holy reading', a complete training for head and heart, for the imagination and all our human capacities. This training, as it begins to reintegrate us, already brings us close to the centre of the Christian life, which is the restoration of the living relationship of our spirit with God and our frequent intercourse with him in contemplation and prayer. The noise and distraction which our untrained powers have inevitably tended to make begin to be quiescent and we then sometimes find ourselves understanding things like the devastatingly honest note of the twelfth-century Carthusian, Guigo, who writes of himself:

You have become attached to just one of the phrases of the great song, and so you are upset when the wise singer continues his singing. The one phrase you loved is taken from you and others succeed in their order. For he does not sing for you alone, or in

129

accordance with your wishes, but his. The phrases which come after are unacceptable to you because they displace the one you loved in the wrong way.[4]

No one to whom thoughts like these never occur is likely to persevere in a life of prayer through all the changes of life or make progress in it. For part of the preparation for the dialogue of prayer is the development of the virtues of a good listener.

St Ambrose, who found himself bishop of Milan before he had had the time he felt he needed to learn what he ought to teach, begins his earliest work with some reflections on this subject.

> For there is but one true teacher, the only one who never learned what he taught everyone. But men have first to learn what they are to teach, and receive from him what they are to give to others. Now what ought we to learn before everything else, but to be silent that we may be able to speak? .... It is seldom that anyone is silent, even when speaking does him no good. He is wise, then, who knows how to keep silent. Further, the wisdom of God has said: *The Lord has given me the tongue of those who are taught, that I should know when it is good to speak.* Justly, then, is he a wise man who has received of the Lord the gift of knowing when he ought to speak? This is why Scripture is right to say: *A wise man will keep silence until the right moment.*

But Ambrose does not content himself with these rather moralizing reflections on the danger of speech as an occasion of sin and on the desirability of being, like Job, protected from the scourge of one's own tongue. He goes deeper and traces the problem to its very root. Quoting the opening words of Psalm 39: *I said I will guard my ways that I may not sin with my tongue,* Ambrose continues:

> Some ways there are, which we ought to follow: others of which we ought to take heed. ... Now, one can take heed, if one is not hasty in speaking. The Law says: *Hear, O Israel, the Lord your God.* It does not say: Speak! But, Hear! Eve fell because she said to the man words she had not heard from the Lord her God. The first word God says to you is: Hear![5]

St Ambrose does not, at this point, develop this very suggestive allusion to the Fall in connection with speech. But it is evident that

130

we must do so if we are to understand the importance that the tradition attaches to an attentive silence that is more than the merely physical absence of noise. We must first note that speech is, of its very nature, a mark of man's dignity as God's creature, in so far as it is the vehicle of man's personal capacity to know and love, in which his likeness to God, as we have seen, chiefly consists. But because of its intimate connection with all that goes on in a man's mind and heart, speech is, in practice, not only one of the means by which he reveals his dignity. It is also the first vehicle by which, whether consciously or not, he expresses the depravity which has resulted in him from the Fall, and normally from personal sin. Thus speech, as it were, either bodies forth harmony, if and where that exists within; or it bodies forth inner discord, if and where discord is found within. As a result of Eve's untimely word, man now says many words which he has not heard from God. This is more serious than a fanciful reflection. For man's words are often not only *not* God's word in the sense that many of them are contrary to the truth of divine revelation, they are sometimes also contrary even to that truth which God has in a different way spoken by creation, in man's own nature and in the nature of things in the world. The shrewd Carthusian, Guigo, notes: 'The truth is not to be defended, it defends. It does not need you, but you need it'.[6] And it is, indeed, certain that, until the work of grace and ascetic effort re-creates some kind of inner harmony based on complete integrity, the story of the Tower of Babel, where people were divided by their tongues, is fulfilled within each one of us. The voices of a hundred warring desires and impulses make themselves heard. We are nudged by vain fears and elated by false and passing hopes. St Gregory the Great has encountered the familiar situation:

> For anybody who either seeks what is forbidden or desires to seem to be somebody or other in this world, is inwardly beset with a countless throng of thoughts. While they stir up a host of desires in their heart, their prostrate spirit is ignominiously trodden by the feet of a crowded market-place. The mind which is disordered by a rabble riot of thoughts suffers, as it were, from over-population.[7]

This particular population problem is more difficult to solve than any other since, as Gregory makes us see, the trouble is less the confusion of thoughts than the compulsive drives that keep them going. The Stoic philosopher Seneca, to whom many Christian thinkers owe a good deal, writes something very similar in one of his letters:

> Here is what Socrates said to someone who was making the same complaint: 'How can you wonder your travels do you no good, when you carry yourself around with you? You are saddled with the very thing that drove you away'. How can novelty of surroundings abroad and becoming acquainted with foreign scenes and cities be any help? All that dashing about turns out to be quite futile. And if you want to know why all this running away cannot help you, the answer is simply this: you are running away in your own company. You have to lay aside the load on your spirit. Until you do that, nowhere will satisfy you.[8]

Incontrovertible reflections like these already shift our attention away from uttered speech to the more mysterious 'words' of the heart, those inward conceivings of desire whose clamour is sometimes loudest in those who try to ensure that they invariably have as much physical noise about them as possible. Such people do everything they can to avoid physical silence even for a matter of minutes. They instinctively know that there will, for them, be nothing in the silence but the unbearable shouts of their frustrations and the shattering disintegration of the false dreams that they strive at all costs to maintain against the tide of reality. Yet it is, naturally, one of the authentic purposes of outward silence, not just to be physically therapeutic, but to provide the occasion for facing the facts about our inward situation and for beginning to reduce the inner noise to a silence which is not just physical, but spiritual. The need to do this, like the reality of the situation described, has been widely recognized by non-Christian religions and philosophies and St Ambrose mentions the frequently reported belief that the pupils of the Greek philosopher, Pythagoras, began with five years of silence so that they should learn to speak by silence alone! In any case, the *positive* purpose of silence is inner attention to reality, to 'the voice of God', understood in the widest sense of that phrase. It thus includes attention to our own God-given nature, to the events which God causes or at the very least permits, to his voice in doctrine or scripture, or in the more mysterious voice of our own hidden prayer.

St Ignatius, the great martyr-bishop of Antioch, reminds us vividly in his second-century letter to the Ephesians of the primacy of *being* over activity, which is the level of thought to which these reflections inevitably lead us. As he says:

> It is better to keep silence and to be, than to talk and not to be. It is a fine thing to teach, if the speaker practises what he preaches. Now there is only one teacher who *spoke and it came to pass*, and the things which he did in silence are worthy of the Father. He that truly possesses the word of Jesus is able also to listen to his silence. Nothing is hidden from the Lord, but our own secrets are near him. Let us therefore do everything, knowing that he dwells in us, so that we may be his temples and he himself be in us as our God.[9]

The foundation of this possibility is, the Christian must believe, the entire God-wrought work of our salvation, not words, but deeds. As Ignatius says, later in the same letter:

> Hidden from the prince of this world were the virginity of Mary and her child-bearing and the death of the Lord—three mysteries to be cried aloud—which were wrought in the silence of God.[10]

To say all these things is not to deny what a common contemporary distaste for physical silence asserts, namely that there is such a thing as a silence which is sub-human and merely bestial. This is, after all, the only kind of silence which is left if physical silence is deprived of the dimensions to which this chapter has referred. These dimensions are always there for those who have the desire and the courage to discover them. It may indeed be said that, if there is one kind of fasting to which we need to find our way back as soon as possible, it is the right kind of fasting from too many words. Over-eating can be damaging to one's physical health and even be the proximate cause of death, as medical science often now reminds us. Talking too much is no less fatal to the life of the spirit. But, naturally, merely to stop talking is too negative a thing to do. A taste for silence is certainly an acquired taste, and one which is only acquired when its purpose is something entirely positive. Since the heart cannot be idle, a fruitful silence can never be the death of evil desires unless it is also the awakener of good ones. This is a notion to which St Gregory the Great loves often to return.

> For it is not our words that make the stronger impression on the ears of God, but our desires. Thus, if we seek eternal life with the mouth, but do not really desire it with the heart, when we cry out we are really silent. But, if we desire in the heart, even

when our mouth is silent, in our silence we cry aloud. This is why the Lord says in the Gospel: *When you say your prayers, you must go into your private room, and shut the door, and say your prayers to your Father who is in secret. And your Father, who sees what is done in secret, will give you your reward in full.* For, when the door is shut, someone prays in his private room when, while his mouth is silent, he pours forth the affection of his heart in the sight of the heavenly pity. And the voice is heard in secret, when it cries out in silence with holy desires.[11]

Such desires are, as St Gregory says in one of his sermons, hidden heavenly treasure. They are normally only found in the field of that genuine ascetic discipline which consists in the gradual restification of our compulsive desires and the freeing of our spirit from its illusions by large doses of the truth about itself and about things. This work of reducing our inner noise to meaningful spiritual silence is normally accomplished more quickly in people who have at least some opportunity of physical silence and solitude, provided they have been training themselves a little to know how to use it. Such opportunities can usually be snatched or found, once we really want or look for them. Even cities fall silent from time to time. There are, naturally, some people who declare that they long for silence and, when they get it, find it unbearable, since it confronts them with matters about themselves or about God on which they are not prepared to change their point of view. For them, and for many others too, it is often only through shattering experiences which seem to be the very antithesis of silence and destroy all their apparent peace that God, if he is allowed to do so, will bring an inner silence which is grounded in the simple truth accepted in love. It can be that only in some temptation or trial the spirit will discover what its truest desires are and at last be prepared to let everything else go. It can be that, before we can find our unobstructed way to God we shall have to face certain aspects of our own inner life which we have studiously tried to avoid or ignore until they force themselves upon us in a breakdown or in some circumstance from which there is no escaping. It is a happy chance thus firmly to be taken into the hands of God and out of our own, if we will consent to it. There is much evidence to show that these are the normal ways of spiritual growth for, as God says through the prophet Isaiah, his thoughts are not our thoughts, nor our ways his ways.[12] It may even be said that the more apparently 'spiritual'

134

the thoughts are, the greater often is the difference between God's thoughts and ours. The point is made with striking clarity by a great nineteenth-century French priest, Henri de Tourville, who helped many others out of the storehouse of his own sufferings. He says in one of his letters:

All souls who seek God with any great depth of desire, all of them, are more or less tangled up in their own aspirations. God means to be content with them for having carried their good will and their search for good thus far. But a time comes when peace establishes itself in a simplicity, humble, reasonable, and confident. It is then that God makes up for things by making the soul whose agonies he has accepted feel, I do not say his *consolations*, but his consolation. One understands that God is good and one never swerves from that position. It is exactly what happened to St Chantal when she met St Francis of Sales; it is what happened to St Teresa too. It is what will happen to you.[13]

It may be that some who read these words will realize that they are still a long way from having reached the point when the inner and outer voices are stilled and the spirit is brought to a deep and stable silence which nothing can really invade. Instead of giving way to incredulity or discouragement they might more wisely remember the words attributed by Bede to one of King Edwin's men when St Paulinus arrived to preach the faith of Christ:

When we compare the present life of man with that time of which we have no knowledge, it seems to me like the swift flight of a lone sparrow through the banqueting hall. This sparrow flies swiftly in through one door of the hall and out through another. Similarly, man appears on earth for a little while, but we know nothing of what went before this, and what follows. Therefore, if this new teaching can reveal any more certain knowledge, it seems only right that we should follow it.[14]

The voices of the Fathers, speaking to us of disciplines which lead to silence, are voices from a past which is also within us, if we are willing to attend to it. It will lead us to the brink of prayer.

135

12

PRAYER

Prayer, all the Fathers agree, has an intimate connection with life and experience. They are quite unable to see it as a special activity going along *beside* the rest of life and apart from it, as many Christians of more recent centuries have tended to do. Prayer is not a kind of optional extra, merely for those who have a taste for it. It springs up spontaneously under the very pressure of living and thinking. Thus it is unlikely that the reader of this book will not already have begun to pray, in some form, before reaching this final section, where prayer is more centrally our concern. But, at the same time, it is not certain that this will have happened since, as it will be necessary to see, spontaneity in prayer is not all there is to it. Hence, the method of the Fathers has been followed in an attempt to make explicit the sort of factors which may be obstacles, either in thought or living, to the kind of activity which prayer is. It will have become clear how positive are the purposes which the traditional ascetic practices are designed to foster. Yet, as with them all, it is necessary—and more than ever necessary—to insist that in approaching prayer, where the mystery of God and the mystery of man meet in discourse, we are venturing to approach a subject whose secrets cannot be mastered by some clever trick or by any amount of mental industry alone. All prayer, even that which is made with an effort, is a gift which must, nevertheless, be sought and waited for, until suddenly it is there. St Ambrose, among others, describes very well the sort of thing that happens:

If the soul desires it, if it longs, if it prays, prays unremittingly and without hesitation, reaching out undividedly to the Word, suddenly it seems to hear the voice of him whom it does not see, and recognizes the fragrance of his divinity in the depths of its being—a thing which many experience who rightly believe. The nostrils of the soul are suddenly filled with spiritual grace and it feels itself to be breathing the air of his presence whom it seeks, and it says: 'So, this is he whom I seek, whom I desire!' Does it not happen that when we are pondering something in the Scriptures and cannot find the explanation, in our questioning, in our very seeking, suddenly the highest mysteries appear to us.[1]

This notion of a close connection between 'holy reading' and holy living, the words of the one shedding light upon the darkness of the other, is an important one. For in this matter of prayer we shall never really learn or properly understand anything we do not try to take seriously with the whole of our being. Doctrine without practice is dead, and the only book which can adequately instruct us in all we need to know is the book of our life. This is a book into whose making written books and spoken words enter, but also many other kinds of 'words', which we learn sometimes painfully to listen to, slowly discovering how to spell them out from the things that God does or permits in us, in others or in the world at large. This book of our life with the mystery of God and ourselves is a book whose pages we can only turn one day at a time and we cannot go faster or further than the limits of each day lead us.

Not that life itself, which is apt to move by fits and starts, and even sometimes apparently to return upon its tracks, will bring us to the things of which we have already spoken, or have yet to speak, in the order in which they can usefully be presented for consideration. Life will rather, ever and again, insist on bringing to our notice some matter to which we really need to attend, either for the first time, or more closely, and rather differently, all over again. If we are so foolish as to imagine that we can refuse to attend to *what* we should *when* we should, we may well be held up in one place for half a lifetime. To say this is to say that things do not always occur in the same order in life as they do in our logical consideration of them. This is as true of our life of prayer as it is of our life as a whole. It would be an illusion to suppose that, if and when we begin to pray, we move in prayer through the stages and states of prayer as technical books describe them, starting, as it were, at the beginning and going on to the end. Indeed, it is much more normal that *some* of the features which appear in the theoretical schemes as belonging to the end show signs of appearing at the beginning, while little bits of the beginning come at the end. In brief, only one broad generalization remains true of any treatment of these matters, and it has been taken as the basis of this book, namely that genuine prayer is necessarily bound into and affected by the rest of our life as it actually is. It is, naturally, not an implication of this generalization that we can set our life in order first, and only then begin to pray. Rather, it implies that we cannot really pray now, as we need to, unless we are prepared to change what we see here and now needs changing in our lives. Moreover, we shall have to be prepared to discover that as we go on praying there will be more things that have to be changed, of which we have not yet become aware.

The same point is admirably explained and emphasized in somewhat different terms in the ninth *Conference* of John Cassian, where Abba Isaac says:

> I cannot enter upon the question of the effect of prayer or its chief purpose, which is the complete development of all the virtues, in a rapid survey, without first discussing individually and in order all those things which need retrenching or developing by way of preparation for it. According to the teaching of the gospel parable, what is needed for the building of this spiritual and exalted tower must be considered and assembled in advance. Upon the living and firm earth of our heart, so to speak, or rather upon the rock of the gospel, the firm foundations of simplicity and humility must be laid, so that the development of the spiritual virtues of this tower may be built upon.... For, if it stands upon such foundations, not only will it not fall, nothing will shake it, though waves of strong passion break over it, though wild torrents of persecution beat upon it like a battering-ram.[2]

Laying the foundations of evangelical simplicity and humility upon the living earth of our hearts is evidently not a matter of conning abstractions. We have to see how all this doctrine applies to us personally. For want of doing this, many people who read books about spiritual things and listen to talk about spiritual matters merely imagine that they desire or have even achieved the things that they find it pleasant or consoling to admire while they are thus engaged. We need not only to make quite sure that we keep our feet upon the ground from which everything in this world must grow, but also that we find the courage to discover our own modest but true way. Even though all are called, it is each individual alone who can know God and speak to him in prayer. The consequence of this relation to any theoretical considerations about prayer is, again, briefly expressed by Abba Isaac, where he says:

> I think that all the different kinds of prayer cannot be understood without great purity of heart and soul and the light of the Holy Spirit. For there are as many kinds of prayer as there are states' and conditions of any one soul, nay of every spiritual being.[3]

These two sentences speak, in fact, of the two poles of our prayer in its beginning, its middle, and its end, namely, the leading and teaching of the Holy Spirit and the nature and changing call of our own very individual soul. If we have dwelt at considerably greater length on the various factors, theological, psychological, and physical, which have a bearing upon our individual situation in spiritual matters, this is because these, though often obscure, are more accessible to our reflection than the movements and formation of the Spirit. This formation of the Spirit is necessarily more mysterious than any formation we can give ourselves, and it involves the entire theology of grace and the supernatural virtues which give us a share in God's distinctive kind of life, and have him as their source and object. We may, however, say that we have found ourselves concluding that the purpose of all our positive efforts, whether in thought or action, in the pursuit of the virtues, is to liberate our capacities and make us, in the depths of our being, responsive to the movements of grace whose horizons, being of their nature boundless, pass in their full significance beyond our ken. Thus, in spite of all that it would be possible to say on the basis of revelation and experience, it can never be too often repeated that there must necessarily be much about the way all these things work out in the concrete which remains unpredictable, even to the wisest of men. A modern Carthusian has written:

> Presence to oneself, faith in him who is that self's secret foundation and gives himself there, silence to everything that is not him in order to be wholly his, that is preparation for prayer. Naturally, such a state of soul does not come about without being itself prepared for by an entire range of circumstances. It is this we do not sufficiently grasp in practice. One prepares oneself for prayer by leading a divine life, and the prayer is, in the long run, that divine life. Everything which conforms us to the image of God, everything which leads us beyond and above the created, every sacrifice which detaches us from it, every glimpse of faith

which shows us in any being him who is, every movement of true, selfless love which puts us in harmony with the Three in One, all that is prayer and prepares us for a more intimate prayer. In us, as in God, there are many rooms. God dwells in the innermost, the most secret. It is there in us, but by sin we left it. Since then, God is in us, but we are no longer there, the preparation for prayer consists in returning there. One must close the door to that which is not, and enter into him who is. The whole secret of prayer is there.[4]

But it may be that passages like this present us with so exalted a view of the entire landscape of prayer as one simple integrated whole that modesty compels us to begin with a more humdrum task, that of examining the notions about prayer which may already exist in our minds. For there is no subject on which it is easier to cover up a great deal of vague and confused thinking with splendid but empty phrases than the subject of prayer. It is necessary to undertake this examination of our own state of mind about prayer because it is evident that, from the earliest times, anyone who wished to give an account of himself as an authentic Christian by the standards of the gospel has invariably been compelled to adopt some position about prayer which looked as though it could be reconciled with the place it obviously held in the life and teaching of Jesus Christ and his disciples. All difficulties of the transmission of the text of the New Testament apart, this place was a notable one. Not only do all the Evangelists speak of our Lord as himself praying a very personal prayer at a number of significant turning-points in his life; Luke, who makes the sight of our Lord at prayer the occasion for a question on the subject by his disciples, even seems to depict our Lord's entire life as governed by the rhythm of withdrawal, prayer, activity. Thus Luke clearly intends to make us aware of prayer as the constant background of the life of our Lord. All three Synoptic Gospels report his injunction to watch and pray, but only Luke reports a saying which appears to command prayer as a constant activity and it was one which, in the form it is given by Luke, made a particularly deep impression upon early Christianity. Luke introduces the parable of the widow and the unjust judge with the words: 'Jesus told them a parable to illustrate the truth that they must always keep on praying and never lose heart'. St Paul, too, tells the Thessalonians: 'You must never stop praying'.[5] Now it must be regarded as very significant that not a single

Christian writer of antiquity, no matter how heretical, ever thought of interpreting these commands to pray *always* as though they could be taken merely metaphorically. It is easy to suppose that we can now safely dismiss this fact as a kind of literal-minded folly on the part of early Christianity. Yet it remains necessary to try to understand what the earlier traditions meant, especially when we consider the preferred solutions of more recent date. It was as obvious to sensible early Christians as it is to us that it is a physical impossibility always *actually* to be praying, but they were not troubled in their resolution of this difficulty by a saying which has been given the colour of an antiquity which it does not enjoy. To work, we are often told, as though the phrase had a long and respectable ancestry, is to pray.[6] Why anyone should find this an easier saying to take seriously than the injunction to pray always will appear mysterious to anyone who is genuinely embarrassed about the problem of how little he actually prays, and a comfort only to those who are already resigned to believing it. 'To work is to pray' can be taken to mean, and doubtless often has been, that to work is as good as to pray any day, even in a life in which one seldom prays at all. This attitude, or its equivalent, is profoundly and understandably unacceptable to any sound tradition about prayer. Indeed, if one wished to draw a contrast between the attitude of earlier centuries and our own, one might perhaps say that Christianity in its first enthusiasm was far more inclined to think that to pray is to work than that to work is to pray. Without referring to the more eccentric views on prayer to which the history of early Christianity bears witness, it may be recalled that in the admirably balanced *Rule* of St Benedict the recitation of the choir office of psalms and prayers is called 'the work of God'. The use of the word 'work' in a transferred sense in this context is not perhaps altogether unconnected with that element of difficulty in the life of prayer which, one suspects, makes work in the more ordinary sense of the term a much more congenial alternative to many people. There is, after all, the memorable saying of Abba Agatho among the *Sayings of the Fathers*:

The brothers asked Abba Agatho: 'Father, which virtue in our way of life needs most effort to acquire?' And he said to them: 'Forgive me, I think nothing needs so much effort as prayer to God. If a man is wanting to pray, the demons infest him in the attempt to inetrrupt prayer, for they know that prayer is the only thing that hinders them. All the other efforts of a religious life, whether they are made vehemently or gently, have room for a measure of rest. But we need to pray till we breathe out our dying breath. That is the great struggle.'[7]

There is no one who has ever tried to pray consistently over a long period who will not be disposed to take this saying entirely seriously. It is really astonishing what a mass of opposition of every kind the attempt to pray with any constancy invariably arouses at all times and in all places, for no reason that appears to have a direct connection with a human activity so apparently harmless in itself. Nor can it be that those who make the attempt are always obviously cranks. It is enough to look through the stories of the desert Fathers to see that they were just as capable as we are of laughing at the kind of people who are apt to imagine that the life of prayer justifies them in depending upon other people to get their lunch. Indeed, the extremists only serve to underline that earnest preoccupation with the problem of unbroken prayer which is common to everyone who tries to lead the full Christian life at any period.

Although the honour of writing the first Christian treatise explicitly on prayer belongs to Tertullian, it is the beautiful third-century work on the same subject by the great Origen which first comes to grips with the matter under discussion and which, when properly grasped in its context, offers what is probably its only satisfactory solution. It is a solution so sound and so rational that most subsequent writers in the tradition of the undivided Church have been more or less directly dependent upon it. Origen compiled his treatise *On Prayer* with a characteristic thoroughness, by making a complex study of the vocabulary and the teaching relevant to the subject of prayer in both the Old and New Testaments, and from this point of view it does not make very easy reading for the modern reader. But the main point he has to make about the relation between prayer and the rest of life is easy to communicate and to grasp. Its consistency with the teaching of the other authorities cited in this book will at once be appreciated. At the point at which we enter his discussion Origen has already insisted that the Christian makes his prayer in and through Christ: 'For the High Priest of our offerings and our advocate with the Father is the Son of God, who prays for those who pray, and beseeches with those who beseech'.[8] This union of praying Christians with their Lord is,

Origen argues, a union of dispositions and desires about divine things. Hence the angels and all God's saints, or holy ones, assist our prayers because of their union with him. Thus, by an extension of the same principle, he will go on to say:

> The man who links together his prayer with deeds of duty and fits seemly actions with his prayer is the man who prays without ceasing, for his virtuous deeds or the commandments he has fulfilled are taken up as part of his prayer. For only in this way can we take the saying 'Pray without ceasing' as being possible, if we can say that the whole life of the saint is one mighty integrated prayer. Of such prayer, part is what is usually called 'prayer', and ought not to be performed less than three times each day.[9]

It is not necessary at this point to launch into the matter of the frequency of formal times of prayer which Origen is clearly about to raise, but it is very necessary to note the essence of what he has to say since it is clearly the doctrine of Scripture and Tradition. Reduced to its simplest terms it comes to this: Prayer *as a specific activity* is a normal part of the daily life of anyone who would be a friend of God is, indeed, its frame. Within that frame, other activities, including work, can be legitimately regarded as in some real sense prayer in so far as they are practical expressions of the same attitude towards the disposing will of God which prayer pre-eminently voices as the ultimate ground of all it seeks. Take away the frame and the theory about work falls to the ground. For someone who never, or hardly ever, prays it is simply not true that his work is part of his prayer. It is manifestly, at best, a substitute for it and it could even be a refusal to take the trouble to have anything directly to do with the mystery of God, and so be a deliberate impoverishment of all that is most human in us. The object of human existence is not productivity. Indeed, all production, all work is, or should be, *for* what is properly human, namely the fullest life of a being who functions through his mind and heart. To withhold what is most intimately human from our relationship with what is ultimate, even though it be a mystery, is as unworthy of us as it is of God.

If considerations like these serve to situate prayer in the context of life as a whole what, it may now be asked, does the tradition think prayer as a specific activity is? St John of Damascus who, in the eighth century, summarizes the tradition of the Greek Fathers in encyclopaedic form, gives the main notions in a single sentence, the first half of which is commonly reported in the West, though the second half is equally a Western commonplace, both notions being passed on through St Thomas Aquinas in his discussion of prayer. The sentence of St John of Damascus thus has the advantage of being both brief and representative. He says that 'prayer is the ascent of the mind to God, the request for fitting things from God'.[10] Looking at the tradition as a whole, there are, indeed, clearly two sorts of definitions of what prayer is. One thinks of it as some kind of petition, request, or entreaty. Those who use English as their language will note the connection between the word *precarious* and this sense of the word prayer. A precarious situation is, naturally, the kind of situation from which one can only hope for a happy issue by supplication or entreaty. The solution to the difficulty does not lie within the situation itself; some outside help must be called in. It will be appreciated that even this most elementary notion of what prayer is implies just a little bit more than the bare idea of entreaty. There is already implicit in it a notion of the relationship between the one who entreats and the one who is entreated. In this case the one entreated is God and consequently, in harmony with the widest use of the word 'prayer' in Scripture, he is asked for the appropriate. He is asked not only for what fits the immediacy of the situation, but also for what is appropriate to his nature and to his plans for the salvation of mankind. Hence it is appropriate to pray to God for anything which it is appropriate to need or desire. Thus it is entirely normal and right that, although prayer is itself a spiritual activity, we should ask in prayer even for physical and material things, in so far as these things may be related to human life and fulfilment. From the soles of our feet to the crown of our head, everything about us is worthy of prayer, just as it is, according to Christian faith, worthy of salvation.

That prayer does include the physical as well as the spiritual is clear enough from the answer of our Lord to his disciples on the subject: 'When you pray you must say: *Our Father*'.[11] While Christians have always gone on saying some form of the words of the model prayer which the Synoptic Gospels report, both in their public liturgy and private prayer, it also seems clear that he was not even telling them necessarily to use any words at all, but rather that he was telling them by the use of these words what sort of a thing prayer was. At least in the context in which St Luke transmits the *Our Father*, it is the sight of our Lord at prayer which prompts the question: 'What is he really doing?' To which Jesus replies: 'This is the sort of thing it is'. One consequence of this circumstance of the transmission of the *Our Father* is that, although all sorts of valuable things about prayer may be found scattered up and down the writings of the Fathers and saints, from Tertullian at the end of the second century to St Teresa of Avila in the sixteenth, again and again the classical spiritual writers choose to write a special treatise on prayer in the form of a commentary on the Lord's Prayer, examining what is involved in it. Without attempting any such commentary here, it will be sufficient to note that, above all, the *Our Father* defines an attitude about the relationship between the one who prays and the one to whom he prays. It begins by establishing an attitude of adoration and worship. Prayer, evidently, is meant, not to change God, but to change us. When it is real prayer, it infallibly does so. Hence we must also notice that mere thinking is not prayer, nor is reflection or meditation prayer, for these activities may be carried on without their ever leading to the attitude which prayer defines. True prayer is a specific change about our kind of relationship to God. This is exactly what is implied in the first of the phrases of St John of Damascus that prayer is 'the ascent of the mind to God'.

Now there are several things to be noticed about this phrase. In the first place, no reputable person has ever thought that the ascent here spoken of is a physical ascent, though beginners in prayer have been known to imagine that it was! God is not 'above' us physically; in fact heaven lies about us. God is 'above' us, in so far as we are his creatures, dependent upon him for even the noblest that we can do. Prayer, above all, is so much *beyond* what we can do of ourselves that there is no true prayer which is not the effect of grace, and is indeed a form of grace itself. This is true, whether the prayer in which we are engaged appears, from the point of view of our own consciousness, to be the result of our own effort, or is something that, as it were, seizes hold of us, and to which we have only to submit by co-operation. Something will later have to be said about both these kinds of prayer, but it suffices for the moment to note that however the 'ascent', which is here spoken of, appears to be accomplished, it is always in reality God who 'raises' the soul which ascends to him. That this is the case is clear from the fact that, as Evagrius, one of the great desert authorities, says: 'prayer is a converse of the mind with God'.[12] The converse referred to is not that which takes place in conversation, but rather that which occurs in the daily to and fro of relationship. But, as we have seen earlier, no one can have such a relationship with God, since the Fall, save in and through the grace of Christ, who re-opened this relationship for us, whether we are directly aware of it or not. Further, when either Evagrius or St John of Damascus use the Greek word here translated 'mind', they refer to the very depths of the human spirit, which we might probably rather better translate by the word 'heart', provided we gave it its Hebrew connotations. It is in continuity with this biblical way of looking at man, which has been discussed earlier in this book, that one school of spiritual writers in the Eastern Church tells us that we must learn to pray with the mind in the heart. This is one clearly legitimate way of interpreting what all the oldest traditions believe, namely that if prayer is to be true prayer it must be the expression of the ultimate depths of man in his totality.

It was when we take *together* the two representative definitions of prayer reported by St John of Damascus that we see that, words or no words, there is no such thing as a prayer which implies no personal involvement *of any kind*. To say this is to say much more than that prayer requires 'attention'. All spiritual writers gradually come to conclude that genuine prayer is quite compatible with even very notable 'distractions', provided these are not deliberately chosen, either in fact or in their causes. But no one believes that one can genuinely pray if one holds back or does not involve that in oneself which one is *free* to involve in this relationship with God. Consequently it is even right to pray that we shall learn to pray. For actually to give ourselves, as far as we can, is already also God's gift.

13

THE APPROACHES TO
PRAYER

If it be true, as the Scriptures and the teaching of the Fathers declare, that prayer of its very nature is an activity that involves us as human beings more completely and more deeply than anything else in which we could possibly attempt to engage, our personal approach to prayer necessarily imposes an unusual problem. On the one hand, it is theologically certain that we are already involved with God and divine things, at least in some way, by the mere fact of our existence, whether we know it or not. On the other hand, we shall never be *humanly* involved with divine things in any significant manner unless we involve ourselves. Unless we approach him who is nearer to us than we are to ourselves, he might just as well not exist, as far as we are concerned. This dilemma explains the difference between the results of that 'theology' which the Fathers practised and that perversion of the activity of the mind about divine things which has often passed for theology or philosophy in those in whom the sense of the tradition of the undivided Church has been either attenuated or non-existent. The older sense of 'theology' has already been discussed to some extent earlier in this book, and it is implicit in the observation of Evagrius that 'if you are a theologian, you will really pray, and if you really pray, you are a theologian'.[1] Whatever reserves the orthodox tradition may have felt about some of the views of Evagrius, it was undividedly behind him in this belief. Moreover, that it commanded the assent of the very finest thinkers of the fourth century, judged by any standard, ought to be a sufficient guarantee that it was not a formula that appealed to the anti-intellectual or the merely empty-headed. For all of them, prayer was a challenge to the very best that was in them, and it is likely to prove so to any who would try to follow in their footsteps. 'I can see', says Gregory of Nyssa in a passage which notes the concerted energy devoted to the pursuit of business and other personal interests, 'that in this present life, in which the mind passes from one occupation to another, everything else is a matter for preferential concern, but the quality of prayer is something about which people do not worry'.[2]

It is to awaken their concern about *how* they are involved in divine things that everyone needs the discipline of reading holy Scripture and other kinds of 'holy reading', for it is only so that they are likely to accept those other personal disciplines appropriate to the fullest human development which will free them to involve themselves with a God who offers himself to those who worship him 'in spirt and in truth'. It is only the truth which frees, and there is no authentic life of the spirit without it.[3] But this truth of doctrine is not meant to stimulate the mind. It is, as St Bernard saw, more like a food, and we have heard him reminding us not to forget to eat our bread, but to take it into the stomach of our mind and let it transform our way of living. The privileged way in which this doctrine is communicated to everyone and embodied in the attitudes of prayer which it implies is in the various liturgies of the Church. The ancient prayers and the scriptural and other texts associated with the commemoration of the mysteries of faith are themselves a school of prayer when, as a Russian theologian has put it, 'the inner memory of the Church brings fully to life the silent evidence of the texts'.[4] Expressed in an alternative way, it may be said that, since the words of the Church's prayers, whether taken directly from the Bible or composed by her saints and bishops, have a natural and proper meaning of their own, they are only actually *given* that meaning, for the one who uses them, when he is really praying 'in spirit and in truth'. In other words, prayers in books, even the official books of the Church, are for the worshipper only 'approaches' to what prayer is, in and of itself. Unless he involves *himself* with them they are profitless as *his* prayer, even when, as in the special case of the priest or the monk, he says them as the delegate of the Church as a body.

To insist that it is only the combination of spirit and truth together that creates the climate of genuine prayer is to say that it is in and by the spirit that God's truth lives in us and leads us to its source in him. Yet, again, to reject, as our Lord does in the Sermon on the Mount, those 'vain repetitions', or 'meaningless phrases'[5] which mark the difference between a superstitious or magical attitude to prayer and its living reality is not, as we must presently see, altogether to reject the value of even the physical habits which are formed by the use of words whose true application to us may be missed, though not deliberately denied. We do not and cannot, in this life, live in a world of pure spirit. Life must have forms and structures, and there is always the possibility that a valley of the driest of dead bones will rise up in the power of the spirit, if only the bones be there. Every beginner in prayer today is likely to need to acquire a healthy distrust of the false contrast that the contemporary world often makes between the value of spontaneity and the danger of habit. The Fathers of the tradition see the need to value both. After all, habit is not necessarily the enemy of the spontaneous, and is often the pre-condition of its fruitful occurrence. As in the other human arts, in the art of prayer training, if it be sound, it is the normal prelude to personal proficiency. Most people would never begin to pray at all if they had simply to depend upon their spontaneous feeling in the matter; and certainly they would never continue it with the regularity which so basic a diet for the life of our spirit requires. Most of us would die from want of this necessary daily bread if we invariably waited until starvation or malnutrition drove us in search of anything we could find to fill the gap. The starving or the underfed are not capable of assimilating a normal, balanced diet. There is every sign in our own period of the universal symptoms of this spiritual malnutrition, and we should do well simply and modestly to acknowledge it.

It is here that the sense of balance reflected by the tradition will profit us, even though we may have to find our own way of applying what it has to teach to our particular circumstances. Thus, if we examine that extraordinary epitome of the old monastic tradition the *Rule* of St Benedict, we shall notice that, for Benedict, the saying of the psalms is a 'discipline',[6] something ascetic, a method of training. Yet when at the same time he tells his monks 'so to sing the psalms that our heart may be in harmony with our voice',[7] we can see clearly that he implies that distinction which later writers will make between vocal and mental prayer, a distinction between the words formed by the lips and the thought which is being entertained by the heart. Benedict clearly teaches, as the Gospel does, that the mere saying of the words is not enough for this particular discipline to be properly carried out, but he does not yet call even this 'prayer'.[8] 'Prayer' he speaks of in the following chapter, and it is evident that it is to this personal exercise that the public discipline of the psalms leads up. Here, what is vocal is less conspicuous. There may, naturally, be words in it, even if they are not necessarily formed by the mouth, but as Benedict says: 'Let us realize that we shall not be heard for our much speaking, but for purity of heart and tears of compunction. And this is why our prayer ought to be short and pure, unless it happens to be prolonged under the influence of the inspiration of divine grace'.[9] Here we have unmistakably the impression of an activity on which the whole inner life of a man is concentrated and consequently, unlike the discipline of the psalms, no arrangements can be made about it. God is the leader and teacher now, and he determines how it all goes and for how long. Another consequence of this conviction is that when the community, as a group, falls to prayer together, at the end of the psalmody, the prayer is to be made shorter still. Benedict, apparently, has no time for anyone being forced to pretend about a matter in which it is, above all, necessary to be absolutely genuine. On this point he is entirely consistent. In his very first mention of prayer in the *Rule*, he speaks of beginning every good work with 'instant prayer',[10] evidently prayer that goes like an arrow shot from a strung bow. The bow is strung, naturally, by the entire life the community is living, the whole discipline, the sum of all the things one can arrange about, and it is these which lead spontaneously to prayer under the movement of the spirit. So it is that the oratory must be a place of physical silence, so that people can linger there to pray, if they want to or if, at other times, they feel the impulse to pray they can, as he so simply and informally says 'just go in and pray'.[11] What could be a happier picture of the combination of habit and spontaneity, of basic structure and unpredictable life?

It is this simple and sure way, the antithesis of false tension and lifeless monotony, that we each of us have to find. As Benedict and the entire tradition he represents know, prayer springs up out of the ground of a whole life, whose structure includes divine things as part of the daily diet which each one has set before him. There are, as we have seen, more immediate preparations, special disciplines, which normally lead us more directly into prayer, but which cannot and should not be identified with prayer itself. Privileged among all these disciplines are the texts of the liturgy of the Church, which owing to physical and social circumstances have in practice become less and less available as part of the structure of daily living for most people. It would be a waste of spiritual energy to regret what cannot be altered. Everyone is at least free to say some of the psalms and the common prayers like the *Our Father* and the *Hail Mary,* all of which are drawn from the inspired text of Scripture, at times which it will profit them to arrange for as part of their daily round of living. These prayers by the very frequency with which they are repeated will tend to keep the attitudes of prayer in our minds and hearts and lead us into a prayer, simpler, deeper, and more intimately personal. They will do this, provided we always remember that none of these words or phrases becomes true prayer simply by being repeated. Their very familiarity which, like all valued things, *could* lead us on to love, can equally well be reduced to a screen of empty sound, a kind of holy distraction, preventing us from entering into the presence of God. While avoiding the folly of expecting our habits to produce fruit without their involving the test of time, toil and patience, we ought not to dismiss the danger of the alternative possibility too lightly, especially if we can give little time explicitly to these disciplines in addition to our 'holy reading'.

Both the Eastern and Western traditions of Christianity have their favourite brief formulas or phrases which are meant to be used as approaches to prayer, and these it will be valuable to discuss at the end of this chapter; but first it is necessary to note that it is not possible to think of anything which can really be called 'prayer' which is *in no way* mental. For prayer is, of its very nature, a human activity, and to deny it that involvement of mind and heart by which spiritual things become our food is to reduce it to something purely animal. The witty protest of St Teresa of Avila on this subject is sufficient to lodge in our memory a fact which ought to be obvious to everyone. Speaking to her nuns, she says:

> You must know, daughters, that whether or no you are practising mental prayer has nothing to do with keeping the lips closed. If, while I am speaking with God, I have a clear realization and full consciousness that I am doing so, and if this is more real to me than the words I am uttering, then I am combining mental and vocal prayer. When people tell you that you are speaking with God by reciting the Paternoster and thinking of worldly things—well, words fail me.[12]

As St Teresa will say elsewhere in the book in which this passage occurs, it is perfectly possible to reach true contemplation while continuing to say the common Christian vocal prayers. But it will be quite evident that both she and the entire orthodox tradition on

151

this subject is concerned that, whatever form the prayer takes, it should be real prayer. And in so far as all the saints and spiritual masters are trying to teach us anything, they are all of them concerned to bring us to the point where they must leave us behind and we are actually praying.

Now, as we have been trying to see all through this book, life itself, if we see it for what it is, is enough to bring us to the point of prayer, so is the proper reading of holy Scripture, so is taking part in the liturgy, where it is accessible to us, so is the practice of turning to God in short phrases of familiar words. But for many centuries, particularly since life in towns became so complex and, through one channel or another, began to fill our minds and our imaginations with so many alternatives often profoundly indisposing for prayer, large numbers of people who really want to pray have increasingly found that they need some more specific help to be brought to the point of praying. Books on prayer have therefore tended to offer 'methods' of prayer and methods of 'meditation' which, though rooted in the psychological processes which have always inevitably gone on in those who pray, have often led to results in those who used them which the older masters would have regarded as most undesirable. None of the classical teachers of methods of meditation—not even the much-maligned St Ignatius Loyola—believes that the method they teach *is* prayer. All methods of 'meditation' aim at drawing our dispersed human powers together, quietening some down and engaging others. But, one and all, they tell us that when we reach the point where prayer begins to flow of itself we should let it lead us. If we need a method to lead us into prayer—and most modern people do, at least when they begin to practise it—we shall find it wise to choose one which conforms to our own psychological and temperamental type. Those whose minds are fairly active, who like to reflect and analyse things, will tend to find they need a method of the Ignatian type, while those who are more intuitive will tend to feel more at home with the methods which stem from the seventeenth-century French Oratory. In either case, they must resolve at the outset that the purpose of the 'method' is not to have beautiful thoughts or striking intuitions about God, but to enter into converse with him.

St Ignatius Loyola himself never wrote a book on the subject of meditation for general use, his *Exercises* being designed to assist those who were guiding others in these matters. But his basic ideas on meditation are clearly and attractively set out in a minor classic of the seventeenth century, which is generally available in one English translation or another, as it normally has been since within a few years of its appearance. In St Francis of Sales, the author of the *Introduction to the Devout Life*, we meet the first great spiritual writer who made it his conscious aim to help and encourage people leading ordinary lives in the post-medieval world to pray, wherever they found themselves and whatever their occupation. His sense of what is relevant and his boldness in adapting the older disciplines to quite new situations and states of mind has never been surpassed or even remotely equalled in its overall sureness of judgement.

> Those who have written about devotion have almost all done so for people very much withdrawn from the bustle of the world, or they have at least taught a kind of devotion which leads to this complete withdrawal, [he writes in his preface to the *Introduction*]. My intention is to instruct those who live in towns, in families, and whose circumstances oblige them to lead, to all appearances, an ordinary life.

With great shrewdness and good humour this is the programme he carries out. His teaching about prayer and meditation occupies the first nine chapters of book two of the *Introduction*. Since he supposes that we shall not necessarily have been helped by the circumstances in which we find ourselves, he suggests four possible ways of placing oneself in the presence of God by way of preparation. First, one might remember that God is everywhere and that therefore he is here *now*, or one might remember that he is in the depths of our own being and therefore very close to us. Again one might reflect that our Lord and all the saints look upon us here and now, or finally one might simply use one's imagination to make these undoubted theological truths more vivid. Naturally, as St Francis remarks, one must not try to use all these methods together, but whichever one seems to help to draw our preoccupations back from their previous involvements and make us ready to ask God's help to make our meditation. These two steps are an invariable feature of each occasion. Then follows a variable element, 'composition of place': he says, 'This is nothing but the use of the imagination about the scene of the mystery on which we wish to meditate, just as though it were a real event occurring'.[13] This is a technique which goes back at least to the twelfth-century Cistercians, St Bernard and St Aelred of Rievaulx. Obviously this third step presupposes the choice of a subject or a passage of Scripture in advance, and those who follow this method will often make the choice the previous day before going to sleep, recalling the subject briefly when they wake up and thereby giving the day something of a frame within which the meditation occurs. St Francis is quite clear about the purpose of this third step. 'By this use of the imagination we confine our attention to the mystery we have chosen for our meditation so that it may not roam all over the place'.[14] St Francis is perfectly well aware that some people will feel critical of this explicit use of the imagination to secure the sense of immediacy to the subject, but his advice is simply to concentrate on the purpose of its use, and not to let oneself get lost in purely fanciful details. In any case, by whatever means the sense of immediacy to the subject is gained, the next step is reflection about it. But this reflection is not just *any* use of the mind about the subject. 'It is', St Francis says, 'nothing but one or more considerations made in order to stimulate our love for God and divine things—which is the way meditation differs from study and from other kinds of thoughts and reflections not made with a view to acquiring virtue or the love of God.'[15] This distinction is an important one and, if it is not observed, the meditation will never arrive at prayer at all. The meditation must be a gentle and simple responsiveness to the subject which leads us on quite naturally to movements of the will and the affections. St Francis is rather insistent that one should not let these desires remain a kind of empty delight but that one should bring them down to something quite concrete in one's own life. The meditation which has thus broken out into prayers and desires is concluded with thanksgiving for the graces received and a restrained return to the ordinary occupations of life, in such a way that the thoughts and attitudes which the meditation has produced in us may not be too quickly or easily dispersed again.

The scheme, then, is a very simple one—awareness of God, reflections on some subject that refers us to him, leading into affections and prayer—an exercise that has thus involved the entire range of our spiritual capacities. St Francis allows us, as every instructor would, to use a book of some kind to help us when we begin to train ourselves. But we should be well advised to see that we never let this become the excuse for spending the time reading what someone else thinks, or expressing someone else's reaction to a subject about which we ought *ourselves* to be reacting in our own way. Until we are brave enough to launch out, we shall never really learn. It is for this reason too that we must not fail to note what St Francis says immediately after he has explained his method of meditation, for it is clearly in a direct line with the oldest traditions.

It will sometimes happen that immediately after the preparation you will find your affection stirred up towards God, then, you must give it the reins, without trying to follow the method which I have given you; for although consideration ought normally to precede affections and resolutions, yet if the Holy Spirit gives you the affections before the consideration, you should not make the consideration, since that is only made in order to stir up the affections.[16]

Here again are habit and spontaneity in happy co-operation.

Père Surin, a great Jesuit director of fifty years later, gives identical advice:

How can one be familiar with God if one is resolved to listen to him on only one subject, and if one cannot behave in his presence with ease and liberty. Just as the lute player keeps his instrument in harmony although he hums a number of different tunes, provided the main chord which sustains the ground-base for the song remains in the same key so, provided union of heart is maintained, one can strike all the chords in one's prayer if they accord with this chief and fundamental key. Yet this variety of thoughts ought rather to come from the spirit of God than the choice of his creature who, left to himself and his own efforts, ought rather to turn to the subject he has proposed than to any other.[17]

The concluding words of this passage deserve to be weighed. We shall never make progress either in prayer or in the practice of the virtues if we give ourselves over to our own instability, either about what we do or how we do it. But, at the same time, the remedy for this instability of heart, mind and mood is not a method or a rule so inflexible that we will not let even God himself disturb it. All the great writers agree about that.

But whereas the Ignatian method tends to concentrate on the training of our psychological processes, the teachers connected with the French Oratory tend to encourage us more explicitly to live at the theological sources of prayer. This is due to the rather special formation of their founder, Cardinal de Bérulle, for whom St Francis of Sales had an admiration which he richly deserves. His

155

is a mind of extraordinary unity and concentration of view. Everything Bérulle wrote and everything he taught is coloured by what his study of the Fathers of the Church had taught him. It is a thought with one simple, luminous centre. Like the great fourth-century champions of Christian orthodoxy, who had become his spiritual heroes, it is the union of the two natures in the one person of Jesus Christ which commands Bérulle's admiration and excites his wonder. Upon the consequences of his vision of the meaning of that union his entire doctrine depends.

> It is no longer the heavens that rule the earth, but it is the earth that rules the heavens; and the first mover is no longer in the skies, but on the earth, since God has become incarnate on earth.... Even the order, state, and situation of the principal parts of the world is reversed by the reversal that God has made with regard to himself in this mystery. For heaven is no longer above the earth, but the earth is above the highest heavens, that is to say, the earth of our humanity living in Jesus Christ.[18]

In this single concentrated sentence is the germ of all Bérulle has to teach. Not a single moment of our Lord's life has been lost; its virtue, its power, its meaning, what Bérulle calls its 'state', is forever present in Jesus Christ in the heavens. Hence it is still available even to those who were not actually present at the events as they historically occurred in that life. Bérulle and his disciples put us, in the Fathers' sense, 'theologically' in contact with that life, whether we imagine it or not. As Bérulle says elsewhere: 'This mystery of the Incarnation, which is the sacrament of sacraments, is a sacrament and mystery full of God'.[19] We have only to approach this mystery, in faith, to be filled, because, as St John's Gospel says, 'out of the Word's complete perfection we have all received, and to us there has come wave upon wave of grace'.[20] A line of disciples, who depended more or less directly on Bérulle's insight and conviction, taught a very simple method of prayer designed to foster it. 'It consists', says M. Olier, 'in having our Saviour before our eyes, in our heart, and in our hands'. Thus we look at Jesus, unite ourselves with him, and work in him. It is adoration, communion, and co-operation. Hence, though it leads us directly into the Christian mysteries by a conscious change of tempo, it leads us back into the ordinary run of life with something to do in the strength of what we have received. This prayer is a food which we digest in order to live.

We must, naturally, note that just as whatever 'method' of meditation we use involves us in a change of tempo, so its digestion must involve us in a change of attitude to the way we live, as far as this is possible in a life of catching buses and answering the telephone. The food of our prayer we need daily. And just as there is a best time for each of us to choose, so there is also a best minimum length of time to spend over it. When we remember in the modern world Benedict's sound instruction that prayer should be 'brief and pure', we ought surely not to understand him as saying that we should do it fast and get it over quickly, like so much else that we do. He means that we should discover a norm for those days when we do not happen to experience one of those leadings of the Spirit which draw us into prayer and hold us there; and the guide as to what the norm should be is, surely, the period of time during which we can normally be genuinely praying. Benedict does not want us to go on simply for the sake of time, but it is tolerably certain that, like all the spiritual masters, he would, conversely, want us to take *enough* time really to pray, however briefly. This means, for most of us, time to lead into prayer and time to lead out of it.

This approach to prayer as the real food of our spirit is not, however, the only one there is. It ought also, especially for those of us who lack the special help of quiet cloisters, to be part of the air we breathe.[21] Both the East and the West know of methods of prayer as brief and regular as breathing, which may, for some people, even become their whole way of prayer, and will certainly be a great assistance to prayer as a daily diet, since they make prayer enter into the very fabric of life. John Cassian reports in his tenth *Conference* that it was the custom of the desert Fathers to use often, at all times and places, the first verse of Psalm 70: 'O God make speed to save me: O Lord make haste to help me'. 'It fits', he says, 'every mood and temper of human nature, every temptation and circumstance'.[22] It is less well-known that St Ignatius Loyola also recommends a method of meditated prayer which he calls 'prayer by way of measure or rhythmical beats'. The idea is that with each breath or respiration prayer should be made, saying one word only of the *Our Father* between one slow breath and another. But undoubtedly best-known of all today is a method which seems to have its lost origins in the desert of Sinai and has been propagated among the Christians of the East with a steadily growing literature since the fourteenth century. A small, anonymous

157

nineteenth-century Russian book called *The Way of a Pilgrim*, now widely available in English and other modern language translations, tells how a simple man who wants to learn to pray goes on his travels with a Bible and an anthology of texts from the Fathers in his rucksack, and saying as he breathes in and out: 'Lord Jesus Christ, Son of God, have mercy on me, a sinner'. All the reputable teachers of this way of praying give a warning that one should not concentrate on developing a technique of breathing, which may, and frequently does, begin to develop of itself.[23] Naturally, prayer is calming because it refreshes us from the very source of life itself, but the beginner needs to bear in mind what the masters of the undivided Church unanimously teach. One should not go to prayer to be calmed, to think splendid thoughts, or to solve difficult problems. One should go to prayer to seek God, and in the seeking one finds everything else one needs. One discovers the fulfilment of the gospel promise that if we 'make the kingdom of God and a life of loyalty to him, the object of all our endeavour, then we get all these other things as well'.[24] The entire tradition is profoundly suspicious of visions and 'experiences', and its attitude is delightfully summed up in the tale from the *Sayings of the Fathers*, which describes how 'the devil appeared to a monk in the guise of an angel of light, and said to him: 'I am the angel Gabriel, and I have been sent to you'. But the monk said: "See whether you were not sent to someone else. I am not worthy that an angel should be sent to me". And the devil vanished'.[25]

This note of humility is, it will be noticed, common to all the ways of praying mentioned in this chapter. The methods of meditation may start with books, and the use of the 'Jesus Prayer' simply with saying words. They aim at impregnating the mind with the food of doctrine which, even in their briefest forms, they contain and imply, and from the mind they ought, if they are being practised properly to descend into the heart where they gradually bring about the conversion or turning of our whole spirit to the God who is the God of our life.

14

CONVERSION OF HEART

It may surprise some modern readers to be told that the time has now come when, if they are still only entertaining what is being said in this book as a curious diversion and doing nothing about it in their lives, it would be wiser for them to stop reading it altogether. To study the question of prayer, without being prepared for what prayer involves, is not only a waste of time; it can be positively harmful. This forgotten truth has often in the contemporary world been replaced by the widespread illusion that everything can in principle be mastered, given time and trouble. But the more this attitude governs our approach to a genuinely spiritual subject, the more dangerous it is. This observation is not meant to be either mystifying or merely frightening. It seeks to draw attention, in the first place, to the fact, of which everyone is aware, that fire can be used to warm and cheer a house and make it a welcoming home. But if one plays with it, or is merely careless about it, it can burn the place to the ground. We should not experiment with God, or even the devil. It can lead to disaster.

'Reverence' is a word we, in some ways rightly, tend nowadays to be rather careful of using, since it often carries conventional overtones of unreality and superstition. But we must be careful that our preference for intimacy—and this is, indeed, one way of expressing what the ultimate goal of prayer is about—we must be careful that our regard for intimacy does not lead us to the opposite extreme of contempt. Even in our relations with each other a crucial moment comes when the first barriers are down and we realize or, often disastrously, fail to realize that whatever code of behaviour we have either learnt, invented or inherited is not going to be sufficient guide to see us through. At this point we can either grow and develop in the way and at the pace that a genuine respect for the mutual realities of our situation defines, or we can try to push ahead regardless of everything that does not conform to our preconceived plans and notions. This normally does *us* infinitely more harm than it does to others. The effects of the wrong that we suffer are, on the whole, at least at the spiritual level, easier to remedy than the effects of the wrong that we *do*. For the wrong that we do, blindly and obstinately, stultifies us at the very root of our being and incapacitates us for making the right and authentic responses to even quite new situations which arise. Indeed, Christians believe that there are some such effects of our own actions so irreparable and self-destroying that only the direct intervention of divine, forgiving grace can rectify them. We ought not to need reminding that just as we can refuse to make the gift of ourselves to each other which the realities of our situation may demand, so we can refuse this gift to God.

This is, naturally, what is ultimately at issue for everyone in the spiritual life, whoever they may happen to be. Probably we ought even to say that it is always the issue at every moment, but this could be a practical exaggeration. It does not seem that God makes every moment a moment of crisis. But, at the same time, as holy Scripture from one end to the other reminds us, the danger of all practices which we should normally call 'religious' is that they can be used as evasions of our true relationship with God, and even as permanent protections against it. If one says prayers and observes ceremonies, but never *really* prays or worships, if one reads books about prayer until one becomes a specialist in spiritual techniques, but never really goes out to meet the God who comes so humbly and simply to meet us in the Incarnation, then all these things, and even our very concern with them, will remove us further and further from the very life they only exist to promote. This life is characterized by what holy Scripture calls 'conversion of heart' and flows from it, and this is the point upon which the thought of the Scriptures and the masters of prayer converge.

We have tried to see at an earlier stage in our discussion why much more is at issue in the Hebrew conception of the role of the heart than the apparent accident of language that the Hebrews associated 'thinking' with one part of their anatomy, whereas we associate it with another. The heart as the centre of a single, embodied being is of very different significance from that 'mind' which we so easily think of as mastering 'matter', and whose progressive distinction from our bodies has made it urgently necessary to try to reintegrate our bodies into the strangely dismembered notion we have of what it is to be ourselves. We cannot afford, on

account of our different view of the anatomical function of the
heart, to feel superior to the firm biblical assertion that man is one
whole living thing, and that his 'thoughts' go right down into his
flesh. They do; and it is to our profound spiritual loss that we no
longer find it easy to adjust ourselves to thinking about man in
this way, as an occasional voice, generally from the field of medicine, needs to remind us.[1]

It is perhaps necessary at this point briefly to recall some of
the biblical expressions of these convictions which may help us to
rethink and readjust our position in regard to them. First, as
roughly in the physical centre of the body, and as the centre of
the circulation of the blood, the heart may not too unsuitably be
regarded as the centre of life. Thus, sometimes the heart is virtually
the equivalent of the 'soul', as in the beautifully neat little parallel
which occurs in a single verse of the psalms:

> My soul longs, yea, faints
>   for the courts of the Lord;
> my heart and flesh sing for joy
>   to the living God.[2]

In this verse it is clear that, whether it is 'soul' or 'heart' that is
being spoken of, it is the whole centre and core of our being that
longs for God. Hence, too, since the life that is in me goes on
even when I sleep, and my concerns and dispositions remain, at
their deepest, essentially the same, I can sleep while my heart remains awake, like the dreamer in the Song of Songs who hears the
beloved knocking:

> I sleep but my heart is awake.
>   Listen! My beloved is knocking:
> 'Open to me, my sister, my dearest,
>   my dove, my perfect one;
> for my head is drenched with dew,
>   my locks with the moisture of the night'.[3]

To talk thus about the heart as the seat and centre of life is,
naturally, not to exclude our more common imaginative association
of the heart with the emotions. For the Hebrews, however, it is not
simply affection and the tenderer sentiments that have their seat
in the heart, but courage and fortitude too. The lad David says to
king Saul about Goliath: 'Let no man's heart fail because of him:

your servant will go and fight with this Philistine'.[4] So, too, it is really the heart that 'thinks', that is faithful or perverse. Today we talk about people being double-minded, but the Psalmist cries out against people who are double-hearted:

Help, Lord; for there is no longer any that is godly!
    for the faithful have vanished from among the sons of men.
Every one utters lies to his neighbour:
    with flattering lips and a double heart they speak.[5]

The contrast to this inner dividedness of the wicked is God's gift to the great King Solomon. Only the older versions tend to remind us explicitly of the original Hebrew. The Authorized and Douai versions read: 'And God gave Solomon wisdom and understanding exceeding much, and largeness of heart, even as the sand that is on the sea shore'.[6] More modern translations give the correct meaning when, like the Revised Standard Version, they read for 'heart', 'mind', or some equivalent. But yet, how subtly this alters the sense of the gift, if one is aware of the Hebrew background. This is wisdom that is here being spoken of and wisdom is not something of the mind and the understanding alone. It is the integral response of the whole man to the reality of the world and of God, a love-knowledge, all-embracing as well as penetrating.

When the New Testament refers, as it often does, to the books of the Old Testament as 'the Law and the Prophets', it is in fact referring schematically to a steady progress towards inwardness. Moses, coming down the mountain after his intimate conversation with God in the clouds, is carrying God's law in the form of commandments written on stone. This law contains rules about things to do and things not to do, ceremonial precepts which will give the desert community some tangible expression of its bond with God. The prophets are going to have to cry out that the trouble about all this—and it continues to be the trouble of those whose religion is only laws and precepts—is that it is the people's hearts that are like tablets of stone. Speaking with the voice and on the authority of God, the prophet Ezekiel will proclaim the coming of the days when God will 'give them a new heart and put a new spirit within them; I will take the stony heart out of their flesh and give them a heart of flesh'.[7] The necessity for this has been declared in the opening chapter of the prophecy of Isaiah in the most unequivocal terms:

Your new moons and your appointed feasts
  my soul hates;
they have become a burden to me,
  I am weary of bearing them.
When you spread forth your hands,
  I will hide my eyes from you;
even though you make many prayers
  I will not listen.[8]

If one recalls this background, then and only then does one see vividly the context in which Jesus warns his disciples:

Be on your guard against the experts in the Law, for they like to walk about in long flowing robes; they like to be deferentially greeted as they move through the market-places; they like the front seats in the synagogue and the top places at banquets. They greedily extract the last penny from credulous widows, and then with their long prayers they try to give an impression of exceptional piety. They will receive all the heavier sentence.[9]

He who himself normally observed all the customary courtesies and ceremonial precepts is ruthless in his condemnation of the kind of religion which is mere external and superstitious show. His positive alternative to all this is bound up with the Hebrew conception of the significance of the heart.

Listen to me all of you [he said] and try to understand. Nothing which enters a man from outside can defile him. On the contrary, it is what comes out of a man that defiles him. When he had left the crowd and gone indoors, the disciples asked him what this difficult saying meant. 'Are even you not able to understand?' he said to them. 'Do you not realize that anything which goes into a man from outside cannot defile him, but goes, not into his heart, but into his stomach, and is then evacuated into the drain by natural processes? It is what comes out of a man that defiles him, for it is from within, from the heart, that there emerge evil thoughts, fornication, theft, murder, adultery, the desire to possess what a man has no right even to desire, wickedness, deceitful trickery, shameless immorality, jealousy, slander, arrogance, folly. All these wicked things come from inside, and it is they which defile a man'.[10]

The inner situation to which our Lord thus draws attention has

163

already been discussed in some detail earlier in this book. The dis-integration that is within us, whether it bubbles up in the primitive form in which the wounds of original sin manifest themselves in our particular personality, or in a form which is actually trained and intensified by sin chosen and premeditated, is not only the root problem of the moral life, it is also the root problem of prayer. But it is, further, a problem for which prayer is the true and only cure. If one says this, one is in effect saying what all the teachers of the approaches to prayer ultimately teach, namely that prayer normally and inevitably *must* lead to conversion of heart, in a sense which understands 'heart' as the Gospels and Hebrew thought understood it. Any and every school of prayer from the tradition of orthodox Christianity is unanimous in saying something like this: Thinking things is not prayer, analysing things is not prayer, discussing things, however holy, is not prayer. Or again, doing things is not prayer, whether they are things done apparently for God or for one's neighbour, however lovingly. But, on the other hand, prayer is *about* all these things, and if you deliberately with-hold any of these things from their natural relation to prayer, then it may be doubted whether you really pray at all. It will be necessary to look a little later at some of the problems that arise from the fact that we cannot always have either the thoughts, or more especially the feelings, that we should like to have in or about prayer. But it remains generally true to say that if we deliberately withhold or try to close off some part of ourselves from its relation to prayer, then our prayer is a mere sham. For prayer is concerned with the very centre of our being, with the very source from which everything about us flows. This is the point made by those Greek and Russian writers who insist that we must learn to pray with the mind in the heart. We must allow, in other words, that undivided engagement with God which true prayer is, to seize hold of the very centre of our being. This in-volvement of the centre of our being with divine things is inevit-ably a gradual process, which is furthered by our own efforts and by the formation which God himself gives us, whether within the specific exercise of prayer itself, or in the course of the events of our lives. We have so far in this book possibly said almost all we can about the formation we can give ourselves, and most of what has still to be said is concerned with the sort of things God does to us, in one way or another. But we shall only be able to understand these two factors together if we understand them in the context of 'conversion of heart', of that purification of the very centre of our being whose steady progress is necessary if we are to co-operate fruitfully with that share in his own kind of life which God alone can give us.

A great seventeenth-century Jesuit, Louis Lallement, says this with pertinent brevity, where he writes:

> The two elements of the spiritual life are the purgation of the heart and the direction of the Holy Spirit. There you have the two poles of all spirituality. By these two ways one arrives at perfection according to the degree of purity one has acquired, and in proportion to the fidelity one has had in co-operating with the movements of the Holy Spirit and following his conduct. Our whole perfection depends upon this fidelity and one could say that the abridgement of the spiritual life consists in attending to these two ways, the movement of the Spirit of God in our souls, and the strengthening of our will in the resolution to follow them, using to that end all the disciplines of prayer, reading, the sacraments, the practice of the virtues and good works.[11]

Looked at from a somewhat different point of view, what Lallemant is saying is that our development in the life of prayer and in spiritual matters in general depends upon the gradual enlistment of all the forces of our being in the love and service of God, whether by our own effort or the formation and leading of grace. Our problem is, we may say, the problem of the conversion or transformation of the forces within us, especially desire and aggression, into forces which build us up, nurturing us in true love and strengthening us to face and to bear what is often difficult with perseverance and courage. In yet another way, we could say that, as in life in general, so in prayer, our gradual growth and development depends upon releasing our capacities from the disintegrating habits of the vices and capturing them by the integrating habits of the virtues, so that we may become submissive to the positive action of God and live a life of true faith, hope and charity.

It is evident that a transformation of this kind is not one which normally takes place in a moment, though it may very frequently be approximately dated from some definitive beginning which could not too inaccurately be called a 'conversion'. The seventeenth-century Carmelite lay-brother Lawrence of the Resurrection, whose lovely little book the *Practice of the Presence of God* has never ceased to enjoy a well-grounded esteem, could look back to just such a day when something definitive happened to him at the mere sight of a tree in winter. The more dramatic and influential conversion of St Paul on the Damascus road has long been celebrated with an annual festival. But perhaps the more usual picture of conversion is that delightfully described by St Francis of Sales in his *Introduction to the Devout Life*, where he says:

> The normal purgation and healing, whether of the body or the soul, occurs little by little, by progressing from improvement to improvement, haltingly and without haste. The angels on Jacob's ladder have wings and yet they do not fly, but they go up and down in a regular way from one step to another. The soul that climbs up again from sin to devotion is like the dawn which, when it comes, does not drive away the shadows in an instant, but little by little.[12]

This is all very good sense, as long as we do not understand St Francis as saying that our way to God through prayer can be mapped out in stages in the way that we sometimes find it mapped out in books about prayer. It is clear that if, for theological, psychological, and even physical reasons, human life is a changing and developing thing, then so is the life of prayer, and hardly less complex to describe. For, although the beginnings of prayer tend to draw our attention to processes of which we can be conscious, it must, like the rest of our life, reach right down into that of which we cannot be conscious, to those deep wells at the very centre of our being which are subsumed under the biblical notion of the heart. We should be deceiving ourselves if we did not realize that as long as we think on the surface, live on the surface, and pray on the surface, we are less than our full and true human selves. Even if, at the stage we have reached, we do not yet know this by experience, there are, in fact, in the depths of the human spirit powerful forces to be captured and canalized in the service of life, if they are not to run to waste and so leave us as an arid and barren desert, a mere empty husk. If our beginnings in prayer seem to do nothing else for us, they ought at least to make us urgently and abidingly aware of what is at stake for us, and hence for everyone with whom we come into contact. When he has spoken of all the other spiritual gifts, St Paul concludes with this advice:

> Set your hearts on possessing the greater gifts. And now I am going to show you the way which is by far the best. Even if I

166

could speak the languages of men and of angels, if I am without love, I am no better than a clanging gong or a clashing cymbal.[13]

St Paul's great hymn in praise of that special form of love, known in Greek as *agape*, in Latin as *caritas*, and in technical English as charity is generally familiar even to those who make no profession of Christianity. But St Bernard's rather longer, though still brief, explanation of the dynamism of Christian love has been allowed to pass into a quite unmerited oblivion. For it may be doubted if any short work on Christian living and the Christian sense of perspective has so firm and clear a grasp of the really basic factors likely to lead to the transfiguration of a life by love as St Bernard's *On loving God*. It also happens to be the last classical expression in a concise, explicit, and accessible form of the unanimous spiritual doctrine of the undivided Church on the destiny of man as a living whole. After St Bernard, even the greatest of Western writers tend to take the resurrection of the body for granted, if they think about it at all. For St Bernard the entire story of our conversion to God is meaningless without it. His thought on this subject therefore deserves our special attention.

The treatise *On loving God* was written in 1125 when the topic of love, in both its sacred and secular sense, was much in the air, as it is once again in many circles today. St Bernard's period happens to coincide with that awakening of self-awareness which is often thought of as characteristic of modern man, and it is certainly to bring about self-awareness in a Christian sense that he is writing. His entire approach is instinct with life and experience.

You ask to hear from me [he writes in his opening words] why and how God is to be loved. And I reply: 'The reason for loving God is God himself; and the measure in which to do it is without measure'. Isn't this enough to say? Perhaps it might be for a wise man. But my duty is also to the less than wise.[14]

When one says that the reason for loving God is God himself, St Bernard's argument goes on, one could mean one of two things. One could be answering either the question: 'What makes God lovable?' or the question: 'What should I get out of loving him?' St Bernard says: 'I am bound to say that I should have to give the same reply to either question. No other satisfactory reason for loving him occurs to me except himself. But let us look at the first aspect first'. Bernard then quotes the New Testament text from the first letter of St John, which is the foundation of all his spiritual teaching: 'He first loved us'.[15] The fact that 'God loved us before we loved him' is the best of all possible reasons for making him lovable. It will also be found in practice that it is the only one which really effectively moves anyone. The Christian life begins not with loving, but with the sense of *being loved*. It may, indeed, be doubted whether anyone arrives at any great capacity for loving, whether at the human level or at the divine, unless they start out from a position of feeling loved. St Bernard is simply reminding us that God speaks to us in holy Scripture from a standpoint which respects this basic psychological fact which he has written into our nature. Not to be loved, even though we are not worth it, is the greatest of human tragedies. No one respects this fundamental need for the security of being loved more than God does. St Paul tells the Romans: 'God proves how much he loves us by the fact that Christ died for us while we were still sinners'.[16] This is the basis of God's claim upon us. He is lovable because he loves.

But, naturally, to feel involved in this love which anticipates us is a question of personal engagement, and the discovery of this involvement is what our prayer is all about. The right kind of self-love is that of someone who feels that he must care for himself *for the sake of another*, and it is the very opposite of the rapacious purely self-seeking love of someone who feels fundamentally insecure. St Bernard respects this complementary psychological fact by going on to confront us with what it is to be a man, and to show that God's claim to be loved is personal and, as it were, built into our very nature. We must begin he will say, with self-knowledge. Food, sunlight, and air, so necessary for bodily health, may be cited as impressive gifts shared by everyone, which do not have their source in us. But nobler and more impressive still are our own inner gifts which St Bernard, following the common view of Gregory of Nyssa, names as the dignity of free choice, and the capacity for knowledge and virtue.[17]

But what is the use of having capacities which one does not recognize? A purely abstract and theoretical self-knowledge is useless. If we do not see ourselves as creatures distinguished from animals by the gift of reason, we begin to be, for all practical purposes, confounded with them. Turning away from our own true glory, which is within us, we are led on by the vice of curiosity to dissipate our energies in the pursuit of everything that is less than ourselves. We must, at this point, notice that what Bernard means here by 'curiosity' is not that sort of curiosity which consists in taking a genuine interest in the facts and wonders of the world which is quite compatible with human dignity. He means rather that perpetual pursuit of the sensational which never amounts to knowledge because it is only interested in experience as an end in itself. St Bernard values experience enormously and, in common with the whole school of writers associated with him, it is one of the words he uses most frequently. But what interests St Bernard is experience seen in a context. Tremendously important for our general spiritual development, and also for our life of prayer, is the capacity to get a sense of ourselves as persisting through a whole succession of happenings.

Later in this book we are going to have to say that one of the secrets of the mature spiritual life is that of being able to live in the present moment. But it is necessary to realize that one cannot live in the present moment *wisely* unless one has a sense of the nature and significance of previous moments. If we are so identified with what we experience in the present moment that we forget that we, in the depths of our being, are not simply and solely *what* we experience, then we learn nothing by living; we do not grow and do not mature. For us there is nothing to do but repeat the same happening over and over again until it wears us out. It is not only or invariably the young who fail to see the possibility of making this mistake. Hence the seriousness for anyone of any age to heed St Bernard's warning that 'this kind of ignorance is to be avoided, whereby we think too little of ourselves; and no less that whereby we think too much, which we do if we imagine that whatever good we find in ourselves comes from ourselves'.[18] In other words, for St Bernard, self-knowledge means the practical and not merely theoretical realization that one is neither a beast nor an angel. And so at least one discovers the truth of one's human situation, and begins to pursue genuine knowledge and virtue. We turn to the life that is properly ours. Thus, too, it is our own endowments of body and soul that teach us to love God for his own sake. If, in addition to this we understand what God has done for us in Christ and him crucified we 'do not mind that we can only offer the little that we are in return for being shown such love and such value. For they easily love the more who realize that they are more loved, while he loves less to whom less is given'.[19]

169

This argument shows us exactly the role that our mediations on the life of Christ and our prayer springing up from them ought to play in our total development. 'And so, if we wish to have Christ for our frequent guest, our hearts ought always to be defended by these faithful evidences of his mercy in dying for us and his power in rising for us'.[20] These mysteries, which occupy those who seek God, do not satisfy them, but rather increase their appetite for what will be ultimately satisfying. The 'little bit of dust' that we are is also steadily inflamed with a desire to return love for love and the awareness that 'in his first creation he gave me to myself, in his second he gave himself to me; and in giving me himself, he gave me back to myself. Given once, then, and then given back; I owe him myself, and that twice over, in return for myself'.[21]

It is, of course, possible to turn this business of loving into a problem, but there is no need to do so. As St Bernard says, God's claim to be loved and our advantage in loving him go inseparably together. For 'true love is its own satisfaction. It has its reward; and that reward is the object of its love'.[22] To seek God for any other reason than himself is to be caught in a vicious circle, longing by nature, as we are, for something to satisfy our appetite, and foolishly rejecting the only means of achieving our end. The wise man chooses the king's highway, turning neither to left nor right. 'Uprightness is the really vital and natural food of the soul that rightly uses it. Wealth, indeed, can no more satisfy the soul's hunger than air can satisfy the hunger of the body'.[23] Yet there is a kind of spiritual hunger which is itself a blessing. 'It is an extraordinary thing that no one can seek you unless he has first found you. And so you wish to be found that you may be sought and sought that you may be found'.[24]

This, then, is the story of our life with God and of our deepening involvement with him. We begin with carnal love, with self-interest, with that recognition of what and who we are, which makes us concerned with ourselves. And so man 'who does not know how to love anyone but himself, begins to love God out of self interest. Frequent experience teaches him that in him he can do everything that it is good to do, and without him nothing. Thus, to begin with, man loves God in a self-regarding way and not yet for himself'.[25] It is the experience of God's mercy in trouble and difficulty that gradually alters all this, if it is to him we turn when troubles come, letting our necessity find its own voice. At this stage, too, our love for our neighbours begins to become a much more real thing and easier to fulfil. Genuinely loving God, we begin to love God's creatures too. So we move towards loving God for himself. Sometimes, as it deepens further still, we get lost in this love. Like a little drop of water in a quantity of wine, or red-hot iron in the burning flame, we take on the character of that in which we are immersed. But this deification which, as we have seen all the Fathers teaching, is our ultimate destiny, can never be complete and permanent in this life. Nor indeed even in the next can our loss to ourselves be complete, until God's total intentions for us are fulfilled in the resurrection of our bodies. The closer we come to loving God, simply and solely for himself, the more we are identified with his wishes for us at every stage of our development.

> He spoke the truth who said, *everything works together for good to those who love God.* To the soul that loves God the body is valuable in its weakness, valuable when it is dead, valuable when it is raised from the dead. In the first condition it serves to the profit of penance, in the second for rest, and in the end for completion. It is right that the soul does not wish to be fulfilled without the body, since it is convinced that in every condition the body has been its servant in good. It is evident that the flesh is a good and faithful friend to the good spirit. For, when it is a burden, it is also a help or, when it does not help, it is an unburdening, and when it undoubtedly helps, it is no burden at at all. The first state is toilsome, but fruitful; the second leisured, yet far from wearisome, the third simply glorious.[26]

And so it is that we come at last to a degree of love that is permanent; 'when God is loved supremely and solely, for we do not even love ourselves except for his sake, so that he is himself the reward of those who love him, the everlasting reward of everlasting lovers'.[27]

Splendidly personal in its way of expressing itself as St Bernard's *On loving God* may be, it voices the unhesitating belief of the undivided tradition of Christianity that the conversion of heart to which the life of prayer summons and submits us is also a return to our true selves, finding ourselves in a God who sees to it that nothing is lost on a journey on which nothing happens in vain.

15

SENSE AND NONSENSE, KNOWING AND UNKNOWING

A complaint that can often, with more or less justice, be levelled against books that once launch into the subject of prayer is that they get so rapidly absorbed in the end of the journey that they forget to tell us enough about the middle. Days often come when we cannot find one which will say anything about the situation where we happen to find ourselves just now. This is not necessarily either their failure or ours. For the middle of the journey is, in many ways, the most difficult to discuss, precisely because it *is* the middle, and therefore shares in a mixture of the characteristics of the beginning and of the end. In this and subsequent chapters it is only possible to talk about some of the factors which have to be borne in mind, once we have actually begun to pray.

One difficulty nearly always dogs those who have been led up to the point of praying, which needs immediate clarification, since it is often a matter in which the books leave us feeling most betrayed. They have all appeared to be telling us with great theological precision Do remember, won't you, that the life of prayer is the life of the theological virtues of faith, hope, and charity. Remember that it is not a question of experiences, of visions and voices, that loving God and one's neighbour is not a question of the emotions. This may be splendid theoretical sense, but if it is taken to imply, as it often is, that nothing I experience, imagine, or feel is of any value in relation to my life of prayer then it is, from both a practical and a theoretical point of view, plain nonsense. We are, as we have been taking great pains to see, one whole thing. Hence we should realize that, since prayer is some kind of a relationship, even though a very special one, there are inevitably going to be reactions to that relationship which affect us *as a whole*.

We have, indeed, seen in our previous chapter that there are some things which we can and should trust about our experience. St Francis of Sales, with the good sense which governs all his writings, has pointed out to us that the angels on Jacob's ladder go up and down by the rungs, even though they have wings.[1] Most of us, especially when we begin, need to be prevented from trying to behave like angels who use only their wings. If we insist on trying to be too spiritual at once, God may very well have to pull us down with a bump. We should certainly be attempting to behave like angels if we expected to go straight from meditation or reflection into a world of pure spirit.

It ought not to need saying that to go to prayer for the experience of doing so is as unworthy of us as it is of God. But, while we have seen that we need to examine our experience and treat it with a certain wise reserve, whether in respect of prayer or of anything else, we must at the same time get a little clearer about which aspects of it to take seriously and to value. It is less the immediacy of experience that must concern us than its long-term effects. St Bernard's English contemporary, St Aelred of Rievaulx, says on this subject in his earliest work: 'No spiritual man can be ignorant of the fact that our love of God is not to be estimated by these transitory feelings, which are far from being in our control, but rather by the abiding quality of the will itself'.[2] In this he is expressing the common view of all the spiritual masters of all periods, to which we must return in a moment. Yet we must, for a little, delay over the fact that sight and sense have *some* part to play in our spiritual formation. Many of the Western masters who try to help beginners to pray, St Aelred of Rievaulx among them, actually encourage us to use and stimulate our imagination in the kind of meditation which leads us on into prayer. In recognizing that imagination and feeling can have some function to fulfil in leading us into the ways of the spirit, these teachers acknowledge the existence of a factor in our formation so necessary that, without its use, some people would never really confront divine things at all. The teachers all warn us, first, not just to pass our time letting our imagination run wild and, second, not to take what we imagine or, naturally, any of the consequences of doing so, for the divine thing itself. These, then, are the dangers of attending to what occurs in our imagination. Can its functions ever be a spiritual asset?

We may consider an example taken from a beautiful fourteenth-

173

century English spiritual classic, *The Revelations of Divine Love* by Mother Julian of Norwich. She writes:

> He shewed me a little thing the size of a hazel-nut, lying in the palm of my hand; and it was as round as a ball. I looked thereupon with the eye of my understanding, and thought: What may this be? And it was answered generally thus: It is all that is made. I marvelled how it could last, for it seemed so little it might suddenly have fallen to naught. And I was answered in my understanding: It lasteth, and ever shall, because God loveth it. And so the world hath its existence by the love of God.[3]

Now Mother Julian, who received the revelations of which she writes on 8 May 1373, insists at the outset that she was 'a simple creature and no scholar'. But, scholar or no scholar, we can see what is happening in this vivid and characteristic little passage. It deserves our attention, not to make us run after visions any more than she did, but to help us understand one of God's normal ways of working. He can, when he wishes, use our imagination to make on our minds an indelible and personal impression of the common truths of faith. This does not need to happen in the form of 'revelations' such as Mother Julian had that day in May, but the work can equally well have its true source in God when suddenly our eye is opened to significances in things we never saw before. Certainly if our grasp of spiritual things is only in our books and in our theories it will hardly be sufficient to move us. The passage quoted shows how, although not a scholar, Mother Julian distinguishes with scholarly clarity between what she sees with her eyes and what she understands in her mind, and does not confuse the one with the other. It is precisely this capacity to distinguish between the visions and what they theologically *imply* that, among other signs, gives Mother Julian's visions their note of authenticity. They stand, in other words, the test of ordinary, common textbook theology. But they also admirably exemplify how the life of the imagination can have a very positive part to play in impressing upon our spirits the deep, impenetrable mysteries of divine things. What Mother Julian is saying, and what God is impressing upon her could, theoretically, be found in a good many books. Yet what matters, in each and every case, is what these truths mean *for us*, and this no book can teach us in the way that God does. In everyone's life, whether in visions or out of them, God uses little, bright, sharp, vivid things to teach us great and ultimately incomprehensible truths. Some will, naturally, need to go by this way more than others. St John of the Cross, when he comes to discuss visions and voices and raptures,[4] will think of them largely as characteristic manifestations which follow in certain temperaments from personal contact with divine things, and consequently as imperfections, even when there is reason to believe that they are authentic in their source. He is doubtless making the same kind of distinction as that which Mother Julian struggles to make between what she sees and what she 'understands', which both know to be something purely spiritual when it is true. But neither would be saying that God cannot and does not teach us by means of these things, especially if we do not despise anything, even though it be as small as a hazel-nut.

This is doubtless an important notion for many people today. Already in 1802 the poet Wordsworth was writing in the preface to his *Lyrical Ballads*:

> The human mind is capable of being excited without the application of gross and violent stimulants; and he must have a very faint perception of its beauty and dignity who does not know this, and who does not further know, that one is being elevated above another, in proportion as he possesses this capability. For a multitude of causes, unknown to former times, are now acting with a combined force to blunt the discriminating powers of the mind, and unfitting it for all voluntary exertion to reduce it to a state of almost savage torpor. The most effective of these causes are the great national events which are daily taking place, and the increasing accumulation of men in cities, where the uniformity of their occupations produces a craving for extraordinary incident, which the rapid communication of intelligence hourly gratifies.[5]

Little can most people have guessed at the date at which they were published what a terrible prophecy these words embodied. With communications by satellite even sensations are reduced to commonplaces, and the blare of advertisements and portable transistors have reduced millions of minds to a torpor more savage than even Wordsworth's worst presentiments can have envisaged. It is possible to retort that none of these developments *necessarily* involves this result. But they certainly mean that we have a greater responsibility than ever to see that, when we can, we really do quite consciously *choose* what we allow to enter into and form our imagination. It is no use complaining that we cannot pray or do anything mentally demanding, if we have not fed our imagination, our emotions, and our feelings with the right food, or have joined in the mad pursuit of gross and violent stimulants, whether intellectual or sensual. Nearly all difficulties in prayer really begin outside it.

But supposing we have done what we can to give our mind and our imagination the right food so that they function freely and happily—and for most of us this will mean the use of poetry, novels, and the works of the creative imagination—even still, there will be days of dark and uselessness, when the rungs by which we have been accustomed to climb seem to break beneath our feet, or not to be there at all. Since we have begun to speak of Mother Julian we may get her to talk to us about this in her own homely way. Even among the revelations of that extraordinary day in May 1373 these familiar alternations of experience occurred. She tells us at one point:

I was filled with the everlasting sureness, mightily sustained without any painful dread. This feeling was so gladsome and so spiritual that I was wholly at peace and in rest; there was nothing in earth that should have grieved me. This lasted but a while, and I was turned and left to myself in heaviness and weariness of my life and irksomeness of myself, that I could scarcely have patience to live. There was no comfort nor any ease to me but faith, hope and charity; and these I had in truth, but little in feeling. And anon after this our blessed Lord gave me again the comfort and the rest in soul, in satisfying and sureness so blissful and so mighty that no dread, no sorrow, no bodily pain that might be suffered should have distressed me. It is helpful to some souls to feel on this wise—sometimes to be in comfort, and sometimes to fail and to be left to themselves. God willeth that we know that he keepeth us equally secure in woe and in weal. But for profit of man's soul, a man is sometimes left to himself, although sin is not always the cause. I deserved not to have had this blessedful feeling, but freely our Lord giveth it when he will, and leaves us in woe sometimes; and both is one love. For it is God's will that we hold ourselves in comfort with all our might; for bliss is lasting without end, and pain is passing and shall be brought to nought for them that shall be saved. And therefore it is not God's will that we follow the feelings of

176

pain in sorrow and mourning for them, but that we suddenly pass over them and hold ourselves in the endless enjoyment that is God.[6]

No one could write with greater precision than Mother Julian does in this matter, or be more clearly representative of the common tradition that, whether things go well or ill at the level at which she is speaking, it is all 'one love' that is the cause of these alternations. Her words should help us to grasp what sort of value we should give to the things of sense, while avoiding any plain emotional nonsense. Just as prayer and experience are not God, though they belong to our relationship to him, so sense and emotion are not useless nonsense, though unless we keep ourselves on the highway of those who have gone before us, they may become so. Time and again in the course of this book we have seen that living a spiritual life in our bodily condition means, not a blind and in fact impossible attempt to fly from that condition *as such*, but rather that it means a re-training and re-forming of all our powers in view of man's true spiritual nature. We have seen, moreover, that this is a re-forming which is in part effected by our own efforts, co-operating with grace, and in part effected by God's formation of us through our total providential relationship to him, in so far as we submit to and co-operate with it. To this providential formation of God, which necessarily sees and goes further than ever we could of ourselves, we particularly expose ourselves when we pray. We must never forget that, as all the traditional masters of the spiritual life believed, the entire attitude of our souls towards God is in its essence indicated in the words of the *Our Father*. If we do not wish God's kingdom to come in us, if we do not wish to be changed in the manner in which God's grace working in us will inevitably and inexorably change us, then we should not pray 'thy kingdom come', since we do not really mean it. We shall find that all the masters of prayer will teach us how prayer itself, as it develops, becomes part of our very necessary education. We have seen Mother Julian telling us how the changes of feeling about spiritual things which occur in us are part of God's plan for and formation of us. One of the reasons why it is perfectly possible for our relationship to God to be just what it should be for the moment, even when it 'feels' most wrong, is that our 'feelings' and our will are not the same thing, and while we can choose with our will, we cannot always make a choice about our feelings. The only appropriate virtue for situations about which we literally cannot do anything is patience. In addition, there is the fact that, as we draw nearer to God, the source of all light and joy, so we learn better what we ourselves are really like. In the light what is dark shows up. This is often very painful and purging. Indeed it is precisely what purgatory is, a condition of being fundamentally united to God by love and, on account of that union, longing to be purged of all that hinders the completeness of our re-formation in God's likeness. As our love grows, so does our cleansing. Naturally, even God's closest friends felt at times ambivalent about this. Mother Julian, among others, remarks: 'If I had known what pain it would be, I had been loth to have prayed',[7] and she goes on to explain that this feeling of reluctance was on the physical side of her being, while in the depths of her soul she was, at the same time, in a kind of dark peace. God does not let his holy ones off purgatory. They simply go through it in this world, and normally in a completely hidden and unknown manner. To be in this condition is much to be desired, for the end of it is the sight of the joy of our Lord. The adjective 'dark' in connection with the kind of peace Mother Julian enjoyed in her purgation has been deliberately used, for there is a long tradition of spiritual writing going back to the earliest years of Christianity which refers to this condition in this way. It is a way of thinking about divine things which has had a very great influence on the theology both of the East and the West alike through the writings of a mysterious, probably Syrian writer, known as Dionysius the Areopagite. This is not the kind of book in which to discuss the problems his writings raise, but it is sufficient to note that there is one aspect of his doctrine which the classical theology of the undivided Church unanimously accepts. It is that, in our condition in this world, however holy we may be, we cannot see divine things directly, but only, as St Paul puts it, as 'bewildering shadows in a mirror'.[8] This means that, although we can learn to speak accurately about God to some limited extent, the living meaning of even what we can correctly say of him is not self-evident to us. What God is, is hidden from us in the darkness of faith. At the same time, if we were to become the sort of 'theologians' who actually approach God in love and service, we should, as we have already seen, actually encounter him whom we cannot see. This is to say that if we were to grow in love in the context of faith, we might come to know God in the way that love can know him, while the full vision of his beauty and glory

178

is still withheld from us. *This* kind of knowledge of God would be what some more recent kinds of talk might possibly call 'anti-knowledge', and what one very great, still personally unidentified, fourteenth-century English mystical writer called 'unknowing'. It is important to begin by understanding what he meant by unknowing. He did not mean that someone who learns to know God in the way that a man who loves him in prayer knows him, will be likely to treat all the theological formulations of the tradition as so much useless nonsense. It is rather the case that, as he encounters the mystery of God in experience, he comes to know in and through that experience how all words fail and falter before the true reality of God. The whole experience in its totality is like that of unlearning, unknowing what, apart from that experience, is perfectly meaningful and sensible, when it is correctly understood. Hence he calls his book *The Cloud of Unknowing*.[9]

Now the author of this little book is perfectly clear that what he is writing is not for everyone. That he should think this is a result neither of prejudice nor of a sort of spiritual snobbery. It is simply a practical recognition of the fact to which not only his book, but this one too, has frequently alluded, namely that everybody's call is unique, that within the universal call to prayer God has one way with some and other ways with others. It follows from this that certain books will help certain people, as corresponding in a general way to the way that God has called them. To others they will not speak, and to meddle with them, once one has recognized this, is only to add to one's spiritual obstacles. Moreover, even the books which suit and help in our case, will not necessarily do so all the time. We shall each of us have slowly to discover which are our books and which are the right times for them. There is only one general word of warning which applies to everyone. By whichever road the Lord leads us, we must gradually become more attached to the Lord than we are to the means which lead, or have led us to him. Nothing, not even prayer itself, is God. All things apart from him are only means. Hence, too, we must be grateful for the way we are led, and not look either enviously or anxiously at the way he leads others. Prayer is a kingdom which cannot be entered by artifice, but only with the simplicity and truth of a child.

It can not infrequently happen that someone who has so far travelled by Mother Julian's way, or something rather like it, who has been using the common means that the tradition offers, the

Scriptures, the Liturgy, ways of meditating and reflecting, the teaching of the great masters, may suddenly stumble upon *The Cloud of Unknowing* and find it, as the old Quaker phrase has it, 'speaking to his condition'. If this should happen, and he has already trained himself in the way that this other book has so far attempted to set out, he will at once find himself listening to a man talking in the language of a recognizable tradition. Like the entire orthodox tradition, this writer says that every life has both its active and contemplative aspects and that consequently these overlap. The active life consists, from one point of view, of praise-worthy activities of a quasi-physical kind; from another point of view, it consists of those sorts of interior activities of a spiritual nature in which we chiefly engage under the impulse of our own decision, reading, reflecting, meditating, thinking about the Gos-pels, the life and passion of Christ, the lives of the saints, and so on. This spiritual side of the active life is also one aspect of the contemplative life, in so far as these kinds of virtuous spiritual activities are designed to bring us into explicit relationship with divine things, and do in fact achieve this, when pursued in humility and faith. But there is another aspect of the contemplative life where God, as it were, draws the soul after him into a kind of activity where explicit reflections cease and where, if anything is said at all, it is only a single word, like, for instance, 'love'. The soul is here rather, as it were, reaching out towards God in the dark. The point the author is making—and it is one that beginners often need brought to their notice quite soon—is that just as it would be wrong, a distraction, to think about one's work while one is supposed to be meditating so, if a time comes when God seems to be inviting one to make simple acts of love of him in the darkness of not thinking about anything specific, although attending to him, it would be equally wrong and equally distracting to go rushing around in one's mind looking for a subject on which to meditate. Work is good, meditation is good, each in their time and place. Indeed, as we have tried to see, we cannot lead a fully human life unless we give each of these activities its proper place. But, if and when a stage of development in the ways of prayer is reached when that love of God, to which meditation is meant to lead, begins to insist upon occupying the whole time of prayer, it is completely mistaken to imagine that we ought to force ourselves to go on meditating. We must take simply to loving, even if it means doing it in the dark of not knowing quite what it is all about save that, as *The Cloud* would say, we 'mean' or 'intend' God by what we do.

Now this, it must be repeated, as *The Cloud of Unknowing* itself insists, is something we cannot decide to begin on a mere presumption, or by way of experiment. However mysteriously, the invitation of God must be recognizably there. When it is, it never creates any problems. For genuinely to confront a mystery is not at all like going out into a state of vacancy of mind. What we are speaking of here is, not just the dropping of thoughts, but our engagement in a special kind of attention. The soul is occupied, although it could not explain to anyone, or even to itself, what keeps it busy, save love.

One last word about this astonishing little book which, as its author says in his preface, should be read all through by those who feel drawn to it. Those who are authentically drawn to this way of prayer are sometimes held back at first by a worry that they are forgetting to be sorry for their sins or meditate on the Passion of Christ and so on. To them our author replies that because the soul experiences God in love, it also inevitably experiences itself as it really is, until it is cleansed of all its impurities. It feels itself, indeed, to be exactly like sin 'congealed in a lump',[10] so general is its sense of sinfulness. Yet it is crazily, inexplicably, and rightly convinced that it will be cleansed if it leaves everything else, even its own most precious thoughts, for God alone. He will certainly not disappoint it.

16

SPIRITUAL GROWTH

It has been possible to see that there are two broad factors which enter into that developing relationship with God of which prayer is, of its very nature, the most vital and intimate expression. There are, on the one hand, those features of our lives about which we can make choices and decisions, and those which emerge of themselves. In either case, we shall have to assess the meaning of what is occurring, not on the basis of the immediacy of our experience, but on the basis of the long-term results on our lives as a whole. From time to time we shall need the help of others, wiser than ourselves, in making this assessment. But, then, as all the great teachers from the desert Fathers onwards agree, there are not so very many wise guides, even in a fortunate generation. In our own times we may well have to depend largely upon the conjectures we can make about ourselves on the basis of the written directives of the classical and accredited masters of the long tradition in these matters. We can be sure that God will not desert us, any more than he deserted those who have gone before us, if we do the best we can in an entirely authentic humility. The marks of an authentic humility are likely to be, first, that we do not reject the help that we could and should ask of others, when a rare opportunity offers; and, second, that we do not set out to achieve our spiritual good upon *our own* conditions. This second point is made with forceful clarity in a letter of the Abbé de Tourville, which is itself a notable expression of the doctrine it teaches.

Perfection does not by any means consist in what is the most certain—sometimes it is exactly the opposite—but in doing the least ill possible, having regard to our condition at the time and the general problems of our temperament. It consists in modestly holding fast to a very straightforward simplicity, giving up any course of action more perfect, either in itself or in appearance, which would overstrain our gift. The saints were not the men for the safest path, but the greatest adventurers in the world, and yet hardly tried to go beyond the ordinary measure of grace they saw and felt convinced was in their souls. Let us enter into this simplicity.[1]

There are perhaps only a few words of caution to be added to this generally sound advice. The circumstances of our own period make it necessary to notice that we are forced to live rather nearer the surface than our ancestors. We may miss giving the various aspects of our personality the training that leads to simplicity, unless we consciously make the attempt to go deeper. Above all, we must see to it that we do not find ourselves leading two, or several, lives, of which prayer is only one. If we are not prepared to live in a way which conforms to the integrity which prayer requires and leads to, then we shall not develop in the ways of prayer. Our growth will be stunted, if it continues at all. Two opposite temptations may ensnare the beginner in these matters. On the one hand, some people will tend to underestimate the importance of their times of prayer, silence, and solitude, provided they can satisfy themselves with a generous display of the active virtues. Others, on the contrary, will plunge so earnestly into the life of prayer and the formation of their habits about it, that they come to think of their spiritual development solely in terms of the graces of prayer. The latter are possibly in less danger of retarded development than the former, since it may be doubted if anyone can persevere in giving time to prayer without being, by the prayer itself forced to do something about developing at least some of the virtues. But both types alike will need to be brought back from time to time to that general Christian sense of perspective which has been our main preoccupation in the first half of this book. Each of us, in other words, has to discover how to achieve that entirely personal equilibrium between action and contemplation which our particular call to conformity with Christ requires. It is, naturally, inevitable that this equilibrium will be to some extent unstable, and the more dangerously so, the less the soul co-operates with the action of God in its prayer and in its life in general. This book has made no attempt to talk about the stages of the spiritual life in a theoretical way since to do this is often a great distraction from what is really important, namely to pay attention to where we

183

actually are. Growth, it is true, does take place by stages, but it is first and foremost *continuity* that gives growing things their healthy character. The most vital continuous factor in our spiritual growth is necessarily our prayer, if it be genuine. For, not only is prayer the chief means whereby we voluntarily open ourselves, as we are, to the cleansing and healing action of God, consenting to and co-operating with that divine action; it is also normally in prayer that we become most profoundly and effectively convinced of our need of the divine action upon us in whatever form is most suited to us.

It is for this reason that our fundamental need is to establish an attitude of complete openness to the divine leading in our prayer. Even the most reputable writers most closely associated by common report with 'method' in prayer and meditation insist upon this point. We may take as a useful example the classical Jesuit writer, Père Surin, who says:

> A good prayer is that in which God works the most, and in which our spirit is most dependent upon his grace. It would seem that one could say that the best prayer is that which brings us the most profit, and which helps us most to correct our failings and advance in the virtues. But this is just the nub of the question, and people ask what sort of a prayer it is which best produces these good effects. It would seem that it is that in which God works the most. For we profit more by the help of grace and the working of God than by our own working. To understand this point properly it is necessary to examine the method and order commonly observed in this exercise.[2]

Père Surin then notes that people are usually taught how to meditate along Ignatian lines but that, although their general intentions are good, they often want to have the best of both worlds and 'reserve to themselves any number of little rights'. As a consequence of this, they put obstacles in the way of the development along which God would like to lead them. Their plea is that 'they stick to what is solid' and avoid the path of illusion. Surin continues:

> It is true that St Ignatius gave a method to form those who come to the service of God in prayer. This method, which consists in the exercise of the three powers of the soul on a mystery or on a truth of faith, is excellent and, according to the intention of

St Ignatius himself, it is a sure way to the prayer of simple regard and repose. Thus it is that, if he co-operates with grace and gives himself completely to God, a man who makes the exercises of St Ignatius will be instructed in the great truths of faith and disposed for a higher prayer, should it please God to raise him to it. But as long as he remains in the ordinary way of meditation, he will never have an understanding so deep and so penetrating as in the gentle repose of the simple regard of God and the truths of faith. This is why good directors try to lead souls that way, as the holy bishop of Geneva did.

Surin is, of course, referring to St Francis of Sales, and he draws a contrast with the kind of directors of whom St John of the Cross equally disapproved, who try to keep those for whom they are responsible busy with their meditations. Surin adds:

If these souls had visions and revelations they would listen to them and examine them without being scandalized. But if they only see a simple attention to God, a gentle repose, they believe that it is time lost; a matter in which they are greatly deceived. Those who always want to keep souls in discursive prayer, judging only that to be good, do a great injustice to the Holy Spirit, laying down limits for him, and taking away his liberty to communicate his gifts in the manner he pleases. Can one believe that the prayer of silence and repose is only for a St Francis or a St Teresa? God gives it freely to the souls he finds empty and well-disposed: he takes pleasure in filling them with his simple and tranquil light, which instructs them in a moment, raises them up and establishes them in a peace and a repose which surpasses anything the mind can conceive. The infusion of this light is a very precious gift, which must be received with respect. Experience teaches that it is useful for everything. It is not reserved for solitaries; it is fitting for all who want to serve God. If we are deprived of it, it is normally because we render ourselves unworthy of it by our want of liberality towards God. If we had it, we should do a hundred times more for God than we do.

This is as clear a statement as any we are likely to find of the way things stand at the frontier where our own activity in prayer tends almost imperceptibly to be invaded by that of God. St Teresa of Avila describes this area of our life of prayer in ways of which the inconsistency is probably best interpreted as reflecting the difficulty, at least for some people, of discerning the degree of passivity which has overtaken them. In the most mature of her works, *The Interior Castle* or *The Mansions*,[3] the necessary distinctions are at least clearly made. Of the activity of the mind she says:

When His Majesty wishes the working of the understanding to cease, he employs it in another manner, and illumines the soul's knowledge to so much higher a degree than any we can ourselves attain that he leads it into a state of absorption, in which, without knowing how, it is much better instructed than it could ever be as a result of its own efforts, which would spoil everything. God gave us faculties to work with, and everything will have its due reward; there is no reason, then, for trying to cast a spell over them—they must be allowed to perform their office until God gives them a better one.

And then, later in the same chapter, she adds:

When instead of coming through conduits, the water springs directly from its source, the understanding checks its activity, or rather the activity is checked for it when it finds it cannot understand what it desires, and thus it roams about all over the place, like a demented creature, and can settle down to nothing. The will is fixed so firmly upon its God that this disturbed condition of the understanding causes it great distress; but it must not take any notice of this, for if it does so it will lose a great part of what it is enjoying; it must forget about it and abandon itself into the arms of love, and His Majesty will teach it what to do next[4]

These developments are, as Père Surin says, 'normal' in those who give themselves unreservedly to God, and they do tend to be one of the most important factors in stabilizing the dispositions of the soul in regard to God.

It will be necessary later to look a little more closely at the question of passivity in contemplative prayer, but for the moment it is useful to delay a little upon the connection between these developments in prayer and the general establishment of the life of the virtues. For all the great teachers agree that there is a 'normal' connection between the appearance of a simpler type of prayer and the soul's overall gift of itself to God, so that it would not willingly refuse him anything necessary for its purification and healing. We also need to note that corresponding to this basic willingness to develop, there is a growth in the virtues which is a characteristic *fruit* of this kind of prayer. Thus there is a constant interaction between prayer and life. A genuine growth in virtue is, indeed, one of the surest signs of the authenticity of this type of prayer. A small point must be added in this connection which may seem, at first, too obvious to need mentioning. It is that our new-found sense of liberty ought not to lead us into the error of being inattentive to little things. This is not, by any means, a suggestion that we should allow ourselves to become absorbed in petty details, but rather that we should value the humility which suggests that we should attend to little things which present themselves as needing to be done. The distinction between this kind of fidelity and mere small-mindedness is made by the Abbé de Tourville in a letter to a troubled correspondent, where he says:

> Let us live content under the best of Masters, whose view is: *Because you have been faithful over little, I will set you over much.* The sense of the words is not, *because you have been faithful down to the smallest detail*, but rather, *because you have been faithful, although in little things.*[5]

This is the kind of necessary observation we should expect from so shrewd a modern disciple of St Francis of Sales. It was, as we have seen, St Francis' preoccupation with integral living that determined the very shape and approach of the *Introduction to the Devout Life*, and it will be useful for our present purposes to look at one or two of the points that St Francis makes about the general setting of the life of prayer as it develops. It will be recalled that the fundamental conviction of St Francis of Sales is that an authentic life of prayer is not the preserve of a few privileged people living under special conditions, but is possible for everyone everywhere, provided always that their will be good and that they are prepared to make the sacrifices which may be appropriate to their circumstances. This is a colourless way of saying what St Francis himself says so much more attractively in book three of the *Introduction*, which contains, as he says 'various counsels concerning the exercise of the virtues'.

> It is [he says,] a great defect in many—and we can all notice this for ourselves—that, when they undertake the practice of some particular virtue, they insist upon producing acts of it on

all sorts of occasions and wish, like those ancient philosophers, either always to weep or always to laugh.[6]

The more sensible and sound way to live is by bearing the following general principle in mind:

> Opportunities for the practice of fortitude, magnanimity, and magnificence do not often occur; but gentleness, moderation, integrity, and humility are virtues with which all the actions of our lives should be coloured. There are virtues nobler than these; but the practice of these is more necessary.

Having said this, St Francis adds:

> Among the virtues we should prefer that which suits our duty best, and not that which is most to our taste and, although everyone ought to have all the virtues, yet not everyone is bound to practise them to the same extent. Each ought to give himself specially to those which are required by the kind of life to which he is called.

This is a principle of adaptation which ought to help us to find, and keep refinding, our personal equilibrium. St Francis has a good deal to the point to say about those divided desires which lose us all the profit of being where we actually are. Writing before the invention of deep freeze had banished the seasons, he tells us good humouredly:

> It is quite normal for us to have the desires of women with child, who want fresh cherries in the autumn and fresh grapes in the spring. I cannot approve of someone, with a particular duty or calling, wasting their time in desiring some other kind of life than that which fits their duty, or practices incompatible with their present condition of life; for this fritters away the energies of the heart and make it weak in carrying out what it ought to do. No, I should not even want anyone to desire to have a greater talent or a better judgement, for these desires are silly, and take the place of the desire which each of us ought to have to cultivate his own talent, such as it is; nor would I have anyone desire a means of serving God he lacks, but I would want him to use faithfully what he has. Now this applies to those desires which preoccupy the heart. As for simple wishes, they do no harm, if they are not frequent.[7]

Many people battle hard and long against accepting the really searching asceticism which the practice of this teaching involves. Clearly it in no way intends to dismiss the kind of reflections which may lead to our deciding that we may have to change our commitments and way of living, if we are free to do so. But it draws our attention to the fact, which all must, in the long run accept, that once we are where we are, we are only half living if we do not make something positive of the circumstances in which we find ourselves. St Francis is consistent in this doctrine all day and every day, as we know from witnesses he personally was in its practice. Thus he has said in the same part of the same book:

> A pursuit of talk and a flight from it are two extremes to be censured in the devotion of ordinary people. Flight from it implies disdain and contempt for our neighbour. Its pursuit suggests idleness and emptyheadedness. You must love your neighbour as yourself; to show that you love him, you must not avoid being with him, and to show that you love yourself, you must be glad to be with yourself when you actually are there.[8]

This is the language of a man writing in a period very remote from that of the Fathers of the Desert, yet parallels from their way of living out these same principles would be easy to quote. Sooner or later everyone has to reach the point where they recognize that the external setting is a matter of comparative indifference.

> I personally could never approve the method of those who, to reform a man, begin with the outside—with deportment, clothes and hair. On the contrary, it seems to me that we must begin with the interior. *Be converted to me*, says God, *with all your heart. My son, give me thy heart*; for the heart being the source of our actions they are such as the heart is.[9]

This insistence upon the primary importance of the gift of the heart is, naturally, the basis of all St Francis has to teach. It makes him consistently more austere than he looks on the surface, as anyone who tries to carry out what he teaches will discover for themselves. He is concerned for what is genuine, and has no time for empty show. Hence his advice that we should aim at cultivating what he calls 'the little virtues', patience, consideration for others, bearing with their imperfections. He includes in the list of the hidden virtues one can practise that humility which makes us love our own abjection, 'abjection' being, as he says 'the littleness, low-

189

liness, and insignificance that is in us, without our thinking of it'.

> There are [he says] even faults in which there is no evil at all except the abjection; and humility does not require that we should commit them purposely, but it does require that we should not be worried about them when we have committed them; such are certain stupidities, and failures in manners and alertness.[10]

This teaching leads on quite naturally to one of the most important pieces of advice St Francis of Sales has to give for those who wish to make progress in spiritual things:

> One of the good uses that we should learn to make of gentleness is in things which concern ourselves, never upsetting ourselves about our imperfections; for though reason requires that, when we are at fault, we should be displeased and sorry, yet we must prevent ourselves from having a displeasure which is bitter, sulky, spiteful and angry. Many people commit a great fault because, when they have given way to anger, they are annoyed for being annoyed and angry at having been angry and upset; for this is the way they keep their hearts preserved and steeped in anger.[11]

In a word, we must have a dislike for our own faults which is 'peaceable, dispassionate and firm'. We must ...

> behave as little children do, who with one hand cling to their father, and with the other gather strawberries or blackberries along the hedges. For just like this, while you are gathering and dealing with this world's goods with one hand, you must always keep the other hand in your heavenly Father's, turning to him from time to time, to see if the way you behave and what you do pleases him.[12]

Here, in fact, is a little image of a way of life lived in intention *for* God, which gradually becomes a way of life lived *with* him. This is the kind of life to which true prayer comes as naturally as breathing.

If we turn to a great nineteenth-century Russian archbishop, Theophan the Recluse, whose way of expressing himself often has an uncanny affinity with that of St Francis of Sales, we shall find him saying something rather similar. His thought has more obvious connections with an older past, derived from studies of the Fathers more thorough and extensive than Francis ever undertook, but the message is essentially the same:

To pray does not only mean to stand in prayer. To keep the mind and heart turned towards God and directed to him—this is already prayer, whatever the position in which one may be. Prayer according to the rule is one thing, and this state of prayer is another. The way to it is to attain the habit of constant remembrance of God, of the last hour, and the judgement that follows it. Accustom yourself to this and all will go well. Every step you take will be inwardly consecrated to God. You must direct your steps according to the Commandments; and you know what the Commandments are. That is all. It is possible to apply these Commandments to every event, and to consecrate all your activities inwardly to God; and then all your life will be dedicated to him. What more is necessary? Nothing. You see how simple it is.[13]

17

FURTHER DEVELOPMENTS
IN THE
LIFE OF PRAYER

'Although he is small, he is, I feel, big in the eyes of God', St Teresa of Avila wrote of St John of the Cross,[1] and no one who comes to know, as a whole, the life and writings of her incomparable 'little Seneca' can doubt that she was right. Some readers may meet him first as a poet and only later discover that, when the moment comes to ask his advice, he has no equal. There is certainly no one to whom we can turn with greater confidence for guidance in the developments in the life of prayer which may now occur to us, and we shall be placing ourselves in the hands of a man of a serene spiritual balance produced by an altogether unusual combination of learning and experience. If we genuinely need his help, he will show us clearly where we are; and if he is not for us, we shall know it equally clearly. But his writings are extensive, and it is doubtless an enterprise of which he would not disapprove to attempt to isolate, as far as possible in his own words, the features of his teaching which may be necessary for us at the point our investigations into the tradition have reached. No one else deals with these matters with quite his firmness and clarity. He was himself a man reluctant to speak and most of his writings were, in fact, drawn from him in response to the need for direction in the ways of prayer. It may, indeed, be best to begin with a passage on the question of direction from what is perhaps the loveliest of his works, *The Living Flame of Love*.

St John has been talking of that process of spiritual purification which has already been discussed to some extent in our previous chapters. He speaks of the emptying of the faculties of memory, understanding and will of everything alien to them, and their preparation to receive the transformation of God's presence. He continues:

> When, therefore, the soul considers that God is the principal agent in this matter, and the guide of its blind self, he will take it by the hand and guide it where it could not go of itself. ... And this impediment may come to the soul if it allows itself to be led and guided by another blind guide; and these blind guides that might lead it out of its way are three, the spiritual director, the devil, and its own self.

With regard to any human spiritual direction spiritual direction sought at this stage, St John insists that

> it is of great importance for the soul that desires to make progress in recollection and perfection to consider in whose hands it is placing itself; for as is the master, so will be the disciple.

He then adds:

> The fundamental requirement of a guide in spiritual things is knowledge and discretion; yet if a guide have no experience of the nature of pure and true spirituality, he will be unable to direct souls therein, when God permits it to attain so far, nor will he even understand it.

Beginners, St John says, inevitably have to start with meditations and discursive acts and the use of the imagination, all of which have been discussed in an earlier chapter in this present book. But when to some extent the desire has been fed, and in some sense habituated to spiritual things, and has acquired some fortitude and constancy, God then begins, as they say, to wean the soul and bring it to the state of contemplation, which in some persons is wont to happen very quickly. This happens

> when the discursive acts and the meditation of the soul itself cease ... And as all the operations which the soul can perform on its own account naturally depend upon sense only, it follows that God is the agent in this state of soul and the soul is the recipient.... If formerly it was given material for meditation, and practised meditation, this material must now be taken from it and it must not meditate; for, as I say, it will be unable to do so even though it would, and instead of becoming recollected it will become distracted. For God secretly and quietly infuses into the

soul loving knowledge and wisdom without any intervention of specific acts, although sometimes he specifically produces them in the soul for some length of time. And the soul has then to walk in loving awareness of God, without performing specific acts, but conducting itself, as we have said, passively.

St John now goes on to describe how God gradually leads the soul into an ever increasing silence and solitude in which it must become detached from all spiritual sweetness so that it may receive only what God wishes to give and teach it in his own way. It is now that the inexperienced director can do so much harm.

Whenever God is anointing the contemplative soul with some most delicate unction of loving knowledge ... there will come some spiritual director who has no knowledge save of hammering souls and pounding them with the faculties like a blacksmith, and because his only teaching is of that kind, and he knows of naught save meditation, he will say: 'Come now, leave these periods of inactivity, for you are only living in idleness and wasting your time. Get to work, meditate, and make interior acts; for it is right that you should do for yourself what in you lies. ... And since such persons have no understanding of the degrees of prayer or of the ways of the spirit, they cannot see that these acts which they counsel the soul to perform and those attempts to walk in meditation, have been done already.

As St John points out, anyone who has reached this stage of development, and tries forcibly to go back, will only become thoroughly distracted and fail to continue in spiritual growth. And so,

Let such guides of the soul as these take heed and remember that the principal agent and guide and mover of souls in this matter is not the director, but the Holy Spirit, who never loses his care for them; and that they themselves are only instruments to lead souls in the way of perfection by faith and the law of God, according to the spirituality that God is giving to each one.[2]

Upon these points, it will be recalled, this present book has insisted from the beginning. The firm conviction of the tradition of the undivided Church is that the Holy Spirit is the primary director and guide of souls. The way in which he leads each one is, as we

have seen, for all kinds of reasons necessarily unique. St John of
the Cross also makes it quite clear that God does not lead every
soul by the paths he describes in his books. But let us suppose that
the reader suspects that he *is* being led in these paths. By what signs
may he judge that the development in his case is genuine? And, if
and when these signs appear, how must he act? For St John's own
answers to these questions we must refer chiefly to the two works
which deal with this subject from rather different points of view.
Looking at the matter from the point of view of the soul's *activity*,
we must refer to the *Ascent of Mount Carmel*, where St John proceeds to explain when the spiritual person may leave the ways of
discursive meditation

> as carried on through the imaginations and forms and figures
> above mentioned, in order that he may lay them aside neither
> sooner nor later than the spirit bids him; for, although it is meet
> for him to lay them aside at the proper time in order that he may
> journey to God and not be hindered by them, it is no less needful
> for him not to lay aside the said imaginative meditation before
> the proper time lest he should turn backward.... We shall there-
> fore here give certain signs and examples which the spiritual
> person shall find in himself, whereby he may know if it is meet
> for him to lay them aside or not at this season.

The reader is recommended to attend to these points particularly
closely, since there are no others of such objectivity and reliability
to be found in any great writer.

> The first sign is his realization that he can no longer meditate or
> reason with his imagination, neither can he find pleasure therein
> as he was wont to do aforetime.... But, for as long as he finds
> sweetness in meditation and is able to reason, he should not
> abandon this, save when his soul is led into the peace and repose
> which is described under the third head.

We should probably note that St John's first point involves two
elements. He is saying, first of all, that the stage in the life of
prayer of which he is speaking may begin by being intermittent,
something which changes from day to day. He is, secondly, talking
specifically about the time of prayer or meditation. In other words,
the imagination of people who have reached this stage may function

perfectly well *except* when they try to pray. Those who think one can always do what one likes in spiritual things are very greatly deceived:

> The second sign is a realization that he has no desire to fix his meditation or his sense upon other particular objects, exterior or interior. I do not mean that the imagination neither comes nor goes—for it is wont to move freely even at times of great recollection—but that the soul has no pleasure in fixing it of set purpose upon other objects.
>
> The third and surest sign is that the soul takes pleasure in being alone, and waits with loving attentiveness upon God, without making any particular meditation, in inward peace and quietness and rest, without acts and exercises of the faculties—memory, understanding and will—at least without discursive acts, that is, without passing from one thing to another; the soul is alone, with an attentiveness and a knowledge, general and loving, as we said, but without any particular understanding and adverting not to what it is contemplating.
>
> These three signs at least the spiritual person must see in himself *all together* before he adventure with security to abandon the state of meditation and sense and to enter that of contemplation and spirit.[3]

All together is the operative phrase in this passage, for as St John explains, if the three signs, of which the third is the most important do not occur *together*, their occurrence may have a purely natural, not to say physical, explanation which might make one glad to remain as he charmingly says 'in that pleasant condition of wonder'. At the same time, it should also be observed that when the condition here described first begins, it is often scarcely noticed because it is so delicate in comparison to that activity in which the soul has been accustomed to be engaged. Some people take a long time to be detached from their conviction that genuine prayer necessarily involves conscious, and even violent, effort.

Now, if we look at the soul at this stage of its development in prayer from the point of view of its *passivity*, we shall realize from what has been said that it will inevitably be starting to undergo a purgation or cleansing of its sense life, a purgation which necessarily carries it further than any amount of active mortification possibly could. St John's great unfinished work on these purifications of the soul by the action of God himself, and the complement

to the *Ascent of Mount Carmel*, is his *Dark Night of the Soul.*
There he says:

> Since these aridities might frequently proceed, not from the night
> and purgation of the sensual desires aforementioned, but from
> sins and imperfections, or from weakness and lukewarmness, or
> from some bad humour or indisposition of the body, I shall here
> set down certain signs by which it may be known if such aridity
> proceeds from the aforementioned purgation, or if it arises from
> any of the aforementioned sins. For the making of this distinction
> I find there are three principal signs.
>
> The first is whether, when a soul finds no pleasure or consola-
> tion in the things of God, it also fails to find it in anything created.
> Hence it may be laid down as very probable that this aridity and
> insipidity proceed not from recently committed sins and im-
> perfections. For, if this were so, the soul would feel in its nature
> some inclination or desire to taste other things than those of God.
>
> The second sign whereby a man may believe himself to be
> experiencing the said purgation is that ordinarily the memory is
> centred upon God, with painful care and solicitude, thinking
> that it is not serving God, but is backsliding, because it finds
> itself without sweetness in the things of God. And in such a case
> it is evident that this lack of sweetness and this aridity come not
> from weakness and lukewarmness.... For the cause of this
> aridity is that God transfers to the spirit the good things and the
> strength of the senses which, since the soul's natural strength and
> senses are incapable of using them, remain barren, dry and empty.
> These souls whom God is beginning to lead through these solitary
> places of the wilderness are like to the children of Israel; to
> whom in the wilderness God began to give food from heaven,
> containing within itself all sweetness, and as is there said, it turned
> to the savour which each of them desired.... If those souls to
> whom this comes to pass knew how to be quiet at this time, and
> troubled not about performing any kind of action, whether in-
> ward or outward, neither had any anxiety about doing anything,
> then they would delicately experience this inward refreshment in
> that ease and freedom from care. So delicate is this refreshment
> that ordinarily, if a man desire or care to experience it, he ex-
> periences it not. For in such a way does God bring the soul into
> this state, and by so different a path does he lead it that, if it
> desires to work with its faculties, it hinders the work which God

is doing in it rather than aids it; whereas aforetime it was quite the contrary.

The third sign whereby this purgation of sense may be recognized is that the soul can no longer meditate or reflect in its sense of the imagination, as it was wont, however much it may of itself endeavour to do so.... With regard to this third sign it is to be understood that this embarrassment and dissatisfaction of the faculties proceed not from indisposition, for when this is the case and the indisposition, which is never permanent, comes to an end, then the soul is able once more to do as it did before. But in the purgation of the desire this is not so: when once the soul begins to enter therein, its inability to reflect with the faculties grows ever greater.

With some people, St John remarks, these aridities are things of a season and, when they are, their purpose is to cleanse and humble souls whom God never in fact intends to lead in the way of the spirit,

for not all those who consciously walk in the way of the spirit are brought by God to contemplation, nor even half of them— why, he knows best. And this is why he never completely weans the senses of such persons from the breasts of meditations and reflections, but only for short periods and at certain seasons, as we have said.[4]

These concluding remarks of St John of the Cross are a reminder of how important it is to see the development of our life of prayer, whether it takes the form St John describes or not, within a total view of the Christian life. This was, it would seem, always the general sense of the personal direction he gave, and in one of his very few surviving letters—written, in this case, to a young woman who was missing his help and advice—he says all this in an unforgettable way:

What do you think serving God to be if not the not doing evil, keeping his commandments and going about his business as best we can? If you are doing this, what need is there of other apprehensions or other lights, or sweetness—whether from here or there, in which ordinarily there are never lacking stumbling-blocks and dangers for the soul, which with its understanding and appetites is deceived and fascinated and its own faculties cause it to err? ... And how can she not err, save by going along the straight path of the law of God and of the Church and living only in obscure and true faith, certain hope and integral charity and waiting for our good things in the life to come, living here on earth as pilgrims, poor, exiles, orphans, desolate, without a road and without anything, hoping for it all there in heaven.[5]

Those who have absorbed the earlier chapters of this book will not fail to note how full of echoes of an older tradition the writing of St John of the Cross is, and it would be tedious to insist upon them now.

But there is a case for being aware of the mature attempt to put all these things into a broader theoretical perspective which St Francis of Sales achieved in his *Treatise on the Love of God*.[6] The *Treatise* is a big book, rather like a huge notebook which kept on growing, and into it Francis stuffed the reflections and insights which his own growing experience and that of others had suggested to him. Although not without a clear and definite outline, it does the *Treatise* no injustice to treat it in a highly selective manner if one wishes since, as the author explains in his preface, this is exactly how he meant it to be used. It is a book that really presupposes some spiritual maturity in its reader—Francis himself could probably not have written it as a much younger man—and, like other books of its kind, much that the *Treatise* has to say will have little meaning for those who have no experience of what it is describing. Yet, at the same time, it is probably less liable to misunderstanding when quoted in isolated fragments than some elements in the general teaching of St John of the Cross can be for those who do not know the man and his doctrines as a whole.

In any case, in St Francis the ascetic frame to his mystical doctrine is always firmly present. The basic conviction of the *Treatise* is that 'salvation is shown to faith, prepared for hope, but only given to charity'. This must be the doctrine of every Christian mystic, just as it is of every Christian theologian. 'Hatred separates us, but love brings us together. And hence the purpose of love is no other thing than the union of the lover and the thing loved'. This, in other words, is where we are going in the life of prayer, in the direction of union. 'It is, indeed, the *man* who loves, but he loves by his will, and so the purpose of his love is of the same nature as his will. But his will is spiritual, and this is why the union at which love aims is spiritual too'. In these opening statements of principle Francis expresses the conviction that original sin has much more weakened man's will than darkened his intellect. The rebellion of the sensual appetite, which we call concupiscence, may disturb the understanding, but it is more troublesome to the will. And yet

> Although the redemption of our Saviour is applied to us in as many different manners as there are souls, it is nevertheless love which is the universal means of salvation, which mingles with everything and without which nothing is profitable. Further, the cherub was stationed at the gate of the earthly paradise with his flaming sword to teach us that no one will enter the heavenly paradise who is not pierced with the sword of love.

In a word, God 'did not leave in us for nothing the natural inclination to love him'. All the early sections of the *Treatise* are careful to build up a picture of the spiritual dimensions of man's activity, as this present book has tried in a rather different way to do, in such a way that the door is always left open for the intervention of God, and so the active and contemplative aspects of our Christian life are held in balance.

This balance St Francis eventually expresses in the following terms:

> We have two principal activities of our love towards God, the one affective, the other effective, or as St Bernard says, active. By the one we conceive, by the other we bring forth. By the one, we put *God on our heart* as a standard of love round which all our affections range themselves. By the other, *we put him on our arm*, like a sword of love by which we carry out all the exploits of the virtues. Now the first activity consists principally in prayer; in which so many different movements occur that it is impossible to speak of them all, not only because of their number, but also because of their nature and quality.[7]

As he continues, St Francis explains:

> We do not take the word 'prayer' here only to mean petition or request for some good, poured out by the faithful before God, as St Basil calls it. But we take it as St Bonaventure does when he says that prayer, to speak in general terms, comprises all the acts of contemplation, or like St Gregory of Nyssa, when he teaches that prayer is a discourse or conversation of the soul with God.

Having said, then, that in this theology, he takes prayer as comprising all the acts of contemplation, St Francis then discusses what he means by contemplation. At first, in a general way, he says:

Contemplation is nothing other than a loving, simple and permanent attention of the spirit to divine things, as you will easily appreciate by comparing meditation with it. We meditate to gather the love of God, but having gathered it we contemplate God and are attentive to his goodness on account of the sweetness which love makes us find in it. In sum, meditation is the mother of love, but contemplation her daughter: and this is why I called contemplation a loving attention.[8]

Evidently we are still in that area where it may be difficult to discern how much of this engagement with God is the fruit of our own effort. But St Francis is soon speaking of a kind of recollection

which is not made at the command of love, but is love itself, that is to say, we do not bring it about by our own choice, since it is not in our power to have it when we want and does not depend on our care, but God brings it about in us when he pleases by his most holy grace. Thus when our Saviour makes his most delightful presence felt in the centre of our soul, all our faculties turn their points in that direction to unite themselves to this incomparable sweetness.[9]

St Francis' advice is:

When you are with our Lord in this simple and pure filial confidence, stay there, without disturbing yourself at all to make sensible acts, either of the understanding or the will. For this simple love of confidence and this loving slumber of your spirit in the arms of the Saviour comprises beyond compare all you could go and look for here and there according to your own taste. It is better to sleep on this sacred breast than to watch elsewhere, wherever it may be.[10]

Valuable in this section of the *Treatise* is what St Francis has to say about the various degrees of the soul's quiet.

Sometimes it is only in the will, in which it is sensible at times and at other times imperceptible. At other times the soul has a certain ardent sweetness at being in God's presence, which is for the moment imperceptible to her. At other times she hears the beloved speak, but she does not know how to speak to him, because the delight of hearing him or the reverence she bears towards him keeps her silent; or perhaps she is in dryness and such a languor of spirit that she has only the strength to hear, but not to speak. But finally, sometimes she neither hears her well-beloved or speaks to him, nor yet feels any sign of his presence. She simply knows that she is in the presence of her God, to whom it is pleasing that she should be there![11]

It is then that Francis comes to one of the most renowned of his illustrations, that of the statue in the niche, which stands there just as it does because it has been placed there, and is content that it should be so, if that is the way the maker wants it. In a word, the highest pitch of loving ecstasy is not to have our will in our own contentment, but in that of God, or not to have our contentment in our own will but in God's.'

To come to this point is, naturally, to come as Francis will say to the point at which love is a pain. But this topic will require a chapter to itself. It will suffice to conclude the subject-matter of this one by citing the two marks which St Francis gives of a good and holy ecstasy:

The first is that sacred ecstasy never so much affects the understanding as the will, which it moves, warms, and fills with a powerful affection to God. I say that he who in his ecstasy has more light in his understanding to admire God than warmth in his will to love him ought to stand on his guard; for there is a danger that this ecstasy may be false. The second mark of true ecstasy is to live in the world and in this mortal life, against all the opinions and maxims of the world, and against the current of the river of this life, by common resignations, renunciations, and abnegations of ourselves. And because no one is able to go above himself out of himself in this way *unless the eternal Father draws him*, this kind of life is a continual rapture and a perpetual ecstasy of action and operation.[12]

This is strong and clear and unmistakably evangelical doctrine and, in spite of all its lavish use of a wide range of secular and ecclesiastical culture, a thoroughly Christocentric account of the hidden life of prayer and its meaning.

18

UNION WITH GOD
IN DARKNESS AND
DIFFICULTY

Our previous chapter led us to the point at which the paths of prayer in individual lives normally branch off into that necessarily uncharted country which is as much a part of the landscape of prayer as it is a feature of every developing human life, even in more mundane matters. Not only does one of us live in Paris while the other lives in Palermo, but we are subject to all the consequences of living in these particular places in their effect upon personalities that were already vastly different in their relationship to a calling whose ultimate secret is known to God alone. This character of mystery about every human life must always be remembered and never lost sight of. Yet to insist upon this, as we have found ourselves compelled to do all through this book, and still more at the point we have now reached, is far from saying that when we are, by whatever means, increasingly submitted to the direction of God, there is virtually nothing more about which we need to reflect. Just as it was necessary to enter into what was involved in the business of praying in order that we might slowly recognize why we must submit to the action of God and how we are to do it so, granted that we are already doing this at least in desire, we shall still need to avoid placing obstacles in the progress of this work to completion through any misunderstandings about what is happening to us. These misunderstandings can easily arise from the fact that every life works out rather differently in the event from the way we envisage it in theory in advance. We shall have been fortunate if we have received the kind of spiritual help and guidance which has enabled us gradually to free ourselves from our inner entanglements and follow our own distinctive path without needless anxiety. But it would be expecting too much for even the most favoured to get through the whole of their journey without any periods of darkness, difficulty, and bewilderment.

St Francis of Sales has pointed out to us what is possibly the one feature common to all the individual paths, in what he has had to say about the notion of that kind of ecstasy which is seen in action and operation. It is the one kind of standing-outside-oneself—for that is what ecstasy is—which is the true mark of all genuine holiness. St Francis expressed, it will be recalled, his suspicions of a prayer which affects one's head rather than one's heart, and then went on to insist that one of the most certain tests of the authenticity of one's prayer is its tangible result in one's life. It will now be useful to hear St John of the Cross talking about this same connection between the love in one's heart and its results in one's life. He has to do this when he is telling us in the *Ascent of Mount Carmel* what he means by union with God:

> It must be known that God dwells and is substantially present in every soul, even in that of the greatest sinner in the world. If union of this kind were to fail them they would become annihilated and would cease to be. And so when we speak of union of the soul with God we speak not of this substantial union which is continually being wrought, but of the union and transformation of souls with God, which is not being wrought continually, but only where there exists that likeness that comes from love: we shall therefore term this union the union of likeness, even as that other union is called substantial or essential. The former is natural, the latter supernatural; and the latter comes to pass when the two wills—namely that of the soul and that of God—are conformed to one another, and there is nought in the one that is repugnant to the other. And thus when the soul rids itself totally of that which is repugnant to the divine will and conforms not with it, it is transformed in God through love.
>
> This is to be understood of that which is repugnant, not only in action, but likewise in habit.... When all that is unlike God and unconformed to him is cast out, the soul may receive the likeness of God; and nothing will then remain in it that is not the will of God and it will thus be transformed in God.[1]

The reader will be able to refer all that St John is saying here to the common doctrine of the Fathers on the notion of man as made in the image of God, without which, indeed, it would not be properly intelligible. In their view, man's likeness to God in his fallen or sinful condition is a possibility rather than an actuality. That likeness to which St John of the Cross is referring when he speaks of 'union of likeness' is the likeness which all the Fathers see as coming into existence when man's possibility of God-likeness is really being brought to life, both in the way he acts and in the virtues which dispose his capacities for action. It is thus of the gradual transformation of man's entire life from its very roots that St John is here speaking. In so far as we all have to travel from unlikeness to God in action and habit in the direction of likeness to him in both our actions and capacities, the Christian life is, when properly understood and lived, a continuously growing life.

> The righteous man [says St Bernard in one of his letters] never considers himself to have arrived; he never says, it is enough.... Jacob saw a ladder and on that ladder he saw angels, but none was sitting down or standing still; all were either going up or coming down. From this we learn that in this mortal life there is no half way between going up and coming down. The soul must either increase or decrease as the body must.[2]

This comparison between spiritual and bodily development is, inevitably, classical. The tradition, as reported by St Thomas Aquinas, is seen as suggesting a comparison between three broad phases of physical and spiritual development, the infantile period, the period which follows the acquisition of speech and the use of reason, and the stage of puberty with the onset of sexual fertility which leads directly into manhood.

> Thus too [St Thomas continues] the different degrees of charity are distinguished according to the different tasks to which a man is brought by the growth of charity. For it is a man's first duty to make it his chief concern to draw away from sin and resist its desires, which stimulate him against charity. And this is the business of beginners, in whom charity must be fostered and nourished lest it should decay. The second preoccupation follows, when a man chiefly concerns himself with his progress in good. And this task is the business of those who are making progress, who are mainly interested in seeing that charity is strengthened in them by growing. But the third preoccupation is that a man

should be chiefly concerned with cleaving to God and rejoicing in him. And this is appropriate to the perfect who *long to be dissolved and be with Christ* [to use St Paul's phrase].[3]

There are, naturally, several other ways of classifying these phases. The Cistercian, St Aelred of Rievaulx, bases his on the different kinds of sabbath found in the Old Testament. There is the first kind of Sunday, the ordinary Sunday, which consists in the inner condition of harmony resulting from the reform of the vices by the virtues. This is a notable relief. The second kind of Sunday, a more special festival, extends this virtuous harmony to include one's neighbour, and the third is the final fulfilment of the soul in the all-embracing charity which flows out from and flows back to the love of God himself. This scheme has the advantage of drawing attention to the fact that one stage does not exclude another, but that they supervene upon each other and interpenetrate, one phase frequently bearing, for a time, some of the features of the other. There is inevitably an element of artificiality in all these schemes but they do remind us of something that is by no means artificial and we must bear them in mind when we notice to what, in modern terms, it is they point.

For there is nothing archaic or obsolete about the observation that each of the phases of ordinary physical and psychological development is marked by a crisis of growth in which the final harmony established arises out of a condition of conflict. What the old masters are saying to us is that the phases of spiritual growth normally have their own characteristic type of crisis. There are, naturally, some people who take it as an ideal never to be, or at least never to admit to being, in a state of conflict. Yet, without conflict, without crisis, there is no growth. The rising temperature of a man who is ill is the sign that his body is trying to cope with the illness and ought to be assisted to do so. The cure, if it comes at all, comes after the crisis. Now all the schemes of spiritual development presuppose the soul's initial conversion from habitual grave sin to a life of seriously and generously fulfilling the commandments. But the story is, inevitably, not quite as simple as that. That conversion should penetrate to the depths of a man's being and the very springs of his action is not the work of a day and, corresponding to the soul's progress in the ways of charity, there are generally, as it were, two levels at which this conversion needs to become effective. Thus, at the point at which the beginner is being purged of his faults, and hence is in what some schemes would call 'the purgative way', he begins to move forward into 'the illuminative way' of those who are pressing forward in the service of charity. As this development continues, he normally experiences a crisis in which the whole of the life of his senses is painfully cleansed. Again, when the love of 'the illuminative way', which has not been without its self-regarding element, begins to lead into 'the unitive way', in which God is loved for himself alone, the whole spirit undergoes a similar purgation. If we find all this incredible, it is because our notions of God are as unworthy of us as they are of him. The men who are not mere theoreticians know better than to confuse their man-centred expectations with the God who is. And it is, above all, St John of the Cross who has described and discussed these two purgations or 'nights' of sense and spirit, as he calls them, in a more complete and masterly way than anyone else. To him, then, again we must turn, if we are to understand what we need to understand here.

In the *Ascent of Mount Carmel* he says:

We may say that there are three reasons for which this journey made by the soul to union with God is called night. The first has to do with the point from which the soul goes forth, for it has gradually to deprive itself of desire for all the worldly things which it possessed by denying them to itself; the which denial and deprivation are as it were night to all the senses of man. The second reason has to do with the mean or road along which the soul must travel to this union—that is faith, which is likewise as dark as night to the understanding. The third has to do with the point to which it travels, namely God, who equally is dark night to the soul in this life. These three nights must pass through the soul—or rather the soul must pass through them—in order that it may come to divine union with God.[4]

The basis of all this in quite ordinary, common teaching from the earliest times ought by now to need no defence or demonstration.

In this passage St John is saying in a summary manner what he proceeds to analyse in detail throughout the three books of the *Ascent of Mount Carmel*. Since it is normally the matter with which this book closes that is too little understood, it is necessary to draw attention to it here. Near the beginning of this final section of the work St John makes the following observation:

It is quite certain and quite an ordinary occurrence, that some persons, because of their lack of knowledge, make use of spiritual things with respect only to sense, and leave the spirit empty. There will scarcely be anyone whose spirit is not to a considerable degree corrupted by sweetness of sense; since, if the water be drunk up before it reaches the spirit, the latter becomes dry and barren![5]

It is then that St John devotes a number of chapters to a discussion of places and methods of prayer and devotion and the right and the wrong way to use them. The substance of what he there has to say, and the best perspective in which to view it, may most conveniently be gathered by looking at what he says at the very beginning of the closely related work, *The Dark Night of the Soul*.

It must be known that the soul, after it has been definitely converted to the service of God is, as a rule, spiritually nurtured and caressed by God, even as is the tender child by its loving mother, who warms it with the heat of her bosom and nurtures it with sweet milk and soft and pleasant food, and carries it and caresses it in her arms; but as the child grows bigger the mother sets down the child from her arms and makes it walk on its feet, so that it may lose the characteristics of a child and betake itself to greater and more substantial occupations. The loving mother is like the grace of God, for as soon as the soul is regenerated by its new warmth and fervour for the service of God, he treats it in the same way; he makes it find spiritual milk, sweet and delectable, in all the things of God, without any labour of its own, and also great pleasure in spiritual exercises, for here God is giving to it the breast of his tender love, even as to a tender child.[6]

All this imagery has a long medieval ancestry. Hugh of St Victor, in the twelfth century, will often talk of grace as 'mothering', and St Gertrude in the thirteenth will be found using almost identical language about mother and child. The idea will return with St Francis of Sales. But to pursue, for the moment, the thought of St John of the Cross, he continues:

Therefore such a soul finds delight in spending long periods—perchance whole nights—in prayer: penances are its pleasures, fasts its joys, and its consolations are to make use of the sacraments and commune of divine things. In the which things spiritual persons (though taking part in them with great efficacy and persistance and using and treating them with great care) often find themselves, spiritually speaking, very weak and imperfect.

St John's argument, then, is that even after our conversion from habits of sin, we still habitually live in the service of our senses, even in spiritual matters—in fact, one might almost say, especially in those, because there we imagine our self-indulgence will be safe. We judge, resolve, and act, not so much by the light of faith, as by our feelings and reactions. We may perhaps have learnt to mortify our passion for the pleasures of the table, but we do not notice that for the sense pleasures connected with spiritual things we have become positive gluttons. The roots of gluttony and of the other six capital, or co-ordinating, sins are thus seen still to be stirring in us, though they have now found another, spiritual-looking, outlet. Such people will never be strong enough to exercise the virtues when they are required to do so under circumstances in which they can discover no attractive incentive. Take from them their favourite corner, place, or time for prayer, and the prayer stops too! This is the reason why they have to be purged from all these 'superficialities and puerilities', as St John calls them, if they are ever to grow up in the spirit. For, as he says:

However assiduously the beginner practises the mortification in himself of all these actions and passions of his, he can never completely succeed—very far from it—until God works it in him passively by means of the purgation of the said night.[7]

This night which, as we say, is contemplation, produces in spiritual persons two kinds of darkness or purgation corresponding to the two parts of man's nature—namely, the sensual and the spiritual. And thus the one night or purgation will be sensual, wherein the soul is purged according to sense, which is subdued to the spirit; and the other is a night or purgation which is spiritual; wherein the soul is stripped and purged according to the spirit and subdued and made ready for the union of love with God. The night of sense is common and comes to many: these are the beginners. The night of the spirit is the portion of very few, and these are they that are already practised and proficient. The first purgation or night is bitter and terrible to sense. The second bears no comparison with it, for it is horrible and awful to the spirit.[8]

For whatever reason we do not know, St John never succeeded in describing the second of these two nights, though he began to do so. *The Dark Night of the Soul* remained an unfinished work. But the first night, that of the senses, he does describe, together with the reasons for its occurrence, in terms such as those which we have already examined. The basic image is that of people being made to grow up and walk on their own two feet 'which they feel to be very strange, for everything seems to be going wrong with them'. It ought probably to be noted that, in a period like our own, when some Christians of the older generation 'feel that everything is going wrong with them', the reason for this feeling is not necessarily a spiritual one, though in some cases it could be. Many of every generation doubtless correctly observe that social circumstances increasingly demand a considerable spiritual maturity if anyone is to attempt to live the Christian life at all, and it would be wrong not to see that the forces which are bringing this state of affairs about are, at the very least, permitted by God. But it would surely be altogether unwise to assume that the requisite maturity can be achieved at one leap by simply rejecting all the help our senses can give us at the period of life when this is the kind of help we need. We have seen St John of the Cross insisting that, even with the best will in the world, we cannot succeed in achieving that purgation of our senses which only God can effectively bring about. That God is in fact often bringing this about under various contemporary social pressures can hardly be doubted. But it can hardly less be doubted that we ought not to try to run before we can walk. Most modern beginners will need to be humble enough actively to cultivate the use of their senses in ways which town life tends either to numb or destroy for, as St John assumes, it is normal for them to need to use their senses in order to begin to lead any spiritual life at all. One can only mortify or cut back something which actually needs pruning, and it would be entirely mistaken to confuse the feeling of strangeness which accompanies the purgation of the senses with the symptoms of a psychological imbalance which may be entirely natural in cause. We have seen St John of the Cross warning us of this latter possibility in our previous chapter.

Returning, then, more explicitly to St John's thought, we have seen him giving three principal signs that the purgation of the senses is actually occurring. We might perhaps frame three simple questions which would cover the points he is making. We could ask first: Is the soul's distaste for the things of God accompanied by a corresponding distaste for created pleasures as well? If the answer is 'Yes', we must bear in mind, as we have just been saying, that both or either kinds of distaste could be the result of some general physical or psychological indisposition. Therefore we must also ask: Does the soul feel a constant anxiety and concern about the things of God, accompanied by the feeling that it is sliding back in God's service? For if this is the case, there will be clear evidence that a concern for the things of God is really alive and genuine and not simply a kind of self-centred scrupulousness. Thirdly, we shall want to know: Does the soul find itself in a permanent (and not just an occasional) incapacity to make meditation on spiritual things, however much it tries to do so?

It is well [St John will comment] for those who find themselves in this condition to take comfort, to persevere in patience, and to be in no wise afflicted. Let them trust in God, who abandons not those who seek him with a simple and right heart, and will not fail to give them what is needful for the road, until he bring them into the clear and pure light of love. This last he will give them by means of that other dark night, that of the spirit, if they merit that he should bring them thereto.[9]

In this purgation, that is to say, the dark night of the spirit, says St John later in the same work, these two parts of the soul, the spiritual and the sensual, must be completely purged, since the one is never truly purged without the other, the purgation which is effective for sense coming when that of the spirit begins.

Therefore in this night following, both parts of the soul are purged together, and it is for this end that it is well to have passed through the corrections of the first night and the period of tranquillity which proceeds from it, in order that sense being united to spirit, both may be purged after a certain manner and may then suffer with greater fortitude.[10]

But of that suffering this book will not attempt to speak any more than St John himself was allowed extensively to do. It is enough to say that all the masters of all the ages are at one in their belief that the soul's purgation or purgatory must come either in this life or in the next, and happy indeed are those to whom it comes and for whom it is over in this present life.

But even about that we cannot, of course, *choose*, for the divine good pleasure is the hidden principle upon which all these developments hang; and that, as St Francis of Sales says in the great Book 9 of his *Treatise on the Love of God*,

> is scarcely ever known save by events; and as long as it is unknown to us, we must keep as close as possible to that will of God which is manifested or signified to us. But as soon as the good pleasure of his divine majesty is made evident, we must lovingly bring ourselves round to obeying it.

This, like the rest of this very impressive section of the *Treatise*, is particularly fundamental teaching and everyone who leads a serious and difficult Christian life will profit by making themselves very familiar with it. Like all the great books, we need to know it so well that we can go back to it when we need it, its ideas and images suggesting themselves to us quite naturally when they are appropriate to our case. It is in this book that St Francis describes the condition of the soul in deep interior anguishes of the kind we have been discussing in this chapter. Of such a condition of soul he says:

> Although she has the power to believe, to hope, and to love God, and in truth she does so, yet she lacks the strength to see properly if she believes, hopes, and cherishes her God. For distress possesses and overwhelms her so powerfully that she cannot return upon herself to see what she is doing. And this is why she believes that she has no faith, or hope, or charity, but only the shadows and useless impressions of these virtues, which she feels almost without feeling them, and as though they were alien and not native to her soul. How the poor heart is afflicted when, as though abandoned by love, she looks everywhere and does not find it as it seems to her. She does not find it in the exterior senses, for they are not capable of it; nor in the imagination which is cruelly tormented by conflicting impressions; nor in the understanding, troubled as it is by a thousand obscure suggestions and strange worries; and although at last she finds it in the summit and supreme point of the spirit where the divine love resides, still she does not recognize it and does not think that it is what it is, for the greatness of the distress and darkness prevents her from experiencing its sweetness. She sees it without seeing it, and meets it without recognizing it, as if it were just happening in a dream or an image of it. In just this way Magdalene, having met her dear master, got no relief from it, because she did not think that it was he, but only the gardener. But what can the soul that is

in this case do? She does not know how to behave in the midst of such distress, and has only the power to let herself die in the hands of the will of God.

Here, then, is another picture of purgation in passivity.

In one paragraph of this same section of the *Treatise* St Francis has compressed his general teaching in two simple images which represent accurately enough the ascetic and mystical aspects of his doctrine:

We ourselves, like little children of the heavenly Father, can go with him in two ways. In the first place, we can go with him, walking with the steps of our own will, which we conform to his, always holding with the hand of our obedience that of his divine intention, and following it wherever it takes us, which is what God requires of us by his signified will. But we can also go with our Saviour without any will of our own, letting ourselves simply be carried by his divine good pleasure, like a small child in the arms of its mother, by a certain sort of admirable consent which could be called union, or rather the uniting of our will with that of God. And this is the way we should try to conduct ourselves in the divine will of good pleasure, since the effects of this will of good pleasure proceed simply from his providence; and without our doing anything, they happen to us.

Here we shall notice how the image of the mother carrying the child is being used to represent something rather different from what it represents in St John of the Cross. For here in St Francis, being carried is the symbolic equivalent of being set down to walk by oneself in St John of the Cross. The two are, in fact, looking at the same thing from slightly different points of view. It is when one is being most completely carried that one feels exactly as though one's mother had put one down and gone away. But this will need elaboration in a separate chapter.

19

SELF-ABANDONMENT TO DIVINE PROVIDENCE

It was by asking the Fathers to explain to us our own continuing human situation that the foundations of this book were laid, and if it has seemed right and necessary to call in the help of later writers to tell us about some things that needed further explicitation, we have always found ourselves reminded of their debt to and contact with an inheritance which never seems to die, wherever the life of the spirit continues. Whatever clothes they wore or setting they came from, it is as though all the men of God always had to learn essentially the same lessons. Here and there a distinctive voice formulates more memorably than another some point we need to understand and remember, but time and date become almost a matter of indifference. Dorotheus, a sixth-century monk living in the desert of Gaza will, for instance, bring us back the full circle to our beginnings if we ask him to tell us about the subject that now calls for our attention. In one of his instructions he writes:

Those who have to swim in the sea and know the technique of swimming, plunge and yield themselves to the wave when it breaks over them until it has gone by, and so continue swimming without difficulty. But if they wish to go against it, it thrusts them back and hurls them a fair distance. When they begin to swim again, a new wave comes over them. If they still fight against it, they are simply forced and thrown back again, and they only get tired without making any progress. But if, as I say, they plunge under the wave and humble themselves beneath it, it goes by without troubling them, and they continue to swim as much as they want and finish their task. So it is with temptations. If anyone endures temptation with patience and humility, it goes by without any harm. But if one delays in distress, upset and on the defensive against everyone, one punishes oneself in making the temptation worse and not only is it unprofitable, it even does us harm. For temptations are very profitable to those who endure them without trouble. Even when a passion disturbs us, we should not get upset. For to be upset because of the disturbance of a passion is ignorance and pride and a failure to recognize our own state and deserting in the face of difficulty, as the Fathers say: This is why we do not make progress, because we do not understand our own limitations and do not have patience in the work we begin, but want to acquire virtue without any trouble.[1]

This, as we shall see at once, is a piece of by no means elementary insight, and evidently belongs to the same world of inner experience as that from which St John of the Cross will be writing many centuries later. Thus, both experience and doctrine always lead us in the same general direction. Christian ascetic principles, when properly understood, inevitably point to the life of prayer as their centre, for it is there that our personal relation with the mystery of God is built up. Yet, as all the spiritual masters make us see, prayer equally inevitably leads us back to asceticism—not, of course, to weird practices of spiritual gymnastics, but to that asceticism which the inner laws of love impose, more searching certainly, but also more sure than any we could devise or discover for ourselves. Dorotheus of Gaza is telling us that we must learn the wise simplicity which enables us to go with the movement of the sea, a sea on whose tides an almost unknown eighteenth-century Jesuit, who knew his classical spiritual source-books, had long meditated. His debt to St Francis of Sales is perhaps nearest the surface in his writings, but his instinct for the tradition of spiritual doctrine is so sure that no one would attempt to isolate all the influences that enter into it. Nor, when the right moment comes to read him, can anyone afford to ignore what he has to say.

When Jean-Pierre de Caussade died in 1751 at the age of seventy-six he had published nothing but a kind of catechism in the spirit of the great preacher Bossuet on various questions connected with prayer. Most modern readers would not be likely to find this book very congenial and there is no reason why they should. But it is, on the other hand, probable that some day the teaching of de Caussade as it appears in a book known in English as *Self-abandon-*

ment to Divine Providence will seem like the revelation of light and truth that it seemed to the nineteenth-century Jesuit, Père Ramière, who put it together from talks that de Caussade had given to the Visitation Sisters at Nancy. This short work, and the letters of de Caussade, place him firmly in the ranks of the truly great spiritual masters. The opening sentences of the treatise on self-abandonment will be sufficient to convince one of this.

> God still speaks as he spoke to our Fathers, when there were neither spiritual directors nor set methods. Then they saw that each moment brings with it a duty to be faithfully fulfilled. That was enough for spiritual perfection. On that duty their whole attention was fixed at each successive moment like the hand of a clock which marks the hours. Under the continuous impulse of God, their spirit found itself turning to each new object as it was presented to them by God at each hour of the day.[2]

We shall notice that de Caussade, who is aware of having a fresh, yet ancient message to convey, is driven by a kind of spiritual diplomacy to draw rather gently, yet still quite firmly, a contrast between primitive simplicity and modern complexity. We may feel that this contrast involves an element of romantic exaggeration if put to the test of history. But it remains true that there is a genuine protest to be made here, and it is one whose true nature should not be misunderstood. When de Caussade says that modern needs require rules and instructions more explicit than those which were once given, there can be no doubt that he means to be taken seriously. His concern is not in fact with beginners in the spiritual life, who, he assumes, will need to be trained in the common ascetic disciplines. But, like St John of the Cross, St Francis of Sales, and all the other great directors, he is undoubtedly concerned to restore to those who are developing in the life of the spirit the liberty to follow the leading of God, which an inexperienced textbook approach to the spiritual life can easily take away. Not only will beginners in the ways of prayer find it almost impossible to understand what de Caussade is saying, but they may, even when they *think* they understand him, be gravely mistaken. Someone who needs to be training himself in the ordinary virtues may easily be dissuaded from doing this by reading de Caussade too early, and failing to see that he is speaking to people in whom he is assuming that a formation of this kind has been given. This is, naturally, not to say that it is easy to determine when the right moment for

216

reading de Caussade comes. We shall see in a moment what he himself has to say on subjects like this. It is merely necessary to note that he is essentially a writer for the spiritually mature. For them he conveys the spirit of the great tradition without embarrassing them with its details. Inevitably, the better we know and understand that tradition the more secure we shall feel ourselves to be in de Caussade's hands. With little historical knowledge or a great deal, it is with the tradition *as alive* that we need to be in touch, and it is de Caussade's special gift to provide us with a sound sense of it, when the right moment comes.

What, then, are the broad outlines of de Caussade's teaching? He sees what he has to say as being symbolized by the mystery of the Annunciation of our Lady. Mary's *'Let it be to me according to your word'* contained, as he says, 'all the mystical theology of our ancestors'. As to Mary, in her humdrum existence, about which there was, if we are to believe the Gospels, nothing in particular to report, 'God reveals himself to the humble in the humblest things, while the great, who only concentrate on the surface, do not discover him even in great ones'. This, in other words, is a doctrine that turns upon our discovering and retaining an abiding capacity to change our point of view, in coming to see that holiness consists in one thing only, namely in faithfulness to God's plan—an *active* fidelity, in so far as we accomplish as best we can the duties of our state of life, a *passive* fidelity in so far as we accept and suffer with love whatever divine providence sends us.

> Here [says de Caussade in a lyrical outburst] is the treasure which we never find because we imagine it to be too far away to be sought. Do not ask me what is the secret of finding this treasure. There is no secret. This treasure is everywhere. It offers itself to us at all times, in all places. All creatures, friendly and hostile, pour it out extravagantly and make it circulate round every power of our body and soul, right down to the depths of our heart. If we open our mouths, they will be filled. Divine activity floods the universe; it penetrates all creatures; it flows over them. Wherever they are, it is there; it precedes, accompanies and follows them. We have only to allow ourselves to be carried forward on the crest of its waves.[3]

This, then, is the basic theological teaching of this doctrine and one which it is of the utmost importance for us to share, that 'divine activity floods the universe', that God as the sovereign director of souls, alone knows what to do to make each soul like himself. We must not contaminate his work with our petty purposes, especially if they be apparently spiritual ones. To be formed by God it is not always necessary to understand what he is doing, provided one submits to it. As de Caussade himself delightfully puts it:

> As it is fire that warms us, and not philosophy or scientific knowledge about it, so it is the plan of God, his will, that produces sanctity in our souls and not inquisitive speculation about this cause and its effects. If we are thirsty, the only thing to do is to leave the books that explain these things, and take a drink. The mere desire to know can only increase the thirst.[4]

It will become immediately apparent, as a result of this notion that apart from God, books are merely useless externals and being devoid of the life-giving power of God's plan, they succeed only in emptying the heart by the very satisfaction which they give to the mind. As we have seen earlier in this book, when speaking of 'holy reading', de Caussade's counsels about how to read a book are in entire conformity with this doctrine. It will be clear that de Caussade is convinced, like John of the Cross, that the obstacle most likely to impede the divine action is that which is found in the soul itself. For, in the case of external obstacles, the divine action can, when it chooses, convert them into useful means.

> Everything is equally useful and useless to it. Without it everything is nothing, and with it nothing becomes everything. Meditation, contemplation, vocal prayers, interior silence, acts of the faculties of the soul may be what they will, but the best of all for the soul is what God wills at this particular moment, and the soul must think of all the rest with perfect indifference as being nothing at all. Thus there is nothing illegitimate in the value and love we give to contemplation and other practices of piety, provided that the value and love are directed wholly to a God of infinite goodness, who wishes to use these means in order to give himself to souls.[5]

By now it will be possible to appreciate that de Caussade's notion of the Annunciation mystery as embodied in what he calls 'the sacrament of the present moment' is a very different thing from that which a man might have who did not realize that Christianity is essentially a life and not a body of theory.

Quietism is in error [says de Caussade] when it despises all use of the senses, for there are souls whom God wishes always to go by this road; and their circumstances and inclinations make this clear enough. It is useless to imagine ways of self-abandonment, from which all personal activity is excluded; when the divine plan prescribes action, holiness lies in activity.[6]

All this implies a view of life which is altogether coloured and transformed by the virtue of faith, a life which 'is nothing other than a continual pursuit of God through everything that disguises, misrepresents and, so to speak, destroys and annihilates him'. Perhaps the most memorable passages of de Caussade's treatise are those which liken this life of faith to that which is communicated to us through the teaching of Scripture.

The written word of God is full of mysteries; his word executed in the events of the world is no less so These two books are truly sealed, the letter of them both kills.... You speak, Lord, to all men in general by general events. Revolutions are only the tides of your providence which stir up storms and tempests in the minds of the inquisitive. You speak in particular to all men by what happens to them from moment to moment. But instead of hearing your voice, instead of respecting the obscure and mysterious character of your word, they see nothing but matter, chance, and the moods of man; they have an answer for everything; they want to add, take away from, or change it; they take the liberty to commit excesses the least of which would be regarded as unthinkable if it were a question of a comma in holy Scripture.... But what God says to you, dear souls, the words which he pronounces from moment to moment, the substance of which is not paper and ink but what you suffer and what you have to do from moment to moment, does this deserve no attention from you? Why in all this do you not respect the truth and the will of God? Nothing pleases you, you criticize everything that happens. Do you not see that you are measuring by the standard of the senses and reason what can only be measured by faith, and that reading, as you do, with the eyes of faith the words of God in holy Scripture, you are greatly in the wrong to read it with any other eyes in his actions.... To the manifestation of the truth of God by word has succeeded the manifestation of his charity by action. The Holy Spirit carries on the work of the Saviour. While he assists the Church in the preaching of the gospel of Jesus Christ, he writes his own gospel, and he writes it in the hearts of the faithful. All the actions, all the moments of the saints make up the gospel of the Holy Spirit. Their holy souls are the paper, their sufferings and their actions the ink. The Holy Spirit with his own actions for pen, writes a living gospel, but no one can read it until the day of glory.[7]

These, then are the big perspectives within which de Caussade writes unmistakably like a master. But when does the right moment come to live within these perspectives?

There is [says de Caussade himself] a time when the soul lives in God and a time when God lives in the soul. What belongs to one of these periods is unsuitable for the other. When God lives in the soul, it should abandon itself completely to his providence. When the soul lives in God, it takes trouble regularly to provide itself with all the means that it can think of in order to attain to union with him. All its paths are marked out. When God lives in the soul, it has nothing more of its own, it has nothing but what he gives it, who is the principle which animates it at each moment. No provisions, no path marked out. It feels its needs and miseries without knowing how or when it will be helped. It waits in peace and without anxiety for someone to come and help it; its eyes look only towards heaven. Other people undertake an infinity of things for God's glory; this soul is often in some corner of the earth, like a piece of a broken pot that no one thinks of putting to any use.[8]

This, as de Caussade sees it, is the source of what such souls do for themselves and for others. They leave God free; they are true instruments of his mysterious work in the world, and it would indeed be a raw and inexperienced disciple who did not realize that to live like this is really only possible to an heroic generosity, springing from a true love that rules the heart in all it does or omits.

Perhaps one more passage will suffice to complete this brief analysis of de Caussade's teaching and it is one which also admirably illustrates the familiar way in which he draws on the mass of sources he has absorbed:

'Truly', said Jacob, 'God is in this place and I knew it not'. You are looking for God, dear soul, and he is everywhere ... he remains with you and you look for him! Oh, you are looking for your idea of God, while you possess his substance, ... you are off chasing your sublime ideas.... God disguises himself to raise the soul to pure faith and to teach it to find him under all sorts of appearances; for once it has learned God's secret he may well disguise himself, it simply says: He is there behind the wall, he is looking through the lattice, he is looking through the windows. Oh divine love, hide yourself, try test after test, bind the soul with your attractions and duties, blend, mingle, confuse, break up like spiders' webs all the soul's ideas and standards. Let it lose its foothold and feel no more roads or paths nor see any light. After having found you in solitude, and after having tried every known method of pleasing you, let it no longer be able to find you in any of these things as it once did. But may the uselessness of its efforts lead it to leave them all aside in order to find you in yourself, and so, everywhere, in everything, without distinction.[9]

Although they would not have written it in this way, how such a passage would have delighted Gregory of Nyssa or Dionysius the Areopagite. It uses the traditional symbolism of Martha and Mary common to all the Fathers, and in a remark about Mary failing to find Jesus according to her idea of him we have the doctrine of St Francis of Sales in the *Treatise on the Love of God*. There, with the reminiscences of the *Song of Songs*, is the spirit of the many mystical commentaries on that book from Origen onwards. In the passage which clearly refers to the soul's successive stripping of its attachments in the twofold nights of sense and spirit it is the teaching of St John of the Cross; and finally comes this passage, using an image from St Teresa of Avila:

Live, then, little silkworm in the dark and narrow cell of your cocoon until the warmth of grace forms you and hatches you out. Eat all the leaves which grace presents to you and do not regret in the activity of your self-abandonment the peace you have lost.... Go on spinning your silk in secret, doing what you can neither feel nor see. Feel throughout your whole being a secret agitation which you will yourself condemn, while you envy your companions their death-like repose who have not yet reached the point where you are. After that, what will become of you little worm? What will be the issue for you? Who could guess what nature does for a silkworm if he had not seen it? All it needs is leaves, that is all. Nature does the rest. In the same way, dear souls, you cannot know where you come from or where you are going, from what divine idea God's wisdom produces you, or to what end it is leading you. But after several transformations the consummated soul receives wings with which to fly to heaven, leaving on earth a fertile seed to perpetuate its state in other souls.[10]

'All it needs is leaves, that is all. Nature does the rest.' When this image is applied to the subject of which de Caussade is here speaking, it is clear that 'nature' must be understood as the Fathers normally understood it, as being that kind of life which is so much in harmony with God's original intentions for the world that it puts everything manifestly right, and it is appropriately called 'grace'. Nature and grace are, on the surface, as de Caussade sees, often indistinguishable, for grace restores nature and brings everything back to its origins. It would, of course, be a grave error not to see that the apparent simplicity of all this is not a position from which anyone starts out. It is rather a simplicity at which we can hope to arrive by co-operating with the grace of God as it is offered to us in the pursuit of our particular calling and as it is indicated to us by all those signs from within and without which make God's will known to us. It is only thus that, in an achieved simplicity, we can become the children who enter the kingdom of heaven. A false childishness, an artful and contrived simplicity is the direct opposite of this condition, being only a cheap and easy evasion of the real cost of true simplicity. For, as de Caussade says in one of his letters, if God does not always make martyrs for the faith nowadays by the shedding of blood,

the Holy Spirit has found a way to make martyrs for divine love by these apparent and painful absences and by countless kinds of actions that cause suffering. Those who undergo these divine torments have only to practise resignation, blind self-abandonment and that unwearied patience the martyrs once practised in their very torments. The same Holy Spirit, who kept them in peace and a wholly divine joy on red-hot gridirons and in the middle of even worse tortures, will maintain peace in your heart too, in spite of all your upheavals of sense and spirit. You have simply to co-operate faithfully with his action by not giving any voluntary consent to the worries which besiege you[11]

The key-words in this passage are, naturally, the words 'voluntary consent'. De Caussade is quite realistic enough to realize that there are some reactions which follow from the pursuit of God *under all circumstances* which we, in our weakness and our limitations, can do nothing to prevent. He is simply, like St Francis of Sales, concerned only that we should not be anxious about being anxious or disturbed about being disturbed. It is in matters like these that he derives his strength from his knowledge of the long tradition behind him, and we can be quite sure that those who follow in that tradition will become like those silkworms who 'leave on earth a fertile seed to perpetuate their state in other souls'. He became such a silkworm himself and there is no reason to suppose that silkworms like this have ceased to propagate themselves even in our own externally unpropitious-looking times. After all, 'all they need is leaves', and to them everything, be it what it may, is equally useful and useless.

20

ANOTHER SELF

This book has been struggling, explicitly and from the first, with at least one insuperable difficulty, and to this difficulty we must return, just as from it we started out. It may be possible to speak of men in general terms, of the way they act and react under given circumstances, and hence it may be possible to speak of their spiritual life and even of their prayer in general terms. But we can never forget that none of us exists in general terms or prays in general terms, for the most incontrovertible of all the general laws of our life and being, natural and supernatural, is our utter particularity. We are all of us different, at the beginning, in the middle, and at the end. There is no escaping this, even if we were so foolish as to wish to do so. Hence, too, no book can reach everyone, and at this stage we may perhaps be allowed to say quite simply that God does not mean that it should. If this book has itself been in part an exercise in the courtesy of listening to a great variety of voices, it may perhaps at least have shown the sort of thing it would be possible to do in some rather different form. God needs all his holy ones for different purposes and we must be grateful for those who are able to say a word to us personally to lighten our darkness as we pursue in our own way the road they travelled in theirs. At the end of every stretch, we are only at a new beginning, with everything, seemingly, to learn all over again and anew. For it is life that matters and not books about it, and the very diversity of holiness is a reminder that when it is authentic it is always fresh and always taking on new forms. Sham holiness is the deadest of all dead things, because it is a caricature of that which, of its very nature, is invariably most alive.

But what is it to be a saint, to be one of God's holy ones? The Christian community which, in so far as it shares in the life of God's grace, is addressed by St Paul as a society of 'saints' or 'holy ones', has never in practice venerated any of its members as a 'saint', in the narrower and more usual modern sense of that word, without conscious reference to the theoretical principles of the Christian life and virtues. Whether 'canonization' has been, as at first, spontaneous or, as in more recent centuries, formal, this theoretical standard of judgement has always been held in mind. Yet, at the same time, it has been clearly recognized from the beginning that these typical virtues may be so diversely realized in any given Christian life that the personality and circumstances of the person who practises them are of the utmost relevance. This notion is at least implicit in the observation of St Paul, where he is discussing the total transformation of the whole man which will occur in the final resurrection, that 'one star differs from another in splendour'.[1] He is making not only an affirmation of continuity and fulfilment, but also necessarily implying an abiding difference within that which is ultimate. These points have, then, been clearly recognized from early times. Hence, although it was the martyrs who first struck their fellow Christians as being characteristically Christian and thus the kind of example that a saint is, it came slowly to be seen that there might be other ways of 'dying to oneself' which could be regarded as setting forth essentially the same virtues as those displayed in the martyrs.[2] It was thus through the contemplation of the concrete embodiment of the saving work of Christ in the person of his saints that Christians were, and are, led back to the fundamental mystery of Christian holiness, Christ himself. 'For', as St Paul says, 'it is in Christ that godhead in all its completeness dwells in bodily form'.[3] This was the startling mystery to which the martyrs, by their death, bore witness, that God was born of a human mother at Bethlehem, died on a cross, and rose again from the dead on the third day, in the flesh which he himself had taken. In the second person of the Trinity, the incarnate Son, that holiness which for the Jews it had been God's alone to possess and communicate, was made accessible to all men.

If this point is to be understood, its background must be realized. In the early part of his prophecy the prophet Isaiah hears the burning seraphim calling out to each other before the throne of God, 'Holy, holy, holy is the Lord of hosts; the whole earth is full of his glory. And the foundations of the thresholds shook at the voice of him who called, and the house was filled with smoke'.[4] In this awe-inspiring presence, the prophet realizes that he is a man of unclean lips. By the ministry of a seraph, he is cleansed with a coal from the smoking altar. In God's choice of Israel, as

225

in his choice of his prophet, there is implied a call to be holy as God himself is holy, a call which is many times repeated in the Levitical books. Nor is it correct to see this as simply a call to a ritual holiness, such as we also find in the religion of the Greeks. For when David commits adultery with Bathsheba, he confesses his moral fault in his psalm of contrition in the following terms: 'Against thee, thee only, have I sinned, and done what which is evil in thy sight'. Now, as he offers his prayer, he has 'a broken and contrite heart', which he is confident that God will not despise. But he must wait for God to create in him a clean heart and put a new and right spirit within him.[5] This most familiar of all the psalms clearly expresses the Jewish idea that it is God who makes holy, and that this holiness, becoming something inherent in the servants of his choice, must be preserved, not by outward ritual alone, but also by moral purity. The Jewish translators of the Greek Septuagint version of the Old Testament actually devised a series of new variants in the language to express this notion by which it is not, as in normal Greek thought, man who makes holy by dedicating something to God, but God who imparts holiness as a result of his free choice.[6]

This Jewish tradition is, naturally presupposed to the writings of the New Testament, and in them it receives an extension scandalous to the Jews. For although the Jewish people as a whole might be called 'holy', and even Aaron, as an individual, is once called 'the holy one of the Lord',[7] still, absolutely-speaking, God alone is the Holy One and Holy is his proper and incommunicable name.[8] Yet this name Holy is twice applied in the Revelation of St John without qualification to Jesus.[9] It is this New Testament usage of the word 'holy' which determines the sense we must give to the word 'saint', as applied to the Christians of the New Testament. The Christians to whom St Paul writes as 'saints' or 'holy ones' are so called because of their relation to the one whom they venerate as their Lord. This is, of course, the relation of which St Paul explores the implications in his letters for, as he insists, 'any one who does not have the Spirit of Christ does not belong to him'.[10] For Paul, the transformation, which the presence and guidance of his spirit brings with it, renews the whole life of the Christian disciple after the image of Christ. It is because Jesus Christ is, as the creeds say, 'true God of true God', *the* holy one, that we can all receive of his fulness. The effect in *this* world of receiving the life of Christ is to conform us to the pattern of his

226

life, death, and resurrection by an imitation that goes deeper than ritual patterns, symbols, and archetypal similarities. It brings about a death to ourselves that does not result from our human efforts at mortification, though they may have their place, but from the gradual triumph of the power of Christ in the midst of our weakness. This passage from death to newness of life is really communicated to us in baptism, when we commit ourselves in faith to Christ as the physician of our souls. If this is done for us and in our name when we are infants, we naturally need to make this commitment explicit for our adult selves when we are capable of it. It is, in fact, by continuing to live the life of faith in Christ that we allow the virtue of our baptism gradually to take complete possession of us, so that we could say with St Paul: 'It is no longer I who live, but Christ who lives in me'.[11]

The New Testament writings are full of the sense that the initiative in this work of holiness is taken by God, but perhaps its most vivid and simple expression is that which is found in the first letter of St John:

> As for us, we have personal knowledge of, and faith in, the love which God has for us. God is love. So then, if a man lives a life of love, he enters into the life of God, and the life of God enters into him. Our love has its source and origin in God's love, for God loved us before we loved him.[12]

This love is that *agape* of God, which has been proved by his undertaking the work of our salvation, and the experience of this love must call forth in the disciples that *agape*, whose praises are sung by St Paul. This love is patient and kind, 'does not insist on its own way'.[13] It is the antithesis of an egotistical love and, as St Paul points out, the most strenuous asceticism would be absolutely valueless without it. In a word: 'Once a man becomes a Christian, whether or not he is circumcised is meaningless. What matters is faith working in love'.[14]

In all this, then, the Jewish conception of holiness has been transformed by the person of Christ. But if it is by him, and with him, and in him that God wills our sanctification, he does not will it without our co-operation. Consequently it is this work of co-operation that the life of a saint, in the narrower sense of the word, displays. It need hardly be said that this is not necessarily true of the *written* lives of saints. For written lives of saints are often so anxious to get to the end of the story before we have had time to get acquainted with the beginning that they deliberately withhold or minimize the evidence which would show us the normal conflict out of which the ultimate harmony arises. Such lives forget that holiness only gradually takes over, and occasionally they only aid and abet that streak of hypocrisy that there is in all of us. We often want to believe the impossible about those we admire as much as we sometimes like to have it believed of ourselves. Inevitably the information necessary to make a saint's life genuinely instructive as a developing process is often lacking owing to their remoteness in time. St Augustine of Hippo and St Teresa of Avila are altogether exceptional in the amount of autobiographical information with which they provide us. It is also necessary to remember that people have not always asked the same kind of questions about themselves as those which we might nowadays be inclined to ask. Even where we possess authentic documents, it is often possible to form rather different impressions of them. How far the sisters of St Thérèse of Lisieux succeeded in modifying the portrait she had drawn of herself in her notebooks, we can now judge from the publication of the full text, which often provides us with just those little touches of character which can be so important and so telling.

It would be entirely mistaken to suppose that mere distance in time or difference of psychological outlook is the only reason why we do not always know all it would often be helpful to know about some of the saints. A respect for every life involves, as we have seen earlier in this book, a respect for something that is ultimately an inviolable secret. These are secrets which, it would appear, God himself often guards with peculiar strictness. Just as it would seem that he wishes us to know of the difficulties of some of the saints for our consolation and instruction, so over the lives of others he draws an almost impenetrable veil. Thus of the comparatively recently canonized Lebanese hermit, Father Sharbel Makhlouf, we know practically nothing. Why it should be that in these particular years, when the hermit life seems to so many people remote and fantastic, the incorrupt body of this man should be unable to be unobtrusively disposed of, but kept on bringing itself to notice through one circumstance or another, is not clear. Unless, of course, it be that we, whose lives are daily consumed with activity, need to be reminded of the possibility that God might call a few to attend exclusively to the 'one thing necessary'. Certainly to attend to God and wait upon his will is the common call of everyone, wherever it may personally lead us. It would seem that sometimes it is the triumph of God in the peace and harmony of contemplation that the lives of the saints set forth, sometimes it is its triumph in spite of darkness and difficulty. Thus, on the one hand, it seems that we were meant to know the real hardness of the life of the little French girl, Bernadette, its simplicity and ordinariness in the ways of prayer as her very conventional notebooks reveal it, and that this mere child, who had to live so courageously with a vocation which included the few visions at Lourdes, was afraid on the day of her death. On the other hand, we know from an equally authentic eye-witness account by a young man who was there that 'all who saw and heard of the death of Bede declared they had never known anyone end his days in such deep devotion and peace'.[15] Thus, to refer back to the last chapter of the Gospel of St John, why it is that St Peter must follow and St John must tarry is the mystery of the difference between one vocation and another and one which only God and each of us whom he calls will ever fully understand. The fact we must accept is that the final mystery of what it is to be a saint is something that is and must remain a secret between each soul and its God. This is a notion clearly suggested by the text in the Revelation of St John, which says:

It is the duty of everyone who can hear to listen to what the Spirit is saying to the churches. To the victor in the battle of life I will give a share of the manna that was hidden away, and I will give him a white stone, and on the stone a new name will be inscribed, a name undisclosed to anyone except the person who receives it.[16]

This idea of the life of the spirit as being a movement towards a new relationship with God, such as the receiving of a new name signifies, is a very profound one. If it be true that our human condition is such as we saw the Fathers believed it to be in the earlier part of this book, then one of the reasons why every human life is so mysterious is because there is, at least potentially, within each of us another self, whom even we do not really know. Occasionally, in moments of reflection, we can be aware that, as Julien Green says in the beautiful first volume of his autobiography, there is always hidden in our own depths someone whose existence we do not suspect, and can never reach. But whom God loves. This person, our true self, can enter into contact with God and speak with him'.[17] It is towards this other self that we move by committing ourselves, with detachment from what we see, to the formation that God sends us through the pursuit of our calling as it unfolds itself to us.

But this is inevitably the kind of story that is better told in symbols and legends, as St Gregory the Great tells us the story of St Benedict in the second book of his *Dialogues*. As we make Gregory's approach to the raw materials of this story our own, it can be profitable to consider what it tells us. The story begins with a conversion in response to an impulse that sends St Benedict on a quest the end of which he cannot possibly envisage. He begins 'instructed with learned ignorance, and furnished with unlearned wisdom', under the guidance of the Holy Spirit, who knows where the journey will lead, even if St Benedict does not. Withdrawing into solitude, into his true self, he remains there until he is drawn out of it by someone who comes to share what he has with St Benedict and evidently also to receive what St Benedict has to give. It is Easter day, as the visitor assures him, and St Benedict, who does not really know the date, replies: 'I know that it is Easter with me and a great feast, having found so much favour at God's hands as this day to enjoy your company'. Benedict, in other words, instantly sees Christ in his neighbour, as he so constantly does in the Rule he was later to write. It is thus a resurrection, an Easter day, in a double sense, and the two share a love-feast together to celebrate it.

Then comes a richly instructive passage. St Benedict, who is himself to become a notable shepherd of souls, is found in his cave by some local shepherds: 'When they espied him through the bushes, and saw his apparel made of skins, they verily thought that it had been some beast'. The pursuit of holiness, we should note, often involves one in living through all the ages and conditions of man and the entire experience of holy Scripture, not simply the edifying portions, but also the more barbaric bits. St Benedict has had, as part of his formation, to come to terms with the animal side of man. Not only has he fought and conquered his carnal temptations. He has come to value the positive side of his animal nature and give it its right place. It is for this reason that the man who looks like a beast is able to convert the shepherds from their bestial habits to a Christian life. St Benedict has the beast inside him, but it is now a tame beast, a friendly animal, and it does not turn and rend him and his neighbours. Thus 'for corporal meat which they brought him, they carried away spiritual food for their souls'. This makes it evident that St Benedict's dependence upon others for his material needs has not in fact been an outrage against justice. He has, all the while, in his solitude been doing for his fellows the best thing one man can do for another. For no one, however hidden he be, can be holy to himself alone.

The first two chapters of St Gregory's life mark St Benedict's development towards maturity and balance. We are only fit to be in charge of others when we have freed ourselves from our own inner compulsive drives. St Benedict is now invited to take charge of a community which, finding that his ways and theirs do not mix, tries to poison him. He is careful not to go beyond the immediate indications of providence and he withdraws again, for 'haply it might have fallen out, that he should both have lost himself, and yet not found them'. Retiring again to consolidate his spiritual strength, St Benedict eventually emerges enriched from all he has had time to assimilate. Now he can even find water on top of a mountain, can discern the disguises of devils and men and learn, as his own *Rule* says, to correct his own faults by correcting those of others. He has now reached the summit of apostolic charity and can cut down the grove of Apollo on the top of the hill of Cassinum and turn it into the mountain of God. The show-down with the forces of evil, which was not possible earlier, is now accomplished. Benedict has thus been formed by inner trials and outward hardships, and through them all he has followed that same Spirit which first led him off to his solitude of Subiaco to learn about himself. He has never anticipated its movements or exceeded its purposes. And now, in the middle of a long night of faith, in which he has toiled ceaselessly over his own soul and those of his disciples, he receives an intimation of truth in a blinding light from heaven 'for, as he himself did afterward report, the whole world, gathered as it were together under one beam of the sun, was presented before his eyes'.[18] Now, his charity made perfect, he is brought to the summit of contemplation. This at least is one way of looking at one man's story, and there are elements in it that have significance for everyone.

It is not a story which can be taken to imply that much heavenly light necessarily comes into the life of every saint, as we know from many of their life-stories. We are nearer the normal facts when St Bernard remarks:

He would be considered to be a perfect man in whose soul these three worked together as harmonious factors, sorrow about himself, joy in God and a capacity to be useful to his fellow-men; pleasing to God, modest about himself, serviceable to his fellows. Would to God that after some years there might be seen in any one of us, I do not say all these qualities, but at any rate one of them.[19]

This may be nearer the sort of thing we could hope for, in times when the giants of earlier days seem rarer. But to worry about such things is not our business, as the delightful stories told of St Francis of Assisi in the *Fioretti* remind us. Particularly in the chapter which describes the conversation about where perfect joy is to be found, we encounter something simply unforgettable. St Francis and Brother Leo are walking one winter's day from Perugia and, at intervals along the route, St Francis asks Brother Leo where perfect joy is to be found. The dialogue goes on for two good miles, with St Francis saying that perfect joy is not in this, and not in that and in the end Brother Leo asks: 'Father, I pray you, for God's sake, tell me wherein is perfect joy'. And St Francis replied to him:

When we shall have come to St Mary of the Angels, soaked as we are with the rain and frozen with cold, encrusted with mud and afflicted with hunger, and shall knock at the door, if the porter should come and ask angrily, 'Who are you?' and we replying: 'We are two of your brethren', he should say: 'You speak falsely; go your way', [Francis even goes on to envisage the possibility of their being physically assaulted if they persist in knocking]—if we should bear all these things patiently and with joy, thinking on the pains of the blessed Christ, as that which we ought to bear for his love, O Brother Leo, write, that it is in this that there is perfect joy. Finally, hear the conclusion, Brother Leo: above all the graces and gifts of the Holy Spirit, which Christ has given to his friends, is that of conquering oneself, and suffering willingly for the love of Christ all pain, ill-usage and opprobium, and calamity: because of all the other gifts of God we can glory in none, seeing they are not ours, but God's. But in the cross of tribulation and affliction we may glory, for these are ours; and therefore, says the Apostle, '*I will not glory save in the cross of our Lord Jesus Christ*'.[20]

This is another man's way, which has something in it for everyone.

As for what links all the ways together, let us give the last word to the great Greek seventh-century Father, St Maximus the Confessor, where he says: 'Let us, then, give ourselves entirely to the Lord that we may receive him entire to ourselves. Let us become gods by his grace, for it was for this reason that he, who is by nature God and Lord, became man'.[21] If we are to listen to words like these and never lose heart, we must remember the words of the angel to Mary on the day of her Annunciation: *There is nothing impossible to God.*

NOTES

Unless otherwise stated:
1. All passages of which the originals are in Latin, Greek, French, or German are given in translations by the author.
2. Quotations from the Old Testament are taken from the Revised Standard Version.
3. Quotations from the New Testament are taken from William Barclay's version.
4. The place of publication of works in English is London and in French Paris.

The following abbreviations are used:
   CV   *Conciliar Documents of the Second Vatican Council* (Biblioteca de Autores Cristianos, No. 252, Madrid 1966)
   CVA   *The Documents of Vatican II*; E. T., ed. Walter M. Abbott, S. J. (1967). (Useful for reference, but some of the renderings should be treated with reserve.)
   NEB   New English Bible
   PG   Migne, *Patrologia Graeca*
   PL   Migne, *Patrologia Latina*
   RSV   Revised Standard Version
   SC   *Sources chrétiennes*
   ST   *Summa Theologica*
   WA   Owen Chadwick, *Western Asceticism* (1958)

CHAPTER I

1. Matthew Arnold, 'Dover Beach' (1867), lines 7-14
2. Lines 21-8
3. 'Stanzas from the Grande Chartreuse' (1855), lines 85-7
4. Jn 7.16-17
5. Heb. 12.29
6. Cassian, *Collationes* 2.2; *PL* 49, cols. 525-7
7. *WA*, p. 38, no. 11; cf. *PG* 65, col. 172, Euprepios, 7
8. Cassian, 24.24; *PL* 49, cols. 1517-19

9. D. J. Chitty, *The Desert a City* (Oxford 1966), p. 6
10. A. King, *Wordsworth and the Artist's Vision* (1966), pp. 20-4
11. Jn. 1.3
12. *WA*, p. 156, no. 1
13. Gertrude of Helfta, *Revelations* 1.1; the best edn, Benedictines of Solesmes (1875)
14. Acts 17.24-8

CHAPTER 2

1. Robert Frost, *Complete Poems* (paperback edn, 1967), p. 18
2. CV, *Gaudium et spes*, para. 14; see also *CVA*, p. 12
3. Ps 8.3-4
4. Cf. Heb. 2.5ff and Jn 10.34-5, where Ps. 82.6 is cited
5. Acts 17.28
6. Gen. 2.7
7. J. Pedersen, *Israel*, I-II (London/Copenhagen 1926), p. 99
8. p. 171
9. Matt. 15.17-20
10. Exod. 35.21
11. Gen. 1.26-7
12. Gen. 5.1-3
13. Gen. 2.7ff
14. Exod. 3.14
15. *de sacr. imag., orat.* 3.26; *PG* 94, col. 1345
16. Col. 1.15 (RSV)
17. I Cor. 11.7
18. I Cor. 15.45, 49 (RSV)
19. I Cor. 15.28, and the argument of the whole chapter
20. The indispensable study is J. A. T. Robinson, *The Body: a Study in Pauline Theology* (1952). From a failure to grasp the continuity of language and thought with Paul in Irenaeus, J. T. Nielsen in his *Adam and Christ in the Theology of Irenaeus of Lyons* (Assen 1968) attempts to sustain a wholly untenable thesis.
21. *adv. haer*; ed. W. W. Harvey (Cambridge 1857), 5.16.1; ed. R. Massuet (Venice 1734), 5.16.2
22. 4.20.7; *SC* (1965)
23. 5, *praef. ad. fin.*; *SC* (p. 14)
24. *de incarn.* LIV.3; ed. F. L. Cross (1939); *PG* 25, col. 192B
25. *Orat. catechet.* 25; ed. J. H. Srawley (Cambridge 1903); *PG* 45, col. 66
26. CV, *Gaudium et spes*, para. 17; see also *CVA*, p. 214
27. *adv. haer.* 4.37.1; *SC* (1965)
28. 4.37.3, 6-7; *SC*
29. 4.38.1; *SC*
30. 4.38.4; *SC*
31. 4.39.2; *SC*
32. Jn. 5.17
33. *adv haer.* 4.41.2; *SC*

34. Matt. 5.44-5
35. 'Not all there', in Frost, op. cit., p. 338

<h1 style="text-align:center">CHAPTER 3</h1>

1. E.g., *Orat.* 32.27; 20.11; *PG* 36, cols. 204-5; 35, cols. 1078-9
2. *Hamlet*, act 2, scene 2
3. K. Clark, *Civilisation* (1969), p. 165
4. *CV, Gaudium et spes*, para. 13; see also *CVA*, p. 211
5. K. Lorenz, *On Aggression* (1966), p. 196
6. 1 Cor. 11.7
7. Rom. 3.23. (RSV)
8. 2 Thess. 2.7. (RSV)
9. Gregory of Nyssa, *de beat., orat.* 6; *PG* 44, col. 1273 AB
10. G. Manley Hopkins, 'Spring and Fall', lines 10-15, in *Collected Poems* (1948), p. 94
11. St John of Damascus, *de fid. orth.* 2.12; *PG* 94, col. 920
12. St Ambrose, *in Ps.* 118, 19; *PL* 15, col. 1459C
13. St Augustine, *Confessiones*, 7.10, 16; 11.9, 11; *PL* 32, cols. 742, 813-14
14. St Bernard *Serm. de divers.* 42; *PL* 183, col. 62AB
15. *in Cant*, 82.2; *PL* 183, cols. 1178A, 1179D, 1180D
16. 84. 2, 3; *PL* 183, col. 1185B-D
17. St Leo the Great, *Serm.* 51, 3; *PL* 54, col. 310C
18. *CV, Gaudium et spes*, para. 22; see also *CVA*, p. 220
19. Lk 9.28
20. *CV, Gaudium et spes*, para. 44; see also *CVA*, p. 246-7
21. A. M. Ramsey, *The Glory of God and the Transfiguration of Christ* (1949), p. 151
22. St Augustine, *de Trin.* 10.5; *PL* 42, col. 977

<h1 style="text-align:center">CHAPTER 4</h1>

1. B. Pascal, *Pensées* (Lafuma edn 1960), no. 84
2. No. 667
3. No. 391
4. *CV, Gaudium et spes*, para. 13; see also *CVA*, p. 211
5. Gregory of Nyssa, *Orat. catech.* 39; *PG* 45, cols. 979, 101C
6. *de vita Moysis II.* 3; *SC* (1968); *PG* 44, col. 327B
7. See p. 29
8. Jn 9.23
9. *Confessiones* 1.6,8; *PL* 32, col. 664
10. *de civ. Dei* 3.14; 14.15 & 28; *PL* 41, cols. 89-91, 422-4, 436
    cf. *Serm.* 112,2; *PL* 887
11. *ST* Ia IIa, Q.82, art.41 ad I um
12. Ps. 139.1; (author's trans.)
13. *Solil.* 2,1; *PL* 32, col. 885

14. An examination of 1a pars Q.116, will display both the sources of embarrassment and the solution suggested by the *de consolatione* of Boethius
15. *Enarr. in Ps.* 83,8; *PL* 37, col. 1061,8
16. *Enarr.* II *in Ps.* 30,14; *PL* 36, col. 238
17. *CV, Gaudium et spes*, para. 14; see also *CVA*, p. 212
18. 'Desmond Morris, who is an excellent ethologist and knows better, makes me wince by over-emphasizing, in his book *The Naked Ape*, (paperback edn. 1969), the beastliness of man. I admit that he does so with the commendable intention of shocking haughty people who refuse to see that man has anything 'in common with animals at all, but in this attempt he minimizes the unique properties and faculties of man in an effectively misleading manner: the outstanding and biologically relevant property of the human species is neither its partial hairlessness nor its 'sexiness', but its faculty of conceptual thought—a fact of which Desmond Morris is, of course, perfectly aware'. K. Lorenz, *Studies in Animal and Human Behaviour*, vol. 1 (1970), p. xiv
19. Gregory of Nyssa, *de vita Moysis* II,2; *SC*, p. 106; *PG* 44, col. 328A
20. 1,5; II,4; *SC*, pp. 48, 108; *PG* 44, cols. 300D, 328C
21. II,243; *SC*, p. 272; *PG* 44, col. 405C
22. 1,10; *SC*, p. 50; *PG* 44, col. 301C

CHAPTER 5

1. 'Why the novel matters', in. D. H. Lawrence, *Selected Literary Criticism*; ed. A. Beal (paperback edn 1967), pp. 104-5
2. Triad 1 2, 1, in *Défense des saints hésychastes*; ed. J. Meyendorff (Louvain 1959), vol. 1, p. 75, 11.1-18. Palamas is citing 1 Cor. 6.19; Heb. 3, 6; 2 Cor. 6.16
3. *ST* IIa IIae, Q.25, art. 5
4. M. Merleau-Ponty, *Phénoménologie de la perception* (1945), p. 231
5. See Lars Thunberg, *Microcosm and Mediator* (Lund 1965), p. 109
6. See discussion in J. A. T. Robinson, *The Body*, pp. 11-16
7. See the excellent note in William Barclay, *The New Testament*, vol. 2, pp. 302-3 under *Flesh*
8. Gal. 5. 19-21
9. Rom. 8.7-8
10. C. H. Dodd, *The Epistle of Paul to the Romans* (1932), p. 125
11. Deut. 8.22-3
12. Lk. 9.3
13. Ignatius of Antioch, *Letter to the Ephesians*, in J. B. Lightfoot, *ed. The Apostolic Fathers* (1907), p. 107
14. Rom. 8.23
15. 1 Cor. 15, 37-8, 43-4, 53
16. 'Futility', in W. Owen, *Collected Poems* (1968), p. 58
17. *WA*, p. 105, no. 1
18. Mk 2.27
19. Lev. 25

20. Irenaeus, *Proof*, 95; E. T., J. P. Smith, in *Ancient Christian Writers*, vol. 16
21. Col. 2.16
22. *WA*, pp. 74-5, no. 40
23. *ST* ia, Q.2, art. 1, ad I um
24. This section owes a debt to J. Mouroux, *Sens chrétien de l'homme* (1945)
25. *in Cant.* 85, 10-11; *PL* 183, col. 1192-3
26. *Regula*, cap. 7
27. Gen. 28. 16
28. *Piété confiante*, ed. F. Klein (1905), p. 98
29. A valuable factor in the discovery of this equilibrium may be the use of various physical techniques of relaxation such as yoga. See J. M. Déchanet, *La voie du silence* (1959); but on this question one should note the reserves of J. Cuttat, *Expérience chrétienne et spiritualité orientale* (1967). The volume 'Techniques et contemplation' in the series *Etudes carmélitaines* (1949) is also useful.
30. *Shorter Rules*, no. 128. For a more detailed study see St Basil, *Les régles monastiques*; ed. L. Lèbe (Maredsous 1969)

Chapter 6

1. *Danish Ballads and Folk Songs*; ed. E. Dal; E.T., H. Meyer (Copenhagen 1967), no. 66
2. *de gen. ad. litt.* 9.5; *PL* 34, col. 396
3. 'Amitiés amoureuses', in M. Lane, *Purely for Pleasure* (1966), p. 231
4. C. G. Jung, *Memories, Dreams, and Reflections* (paperback edn 1963), p. 124
5. See esp. *de Trin. 14*; *PL* 42, cols. 1035-58
6. A. Storr, *The Integrity of the Personality* (paperback edn 1963), p. 124
7. See especially *de civ. Dei* 14. 7; *PL* 41, cols. 410-11
8. *Confessiones* 13. 9; *PL* 32, col. 848
9. *Enarr.* ii *in Ps.* 31.5; *PL* 36, col. 260
10. *de nom. div.* 4. 11ff; *PG*3, col. 708Bff
11. Cf. H. Davenson, *Les troubadours* (1961)
12. Scheme in St Bernard, *Serm. de div.* x; *PL* 183, col. 568
13. Gregory Nazianzen, *Orat.* 11. 16; *PG* 35, col. 425A, and William of St Thierry, *de nat. et dign. amor.* 1; *PL* 184, col. 379. (For critical edn see M-M. Davy, *Deux traités de l'amour de Dieu*, 1953)
14. *de civ. Dei* 14.15; *PL* 41, cols. 422-4
15. *de doct. Christ.* 1.27, 28; *PL* 34, col. 29
16. *de Trin.* 8.8; *PL* 42, cols. 957-8
17. *Retract.* 11. 15; *PL* 32, col. 636,2
18. *Capita gnostica*, no. 15; *SC* 5 bis (1966), p. 92
19. *Collationes* 16.3; *PL* 49, cols. 1014-19
20. For a fuller account, see A. Squire, *Aelred of Rievaulx* (1969), ch. 5
21. From *de spirituali amicitia*, cited on p. 108 of the above book

CHAPTER 7

1. C. G. Jung, *Analytical Psychology: its Theory and Practice* (1968), p. 33
2. R. D. Laing, *Self and Others* (revised edn 1969), p. 117
3. Lk. 10.38-42
4. *de vita Moysis* II. 200; *SC.* p. 242
5. *Moralia in Job* 6.57; *PL* 75, col. 760
6. *de Trin.* 1.10; *PL* 42, col. 834
7. *contra Faust.* 22.52; *PL* 42, col. 432
8. *de civ. Dei* 19.19; *PL* 41, cols. 647-8
9. *Collationes* 14.5, 6; *PL* 49, cols. 959-60
10. As above
11. As above
12. *in Cant,* 57.9; *PL* 183, col. 1054C
13. 'Stopping by Woods on a Snowy Evening', in Frost, op. cit., p. 250

CHAPTER 8

1. M. Lane, *Purely for Pleasure*, p. 7
2. 'Arbeit, Freiheit, Macht', in *Auf den Spuren der Wirklichkeit* (Hamburg 1968), pp. 194-250
3. Gen. 2.15
4. *ST* Ia pars, Q.102, art. 33
5. Ia IIae, Q.91, art. 22
6. *CV, Gaudium et spes,* para. 36; see also *CVA,* p. 233
7. E. Fischer, as above, p. 204
8. J. K. Galbraith, *The Affluent Society* (paperback edn 1962), pp. 273-4
9. E.g., *Work: Twenty Personal Accounts;* ed. R. Fraser (1968)
10. C. Day-Lewis, *Collected Poems* (1954)
11. M. Rose, *Computers, Managers, and Society* (1969), p. 10; see also Rose's letter to the *Times Lit. Supp.,* 7 May 1970, p. 511
12. As above
13. p. 255
14. M. Harrington, *The Accidental Century* (paperback edn 1967), pp. 208-9
15. *Regula,* cap. 31. A convenient edn with Latin text and E.T., is *The Rule of St Benedict;* ed. J. McCann (1952)
16. *PL* 15, col. 1531

CHAPTER 9

1. A. Tennyson 'In memoriam', vii, 11-12
2. *The Way of Perfection,* ch. 21; E.T., E. Allison Peers, in *The Complete Works of St Teresa of Jesus* (1946), vol. 2
3. Matt. 26.8-9
4. *Speculum fidei;* ed. (as *Le miroir de la foi*), J. M. Déchanet (Bruges 1946), p. 116
5. Eph. 1.10
6. Mk. 8.36-7

7. Eph. 6.10-12
8. See 1 Cor. 9.25; 2 Tim. 2.4-5; 1 Jn 4.1; 2 Cor. 11.14
9. *PG* 12, Cols. 886-7
10. Col. 892
11. Col. 848-9
12. Col. 933
13. Col. 658A
14. Col. 677-8
15. Col. 786 BC, quoted by Jerome, *Ep.* 78
16. Col. 790C
17. *Collationes* 1.5; PL 49, cols. 486-7
18. *WA*, pp. 38-9, no. 11
19. J. Wellard, *Desert Pilgrimage* (1970), p. 80
20. *in Eccles., hom 1; PG* 44, col. 624B
21. *Vita* 47; for an E.T., see R. T. Meyer, *Ancient Christian Writers*, vol. 10 (1950)
22. 14
23. *PG* 35, col. 1088
24. See Jn 1.10; 18.36; Jas 4.4
25. 2 Cor. 5.7
26. *in Ps.*, cap. 6; *PG* 44, col. 508BC
27. *PG* 63, cols. 201-2
28. *de virg.*, para. 2; *PG* 46, col. 324
29. *Ethics* I, ch. 10, line 84ff; *SC*, no. 122 (1966), p. 258

CHAPTER 10

1. L. van der Post, *The Heart of the Hunter* (paperback edn 1969), p. 161
2. *CV, de div. rev.*, cap. 2, para. 10; see also *CVA*, p. 117
3. *PL* 176, col. 186D
4. 1 Cor. 10.11
5. On the original sense of *lectio divina*, see C. Dumont, 'Lectio divina : la lecture de la parole de Dieu', in *Bible et vie chrétienne*, no. 22 (1958), pp. 23-33
6. *Vita* 2
7. *in Ioann., tract.* 30, pars 1; PL 35, col. 1632
8. *in Exod., hom.* 13.3; *PG* 12, col. 391
9. *PL* 167, col. 1017
10. *Moralia in Job* 2.1,1; *PL* 75, col. 553
11. *Collationes* 1.18; *PL* 49, cols. 507-8
12. *PL* 184, col. 327, para. 31—col. 328A
13. As above
14. A valuable attempt by a modern monk to suggest an approach like this is made by Dom C. Charlier in *The Christian Approach to the Bible* (1958)
15. *Letters* III.10
16. *Selected Literary Criticism*, pp. 7-8
17. *in Adv., serm.* 5; PL 183, col. 51BC

CHAPTER 11

1. Gregory Nazianzen, *Orat.* 43.11; *PG* 36, cols. 508-9
2. *de musica* 6.14,45; *PL* 32, col. 1186-7. For an analysis of the whole work see A. Squire 'The Cosmic Dance' in *Blackfriars* (1954), pp. 477-84
3. *ST* IIa IIae, Q.168, art. 2
4. *Meditationes Guigonis*; ed. A. Wilmart (1936), no. 149
5. *PL* 16, cols. 28.2.5-29.7
6. Guigo, no. 203
7. *Moralia in Job* 4.30; *PL* 75, col. 667
8. Letter 28 in E.T., *Letters from a Stoic*, R. Campbell (1969), pp. 75-6
9. St Ignatius of Antioch, in J. B. Lightfoot, *The Apostolic Fathers*, pars 15
10. Pars 19
11. *Moralia in Job* 22.17,43; *PL* 76, col. 238
12. Isa. 55.8
13. *Piété confiante*, pp. 307-8
14. *History of the English Church and People*, ch. 13; there is a modern E.T., by L. Sherley-Price (paperback edn 1955; 1968)

CHAPTER 12

1. *in Ps. 118, serm.* 6. 8-9; *PL* 15, col. 1337
2. *Collationes* 9.1; *PL* 49, cols. 780-1
3. 9.7; *PL* 49, col. 781
4. *Hauteurs sereines*; textes choisis de Dom A. Guillerand (Rome 1959), pp. 210-12
5. Lk 18.1; 1 Thess. 5.17
6. For a discussion of this misleading saying see *Notes and Queries*, ser. 6, XI, p. 477
7. *WA*, p. 141, no. 2
8. Origen; *Treatise on Prayer*; E.T., E. G. Jay (1954), ch. x.2
9. Ch. XII.2
10. *de fid. orth.* 3.24; *PG* 94, col. 1089. The two phrases are cited in *ST* IIa IIae, Q.83, art. 1, corp. et ad II um
11. Lk 11.1; Matt. 6.9
12. See I. Hausherr, *Les leçons d'un contemplatif* (1960), p. 16, no. 3

CHAPTER 13

1. Hausherr, p. 85, no. 60
2. *de orat. dom.* 1; *PG* col. 1120C
3. Cf. Jn 4.23; 8.32
4. G. Florovsky, cited by A. Schmemann, *Introduction to Liturgical Theology* (1966), p. 13
5. Matt. 6.7

6. *Regula*, cap. 19
7. As above
8. Cap. 20
9. As above
10. Prologue
11. The final phrase is cited from E.T., Dom J. McCann (1952)
12. *The Way of Perfection*, ch. 22; E.T. Allison Peers, in *The Complete Works of St Teresa of Jesus* (1946), vol. 2
13. *Introduction à la vie dévote*, II.4
14. As above
15. II.5
16. II.8
17. Cited in L. Cognet, *La lumière dans les ténèbres* (La-Pierre-qui-vire 1957), pp. 78-80
18. *Discours des grandeurs* (1644) 4.8
19. 7.9
20. Jn. 1.16
21. In this matter the writer owes a great deal to the teaching of the late Bishop Kovalevsky of the Institut orthodoxe français de Saint-Denys.
22. *Collationes* 10.10; *PL* 49, cols. 831-6
23. There is considerable available literature on the Jesus Prayer: e.g., *The Way of a Pilgrim*, E.T., R. M. French (SPCK repr, as 2 pts in 1 vol. 1954); pt 1 also in G. P. Fedotov, *A Treasury of Russian Spirituality* (1950; paperback edn 1952) and repr. by SPCK 1972; *Writings from the Philokalia or the Prayer of the Heart*; E. T., ed E. Kadloubovsky and G. E. H. Palmer (1951); *Early Fathers from the Philokalia*; E.T., ed. Kadloubovsky and Palmer (1954). On the question of the breathing technique accompanying the Prayer, Bishop Brianchaninov in *On the Prayer of Jesus* (E.T., Father Lazarus, 1952) is particularly useful and important as being a word of caution from a wise master.
24. Matt. 6.33
25. *WA*, p. 171, no. 68

CHAPTER 14

1. e.g. M. Muller Eckhard, *Die Krankheit nicht krank sein zu können* (Stuttgart 1954)
2. Ps. 84.2
3. Song of Songs 5.2 (NEB)
4. 1 Sam. 17.32
5. Ps. 12.1-2
6. 1 Kings 4.29
7. Ezek. 11.19
8. Isa. 1.14-15
9. Mk 12.38

10. Mk 7.14-23
11. *Doctrine spirituelle* IV.2, art. 1.
12. *Introduction à la vie dévote* 1.5
13. 1 Cor. 12.31-13.1
14. *de dilig. Deo* 1; PL 182, col. 973ff, but the best Latin text is in *Sancti Bernardi opera*; ed. Dom L. Leclercq, vol. 3 (1963). For E. T., see H. Martin, *On loving God* (1959)
15. 1 Jn 4.19, (RSV)
16. Rom. 5.8-10
17. *de dilig. Deo* 2,2
18. 2,4
19. 3,7
20. 3,9
21. 5,15
22. 7,17
23. 7,21
24. 7,22
25. 8,25
26. 11,30-31
27. 11,33

Chapter 15

1. *Introduction à la vie dévote*, 1.2
2. A. Squire, *Aelred of Rievaulx* (1969), p. 37
3. Julian of Norwich, *Revelations of Divine Love*, ch. 5; modern E.T., C. Walters, (paperback edn 1966)
4. e.g., in *The Ascent of Mount Carmel*, Bk II, ch. 23-32; E.T., E. Allison Peers (1934) vol. 1
5. W. Wordsworth and S. T. Coleridge, *Lyrical Ballads*; ed. R. L. Brett and A. R. Jones (1965), p. 249
6. Julian of Norwich, ch. 15
7. Ch. 19
8. 1 Cor. 13.2
9. *The Cloud of Unknowing*, ch. 8; modern E.T., C. Wolters (paperback edn 1961)
10. Ch. 36

Chapter 16

1. *Piété confiante*, p. 86
2. This and the two subsequent quotations from Père Surin are cited by L. Cognet in *La lumière dans les ténèbres*, pp. 110-12
3. For a long discussion of St Teresa's terminology, see E. W. Trueman Dicken. *The Crucible of Love* (1963), ch. 7

4. *The Interior Castle*, Fourth Mansion, ch. 3; E.T., E. Allison Peers, *Works of St Teresa of Jesus*, vol. 2 (1946)
5. *Piété confiante*, pp. 305-6
6. This section is substantially an analysis of Bk III of *Introduction to the Devout Life*, of which there are many E.T. This passage and the next two quoted are from III.1
7. III.37
8. III.24
9. III.23
10. III.6
11. III.9
12. III.10
13. In *The Art of Prayer: an Orthodox Anthology* (1966), p. 122

CHAPTER 17

1. St Teresa, *Letters*, 1.16, cited by Padre Crisógono de Jesus in *The Life of St John of the Cross*; E.T., K. Pond (1958), p. 308
2. *The Living Flame of Love*, III.27-46, analysed; E.T., E. Allison Peers, *Complete Works of St John of the Cross*, vol. 3 (1935)
3. *The Ascent of Mount Carmel*, II.12-15; E.T., Peers, vol. 1 (1934)
4. *The Dark Night of the Soul*, 1.9; E.T., as above
5. *Letters* 18, cited by Padre Crisógono de Jesus E.T., Pond, pp. 207-8
6. This section is an analysis, largely in St Francis' own words, of Bks I and II of the *Treatise on the Love of God*; E.T., H. B. Mackey (1884)
7. This quotation and the next are from Bk VI.1
8. VI.3
9. VI.7
10. VI.8
11. VI.11
12. VII.6

CHAPTER 18

1. *The Ascent of Mount Carmel*, II.5
2. *Letter* 254; PL 182, col. 460
3. *ST* IIa IIae, Q.24, art.9
4. *Ascent* 1.2
5. III.33
6. *The Dark Night of the Soul*, 1.1
7. 1.7
8. 1.8
9. 1.10
10. II.3

CHAPTER 19

1. *Instruction* 13.140-1; ed. Régnault and de Préville, SC (1963), pp. 406-8
2. J. P. de Caussade, *Self-abandonment to the Divine Providence*, 1.1,1; E.T., A. Thorold (1959; paperback edn 1971). The next quotation is from the same passage
3. 1.1,3
4. 1.1,4
5. 1.1,6
6. 1.1,8
7. 1.2,4 5
8. 11.1,1
9. 11.3,5
10. As above
11. *Letters*, IV.9

CHAPTER 20

1. 1 Cor. 15.41
2. Probably the most useful study of texts and theories on this theme is E. E. Malone, 'The Monk and the Martyr', in *Studia Anselmiana* no. 38 (1956), pp. 208-28. See also M. Lods, *Confesseurs et martyrs*, (Neuchâtel/Paris 1958)
3. Col. 2.9
4. Isa. 6.3-4
5. Ps. 51
6. The writer owes this point to A. J. Festugière, *La sainteté* (1949)
7. Ps. 106.16
8. Isa. 57.15
9. Rev. 3.7,14
10. Rom. 8.9 (RSV)
11. Gal. 2.20 (RSV)
12. John 4.16,19
12. 1 John 4.16,19
13. 1 Cor. 13.5 (RSV)
14. Gal. 5.6
15. See Bede, *History of the English Church and People*; modern E.T., Sherley-Price, p. 20
16. Rev. 2.17
17. J. Green, *Partir avant le jour*, (1963), p. 262
18. *PL* 6, col. 126ff; passages here are quoted from an old English translation published in Paris in 1608; 2nd edn of this, E.T., Gardner (1911)
19. *in Cant., serm* 57.11; *PL* 183, col. 1055
20. *Fioretti*, ch. 8; E.T., T. Okey (1899), and a paperback edn (1965)
21. *Liber asceticus*, para. 43; *PG* 90, col. 953

INDEX

Heart, Hebrew conception 18-19, 54-5, 160-4
hermits, significance of 113-16
Hugh of St Victor 120-1
Hopkins, Gerard Manley 30

Ignatius Loyola, St 152, 157
Ignatius of Antioch, St 56, 132-3
Image of God: man as 10, ch. 2 *passim*, 30, 43; Christ as 21-3
Irenaeus of Lyons, St 22-5, 60

'Jesus Prayer' 157-8
Julian of Norwich 174-8
Jung, Carl 68-9, 82
John Chrysostom, St: spiritual virginity 115-16
John of Damascus, St: 21, 30; prayer 143-6
John of the Cross, St 175, 185, 192-9, 204-5, 207-11

King, Alec, prof. 8
'know yourself' 27, 35, 43

Laing, R. D. 82
Lallement, Louis 165
Lane, Margaret 68, 90
Lawrence, Brother 165-6
Lawrence, D. H. 51-2, 56, 126
Leo the Great, St: on Transfiguration 33-4
Lorenz, Konrad 28, 45n
love and aggression: 103; *see also* Augustine, St

Martha and Mary ch. 7 *passim*
Marx, Karl 91-4
Maximus the Confessor, St 53, 233
Merleau-Ponty, M. 52-3, 68
mirror symbolism 10-11
Morris, Desmond 45n
Mouroux, Jean 63n

natural and supernatural 46

Origen: desert symbolism 106-9; Scripture 122; prayer 142-3
original sin ch. 3 *passim*, 46

Owen, Wilfrid 58-9

Pascal, Blaise 36-7
Paul, the Apostle, St: in Athens 14; Christ as image 21-3, 102; original sin 28; the body 53-4, 58, 65-6; dark knowledge 178; holiness 224-7
Pedersen, J. 18-19

Ramsey, Michael, abp 35
Robinson, J. A. T., bp 22n, 53n
Rose, Michael 95-7
Rosenborg Palace 9-10
Royal Road (*via regia*): traditional significance 4-7, 49
Rupert of Deutz 122

'Sayings of the Elders' see Verba Seniorum
Sermon on the Mount 25-6
Shakespeare, William 27
Sharbel Makhlouf, St 228
Simeon the New Theologian, St 116
sin, kinds of 29
Socrates 132
Storr, Anthony 69
Surin, Jean-Joseph 184-6

Teresa of Avila, St 101, 135, 145, 151, 185-6, 192, 221
'theologian', traditional notion of 11-13, 147
Theophan the Recluse, abp 190-1
Thérèse of Lisieux, St 228
Thomas Aquinas, St 42-4, 52, 62, 92, 129, 144, 205-6
Thunberg, Lars 53n
Tourville, Henri de 64, 135, 182-3, 187
Transfiguration of Christ 33-5

van der Post, Laurence 118n
Verba Seniorum (Sayings of the Elders) 6, 11, 60-1, 110, 141-2, 158
virtues 47-50

William of St Thierry 72-3, 102, 124-5
Wordsworth, William 8, 175
work and prayer 140-3

ACKNOWLEDGEMENTS

Thanks are due to the following for permission to quote from copyright sources:

Burns & Oates, Ltd: *The Complete Works of St John of the Cross*, tr. E. Allison Peers.

Cambridge University Press: New English Bible, second edition © 1970 (by permission of Oxford and Cambridge University Presses).

Jonathan Cape, Ltd, and Rinehart and Winston, Inc., New York: *The Poetry of Robert Frost*, ed. E. C. Lathem.
—and Harold Matson Co., Inc., New York: *Collected Poems* (1954), by C. Day-Lewis.

Chartreuse de la Valsainte, Fribourg: *Hauteurs sereines*, by A. Guillerand (translation).

Collins Publishers: The New Testament, tr. William Barclay.

Hamish Hamilton, Ltd: *The Affluent Society*, by J. K. Galbraith.

William Heinemann, Ltd, The Viking Press, Ltd, New York, and the estate of the late Mrs Frieda Lawrence: *Hymns in a Man's Life*, by D. H. Lawrence in *Phoenix II*.

Hutchinson Publishing Group, Ltd: *Desert Pilgrimage*, by James Wellard.

Thomas Nelson & Sons, Ltd: Holy Bible: Revised Standard Version.

Oxford University Press: *Israel*, by J. Pedersen.

Penguin Books, Ltd: *Computers, Managers, and Society*, by Michael Rose.
—: Seneca, *Letters of a Stoic*, tr. R. Campbell.

Rowohlt Verlag, GmbH, Reinbek bei Hamburg: *Auf den Spuren der Wirklichkeit*, by E. Fischer (translation).
Routledge & Kegan Paul, Ltd, and Humanities Press, Inc., New York: *The Phenomenology of Perception*, by M. Merleau-Ponty (translation).

SCM Press, Ltd, and Westminster Press, Philadelphia: *Western Asceticism*, by Owen Chadwick.

Sheed & Ward, Ltd, and Sheed & Ward, Inc., New York: *The Complete Works of St Teresa of Avila*, tr. E. Allison Peers: U.S.A. edn, tr. from critical edn of P. Silverio de Santa Teresa, C.D., 3 vols.

Spicilegium Sacrum Lovaniense Louvain: *Greégoire Palamas*: *Défense des saints hésychastes*, tr. by Meyendorff.

George Weidenfeld & Nicolson, Ltd, and Macmillan, New York: *The Accidental Century*, by M. Harrington.

The author would like to acknowledge with gratitude the continuous encouragement that he received from his friend, the Reverend A. M. Allchin, whilst the book was being written, and the co-operation of the Sisters of the Love of God who typed the text.